INFORMATION SYSTEMS SERIES

SYSTEMS ANALYSIS, SYSTEMS DESIGN

David Mason
Victoria University of Wellington, New Zealand

and

Leslie Willcocks
Templeton College, Oxford University

ALFRED WALLER LIMITED
HENLEY- ON -THAMES

Published by
Alfred Waller Ltd, Publishers
Orchards, Fawley, Henley-on-Thames
Oxfordshire RG9 6JF

First published 1994

Reprinted 1994

Copyright © 1994 Alfred Waller Ltd

British Library Cataloguing-in-
Publication Data
A catalogue record for this book is
available from the British Library

ISBN 1-872474-09-8

Produced for the publishers by
John Taylor Book Ventures
Hatfield, Herts

Printed and bound in Great Britain by
Hollen Street Press,
Berwick-upon-Tweed

Table of contents

Chapter 1 The context of systems analysis

Introduction

The widespread use of computers in business is about thirty years old. In that time computers have evolved from clumsy adding machines to sleek personal information tools. However, it is questionable whether the methods of designing computer applications have kept pace with the changes in technology.

The basic premise of this book is that the application determines how an information system should be developed. Different types of application, different end user requirements, respond best to different approaches. No one methodology or technique can be optimum under all circumstances: Prototyping is a useful technique, but it is possible that there are some better ways than trial and error to build the control system for a nuclear power station. Structured systems analysis has many powerful features but it has severe limitations too.

So the modern systems designer needs a range of techniques. And the skill to deploy the appropriate techniques as required. However, this does not mean that systems analysis is nothing more than an ad hoc approach to a succession of unique situations. Applications can be categorised to give a good indication in advance of which technique or combinations of techniques to use.

The challenge for the analyst is to recognise where, and when, to apply the right technique. A computer information system consists of three elements: hardware and software and people. Each brings a vital function to the application solution. The balance between each of the elements differs according to the situation.

Producing an application first of all requires analysis, and then requires design. Analysis is largely a matter of applying well-understood and reliable tools to investigate a given situation. Design is matter of intuition and experience, of seeing the application through the users' eyes and trying to combine all the elements into an effective and efficient solution. There are no guaranteed methodologies for design, no techniques which will inevitably produce the insight which crystallises the problem. But a good set of analysis tools combined with a well chosen methodology will always suggest design alternatives.

1

This text is about the methods of analysing the perceived and actual requirements of information systems users. It considers the appropriate hardware and software types only in as far as they have a bearing on the design possibilities open to the analyst. Systems analysis is a broad concept falling somewhere between programming and operations management. On one day an analyst may be required to improve the efficiency of a routine operation at the core of the organisation's activities and on another they may be asked to develop some application never previously attempted by the organisation.

This text will help managers understand the process of systems analysis, to appreciate the parameters limiting the designer. It will assist information systems people in planning and managing systems proposals. It can help users understand how their information needs are translated into a working computer system and give programmers a better appreciation of the activities they support. It will aid users who want to develop their own systems or who just need to know how to formulate their own requests to analysts more clearly.

For the purposes of this text, the terms *systems analyst* and *systems designer* are used interchangeably, an analyst or a designer being defined loosely as any person who transforms an end user's requirement into a practical and efficient working reality. This definition therefore includes much of the work variously done by a number of people: programmers, business analysts, systems analysts, data architects, database administrators and the like. The work of the analyst is so varied that trying to tie it down to single form serves no useful purpose.

Of systems analysis and systems design

The end product of systems analysis and design will be a working, effective and efficient application which meets the user's needs. This necessarily means that a non-computerised system must be considered in some cases and that conversely in other cases highly sophisticated computer systems must be employed. Since the first mainframes appeared, the range of computer hardware has increased dramatically and the convenient labels of mini, mainframe and micro no longer make much sense.

Similarly the range of software available merges imperceptibly from third generation languages like COBOL through sophisticated database manipulation languages to customisable end user applications. The need to mix personal computers and share files has led to the emergence of communications and networking software. No one analyst can hope to master the details of all of these. The work of the analyst is today more like the work of a film director, using specialists to pull together the separate parts needed to realise a personal vision.

The analyst today is typically more involved in ensuring that business needs are met than in the detailed workings of the hardware or software. Systems analysis and design continues to evolve away from a concentration on the technology towards a more business oriented stance. As the concept of open systems becomes a reality, more imaginative combinations of hardware and software can be applied in more flexible work groupings.

The analyst used to be someone who had learned their trade the hard way, coming from some other discipline and learning on the job and by trial and error. They seldom had formal qualifications. In the modern setting this is no longer acceptable. Analysts need a qualification in a specialist discipline to give an informed perspective to their daily work.

Systems analysis and other disciplines

Systems analysis in theory is a logical approach to determining the information requirements of a user and devising the cheapest way of delivering that information. In practice systems analysis is a creative blend of psychology, politics, management and computer science. The skills of the analyst are less in the technical aspects of the computing machinery and increasing lie in understanding the fundamentals of business and the needs of its people. This means greater interaction with other professionals and an emphasis on educating others to appreciate the potential of information technology and in appraising priorities from the user's point of view.

The environment of the systems analyst has also changed. The end user of computer systems are today fairly sophisticated in the uses of the technology. Many expect to able to drive the system rather than act as passive receivers of predetermined output. Systems analysis is now much 'softer', the action has moved away from accounting type data towards applications using less easily quantifiable elements. The focus of corporate computing is moving upwards, with the analyst expected to contribute solutions which will generate revenue directly rather than merely attempt to make cost savings. The emphasis is on the strategic use of computer technology, taking a company wide vision.

Managing analysis and design

This section looks at ways of classifying current applications, of evaluating the current DP position of an organisation, of identifying strategic applications and of producing a balanced applications portfolio.

The evolving role of systems analysis

In any organisation there are many possible uses of information technology. What new applications should be supported? And which not? How do you

3

judge the potential of any proposed application? In IT terms, where is the organisation now, and where should it be going?

These are difficult questions which every analyst must address. And there are no simple answers. But there are ways available to make sense of the jumble of applications found in every organisation.

The problem

Almost since its inception, the computing industry has fallen behind the demand for applications. An applications backlog is the norm in every industry. At the root of the problem is a poor conceptual model of the nature of information systems (IS) work and its role in the wider organisational context. IS professionals need to stand back from their day to day activities and take a broader view. The structure of the typical IS department reflects an evolution driven by reaction to internal demand and by technological opportunity. Typically, the IS structure of any given organisation is the result of a series of short term decisions made under pressure, not the outcome of long term planning.

Systems designers are often too preoccupied with daily pressures to think strategically. And where strategy is considered, it is usually confined to internal strategy, addressing hardware replacement schedules and software policies, not corporate objectives. Systems designers recognise their role as a service centre and are committed to aiding the revenue generating activities of the organisation, but seldom get directly involved in the strategic thrust of the business.

The analyst-designer needs to recognise the contribution which IT can make to corporate goals and actively manage the process of application selection and development, rather than be driven passively by user demand or technological developments.

Models of corporate computing

The first step towards being a proactive planner, and not merely reacting to events, is to have a grasp of the nature and scope of the applications within the organisation. The easiest way to make sense of a collection of computer applications is to find a way to classify them, which in turn depends on understanding models of corporate computing.

Stratified models

The development of computers has been unplanned and unpredictable. The giants of the 1950s gave way to the mainframes of the 1960s and the minis of the 1970s. At the time there was no coherent or co-ordinated view of computer operations. The model current at that time was a general model of organisational behaviour developed by Richard Anthony.

This put forward the view that there are three basic types of decisions made in organisations: strategic, tactical or control and operational decisions (see Figure 1.1).

Figure 1.1 Anthony's pyramid

Strategic decisions focus on the interaction between the organisation and its environment, involve setting organisational objectives and policies and determining the means of achieving them. **Control decisions** are aimed at ensuring resources are used effectively and that the operations basic to the organisation's function are carried out efficiently. **Operational decisions** relate to the performance of day to day operations and are limited to ensuring that specific tasks are done properly, in the right sequence and at the right time.

For example, an organisation may have a transport division for delivering its goods. At the operational level, managers have to know which loads are going where, when they must get there and what the best route would be. At the control level, managers need to know if loads are reaching customers in time and in good condition, if there are particular parts of the system causing problems and whether this month's figures are better or worse than last month's. At the strategic level, managers need to decide what type of transport service is best, whether the organisation should have its own transport division or contract out all services to specialist trucking companies.

Anthony's Pyramid

Each of these types of decisions has distinct information requirements. Strategic decisions are usually based on information which has long time periods, is not easily quantifiable, originates outside the organisation, is ill defined and often arises unexpectedly. Control decisions have more concrete information needs. Control information usually operates on a regular time cycle, is fairly clearly defined, mostly arises internally and is fairly predictable in nature. Operational information is usually tightly defined, has a short time scale, is predictable and arises entirely from internal operations.

In the normal course of business, operational activities give rise to information which is passed up to managers for control purposes. They use it to monitor operational activities, summarise it and pass it on up to managers at the strategic level. These managers merge the summaries with externally generated data and base their strategic decisions on the results.

This model had (and still has) immense influence on the thinking of managers. All functions of the organisation can be fitted into a hierarchical progression from Operational, through Control (tactical), to Strategic activities. The basic idea includes a natural progression of activities starting at the operational level and moving upwards into the organisational heights.

IS managers internalised the Anthony model and concentrated on applications at the operational and control levels of management. It was felt that the correct progression for computer support of organisational activities was therefore to introduce computer applications at the operational level first, then provide summary information for control purposes to middle managers as part of a higher level Management Information System. Once the MIS was in place the next applications would be aimed at supporting strategic decisions.

So a typical applications progression might be order entry and inventory tracking, leading to budgeting or sales analysis for middle management, and in a mature organisation, market forecasting as a strategic application.

Growth models

Nolan's stage model

The idea of a natural progression from simple low level systems has a lot of appeal and once there were enough examples to analyse several 'growth' models were proposed. Of these the best known is the Nolan Stage Model (Figure 1.2). It went through several revisions, originally a four stage model,

6

then six stages and has been subject to constant refinement and argument since.

Nolan's model implies that every organisation goes through recognisable stages and the appropriate management responses to managing and controlling IT activities will depend entirely on where in the progression a given organisation is at any point in time. An objective examination of the organisation will reveal which stage or transition between stages is current, and this in turn will predict what managerial action is appropriate.

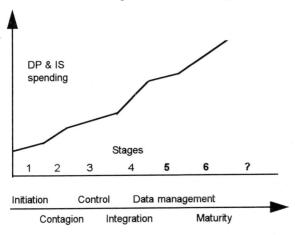

Figure 1.2 Nolan's stage model

Nolan's stages
The individual stages can be distinguished by testing a number of variables. These are:

The rate of expenditure. This is shown by the slope of the line. It varies depending on which stage the organisation is in and is a guide to predicting the future spend needed in the subsequent stages.

Technological configuration. Each stage typically is associated with particular hardware and software combinations. For example, early stages are likely to be batch oriented, more mature stages will have on-line working, and the data management stage will typically be based around a corporate data base.

Applications portfolio. The stage of an organisation can be judged by comparing the types of application in use with the levels of Anthony's model. An information system which only caters for operational activities would be at one of the lower stages.

The DP organisation. Is control of the data processing function under accounting, or run by an independent DP section, or directed independently by the general management? Is there an ad hoc approach with applications built on demand, or are applications pre determined on the basis of a business plan, functional based?

User awareness. In general, is the typical user naive, familiar with the technology, or actually driving the development process?

Strengths and weaknesses
The Nolan model in practice has its strengths and weaknesses.

Strengths. The Nolan model is intuitively appealing, and certainly accords in general with most people's actual experience. It is easily grasped by non specialists and is useful as a shortcut in explaining computer development strategy.

Weaknesses. In practice the model is over simplistic. It cannot explain or guide strategic opportunities. It is too finely detailed and attempts to check the model with empirical data has led to inconsistent results.

Problems with the Nolan model
It also leaves some things unexplained which should be explained (Benbasat, 1984). How is it that some organisations exhibit several stages at once? How come some organisations go backwards? How fast should we go from one stage to the next? Where do we go after stage six?

A further criticism of the stage hypothesis is that there are not in fact six stages (King and Kraemer, 1984). If there really is a progression then there is an infinite number of stages and the number six is quite arbitrary.

The model was quite useful in the seventies and early eighties. But once computing evolved away from centralised, mainframe-based configurations it became less applicable.

Transition models

The stage hypothesis theory generated further empirical studies of the behaviour of information systems departments. One of the more recent, summarised by Ward (1990), introduces the idea that information systems develop phases rather than stages. In Nolan's model, stages run into one another; in Ward's version, there is sudden sharp break between phases, The transition can be traced through the changing role of the management of IT.

8

Three stage model

Hirschheim describes a three stage evolution of the IS function (Hirschheim, 1988). In **stage one** the problems centre round managing internal data processing activities. The emphasis is on the control and management of operations, programming and data preparation. The issues are mainly internal, to improve the IS department's ability to deliver and to gain credibility with top management.

In **stage two** the emphasis shifts to managing the DP department itself. This involves integrating diverse applications, and coping with technological change. Issues change to managing relations with other departments and to an attempt to improve the level of service to departments. IT capabilities are spread throughout the organisation on an ad hoc basis. The criteria for applications is ease of implementation with a cost/benefit bias. Business areas are computerised regardless of whether their function is critical or not. Typically in this stage the functions exhibiting the greatest degree of sophistication are the accounting functions.

The **third stage** involves a radical realignment of the IS function along organisational strategic lines. There is an awareness of local and central organisational issues and the overall management of IT moves away from the IS department. The key objective is balancing business needs with the IT capability.

Organisations today have effectively mastered the problems of Hirschheim's initial two stages but seem poorly equipped to make the transition to the final stage.

Corporate analysts now suggest that there are in practice only two stages for medium to large organisations. The first stage is characterised by a concern for management of the DP technology, the second by a change to Information Management.

There are any number stages of change in organisations but there is one major change point which differentiates the two types. They can be distinguished by asking the questions - Who manages IT? For whom is it organised? What is the role of IT in the organisation? Is there IT resource management?

Towards a strategic model

Progressing to the third stage means reorganising the IS function to reflect the changed realities of the corporate information environment. Departments on the Hirschheim stage three boundary have the ability to deal with two basic types of applications. At the **operational level** applications are concerned with monitoring and exception reporting of transaction processing systems.

Data of this type is typically predetermined and consistent. This type of application categorised what has been called the *DP era* of organisational computing.

At the **tactical level** applications are mainly of the enquiry and analysis type, drawing on data generated in lower level applications. Applications are typified by a short life span, ad hoc nature and a rapid development cycle. These applications collectively define the *MIS era*.

Beyond both of these is the **strategic level**, where the *SIS era* is gathering force and the IS function is charged with developing Strategic Information Systems.

Characteristics of the three levels
The DP era was characterised by improvements in operational efficiency brought about by automating business systems. The MIS era sought to provide better information to improve management effectiveness. The MIS era is characterised by relational databases, fourth generation languages and the widespread use of spreadsheets.

In the SIS era, the thrust is to improve organisational competitiveness by changing the nature or conduct of the business. By this analysis, DP and MIS functions are a subset of SIS functions.

It must be emphasised that, although entering the SIS era represents a break with previous practice, SIS does not replace DP or MIS applications. Both are fundamentally different from the SIS applications and still have a long way to go in terms of development. Existing systems have to be supported, improved and replaced while future opportunities are explored.

Even where an organisation has progressed fully to the SIS era, only about 20% of the IS budget will go on developing SIS applications directly: the rest will be devoted to increasing the efficiency of basic operations and refining management effectiveness. In addition it is worth bearing in mind that the SIS outlook is not in fact different in kind from DP and MIS working: it is just that its potential impact on the organisation is greater.

Future IT spend
Applications in all three areas will continue to be developed. Ward estimates the level of spend in the future to be in the order of DP 50%, MIS 30% and SIS 20%. (Ward, 1990). The leverage however, the effect on corporate performance, may be reversed.

Portfolio models

By the 1980s, computer applications for operations and control were, in general, in place and well understood. Computer applications by and large had migrated from operational, to control, to planning functions, spreading slowly through the organisation at different rates, gradually moving upwards. The normal process was to computerise a particular function, then move sideways and computerise another independent function at the same level. When several of these had enough data in common, control and analysis applications were written to access the data for middle management. Every organisation had a collection of applications of various ages and functions.

Managing the applications portfolio
One consequence of entering the SIS era is that the outlook of the IS function becomes more external, more aligned with the aims and strategies of the organisation. This in turn means that the IS function needs to be familiar with the strategic tools used by general management to set the organisational strategy. A useful analysis tool is the strategic grid developed by Cash, McFarlane and McKenney (1983) which sees organisations operating in one of four quadrants depending on the strategic significance of its existing applications and those under development (Figure 1.3).

The grid classifies applications as being high or low in terms of strategic impact with existing systems on one axis and proposed or current development systems on the other. This allows the classifications of organisations into four broad areas Factory, Support, Strategic and Turnaround (McFarlan and McKenney, 1984).

Factory organisation would have existing applications of strategic impact but not be developing any future systems. An airline might have a strategically important booking system but only support applications under development.

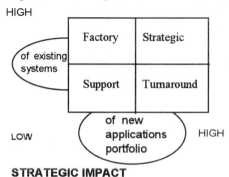

HIGH

| Factory | Strategic |
| Support | Turnaround |

of existing systems

of new applications portfolio

LOW   HIGH

STRATEGIC IMPACT

Figure 1.3 Strategic impact of new and existing systems

11

Support organisations have no strategic applications in place or under development. A retailer or restaurateur may be in this position and still be competitive (and immune from technological failure.)

Strategic organisations have both existing and developing applications of strategic importance; for example a bank might see its quality of service as a strategic tool and be updating applications with this in mind, to maintain competitive advantage.

Turnaround organisations are those with only support applications at present but which are working on developing strategic applications designed to change the way they do business.

It is always instructive to analyse an organisation in this way to see if their practice matches their stated objectives.

Analysing the matrix

Using the matrix allows any organisation to map its current activities and functions into one of the four quadrants, Strategic, Turnaround, Factory or Support.

The **strategic** quadrant shows those activities which are judged to be crucial for the organisation's future success. **Factory** activities are crucial for maintaining current success. Activities in the **Support** quadrant are not carried out for their own sake but to enable the factory activities to carried out. The final quadrant, **turnaround** activities, maps activities which are speculative, which may or may not develop into applications contributing to the factory, support or strategic roles. A completed matrix for a typical company is shown in Figure 1.4.

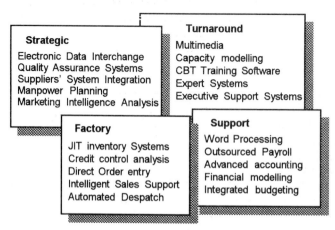

Figure 1.4 Matrix analysis for a typical company

Mapping the portfolio

The McFarlane matrix can be adapted to show a similar distribution for individual applications. Applications can be classified on a scale ranging from absolutely critical to useful but not essential, and on the other axis from day to day operational to intended for future strategic impact (Figure 1.5).

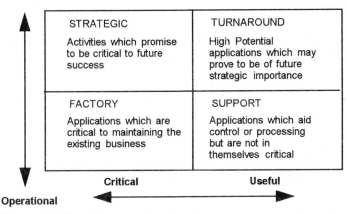

Figure 1.5 Classification of applications

The user matrix

Each of these areas has its own type of user. Similar matrices can be drawn up to analyse the needs and functions of these end users. In Figure 1.6, users form a continuum ranging from end users with limited interaction, through users who have flexible needs and considerable discretion, to users at the very highest levels who plan, initiate and drive new applications. The other axis shows types from isolated applications to company wide systems.

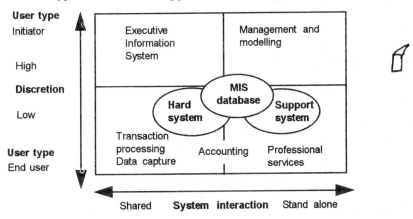

Figure 1.6 User/application matrix

According to this analysis, innovative ideas can be expected from the two upper quadrants. Users involved in the 'hard systems' area will generate ideas but these will in the main be for incremental improvements, slightly better operating procedures or closer matching of client demand. Users in the 'service systems' quadrant will be looking for ways to automate existing systems rather than proposing radical new approaches. In the centre of the user action space is the MIS function which serves both the transaction processing and professional services sectors. Most sizeable organisations have reached the stage of providing a centralised database to support the mainstream 'factory' functions and many have integrated most of the professional services functions as well. However, the strategic function is typically poorly provided for and the management and modelling quadrant in practice consists almost entirely of non integrated applications outside the main database.

Forces driving change

Figure 1.7 shows an alternative view of the data in Figure 1.6, emphasising the forces propelling systems demand.

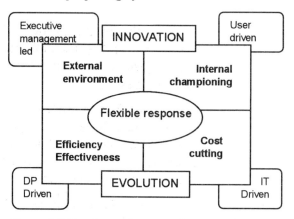

Figure 1.7 The forces that propel systems demand

Transaction processing systems are characterised by a drive towards efficiency. The effectiveness of the systems in this quadrant is largely a reflection of the quality of the data processing department. These systems will be the major concern of the DP department and changes to the system will be driven by DP department initiatives.

The **professional services** sector is characterised by a constant need for cost cutting and the most common cause of change is likely to be shifts in the price and functionality of IT products. Cheaper hardware, communications products and innovative software packages make possible the computerisation and automation of existing procedures.

The **management and modelling sector** is user driven, characterised by product champions. These can be specially set up project teams or individual managers developing new ideas on their personal machines. The applications in the area tend to arise from one individual's attempts to do something better, quicker, cheaper, differently. Applications are experimental, ad hoc, often the result of serendipity and are not always properly thought through.

Initiatives in the **Executive quadrant** are instigated by senior managers taking a personal interest in IT matters and accustomed to thinking strategically. However, these initiatives are not always the result of conscious planning efforts. They are often responses to external threats.

Portfolio analysis: changing the emphasis

If the analyst considers all existing and potential applications in the matrix, then a reassessment is needed to align resources with the demands of each type of application and its users.

One of the first outcomes of this analysis is the realisation that IT applications can no longer be supplied on demand, nor are they just a function of resource availability. Rather, they need to be justified in terms of their actual or potential contribution to the organisation's mission.

Another common observation is that the strategy quadrant as a whole has too little support. IS departments' efforts and resources have in the past concentrated in the lower two quadrants, computerising factory and support functions only. Usually there is little systematic support for strategic functions and only patchy support for activities in the turnaround sector.

Analysis of applications in the turnaround quadrant usually reveals first of all a surprising total number of current applications, and secondly that a few applications take the lion's share of the resources allocated to that sector. The large number of applications in this sector arise as a result of their being developed by individual managers with minimum resources on standalone computers. Without matrix analysis most of these small, potentially valuable applications would be considered as outside the direct control of the IS function, and therefore invisible.

A further consideration is that although future strategies are heavily dependent on innovative use of IT, they are being left to senior management who typically are poorly briefed on new technology, have little personal experience of computing and receive little in the way of direct support from the IS function. This finding shows little has changed since Aguilar's early work (Aguilar, 1977).

Dynamic applications

It will be apparent that an application which is currently a support function could in time become critical to the organisation. Or that what was once a leading strategic application will in time be adopted as standard by the whole industry and become a factory application. This means that any applications development plan is really a dynamic system with applications migrating from one area to another over time.

This in turn means that applications in different quadrants will have different attributes and different support needs. Some applications are primarily for users who are offered no discretion in their use. Other application users can chose to use or not use them, and can use them in different ways. Again some applications are designed to be shared and some are intended for standalone use.

An interesting analysis can be made by putting applications into a matrix using these axes.

Anthony's pyramid correctly points out that people at the top have more discretion than people at the bottom. In DP terms, people up the hierarchy are more likely to initiate application requests than those lower down, and will have more power to insist on some sort of delivery. Who then initiates requests at the lower levels, especially since IT knowledge is often quite limited?

Portfolio analysis budgeting

Each current development can be mapped into one of the quadrants and an estimate made of the cost so far and the likely total spending.

This gives another opportunity to balance the actual portfolio against the organisation's stated aims. It also raises the question of how much should be spent in each area and whether the IT budget is adequate overall.

Education as a portfolio response: educating the end users

One consequence of corporate computing is that the DP department or the IS department inevitably finds itself in the business of educating users. The need for training end users has never been in doubt. Where end users are operating an isolated, stand alone system, the amount of knowledge they need is relatively small, essentially just enough to carry out their own particular task. All they need is some basic computer training.

But where you have any form of corporate wide systems, the knowledge level requirements increase exponentially. If users do not have the right background information about commercial processes, about the products, about the procedures associated with their own job content, they will be unable to use the information system properly. And these information system failures are always blamed on the IS department.

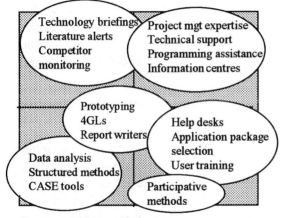

Figure 1.8 The analyst's options

Applications development support and control

Given that there are different forces driving each of the quadrants, how are they to be supported by the DP department and how are they to be controlled? The appropriate response will depend on the needs of each development activity. Figure 1.8 summarises some of the options open to an analyst working within a portfolio framework.

IS responses and tools

The first thing which should be apparent is that there is no one response appropriate to every situation. IS departments need to be flexible in their practices and be willing to provide totally new facilities to their clients.

17

Serving the strategic sector

The least well provisioned area is that of strategic policy setting and applications. Information systems designers need to provide executives with details of the factors influencing strategic use of IS. These include publicising the capabilities of the technology, the economics of using the technology, the feasibility of application ideas, the availability of skills and the potential to improve organisational effectiveness (Ward *et al.*, 1990)

At present computerised support for this sort of information is almost totally absent. Few organisations provide any sort of enabling technology for their executive such as access to remote databases or regular reviews of the current system capabilities. The requirement to provide information to board members is largely ignored. If organisations are to get the most from their senior managers, then the analyst must adopt a much more proactive approach.

Executives

Executives should get a regular series of technology briefings as a matter of course, to keep them abreast of broad developments in IT. The IS function must take responsibility for eliminating the ad hoc nature of executive data gathering. Stubbact (1982) found that managers were handicapped in scanning the environment when dealing with concerns outside their own area of expertise. This means the analyst must take responsibility for conducting systematic literature searches, sifting the press and media generally for items relevant to the organisation and making these available in non directive fashion to senior executives. A specific charge on the IS function should be to monitor the activities of competitors, to watch for announcements of hardware contracts and statements of intent for example. A watching brief is needed to make sure that competitors do not achieve strategic dominance in IT. Regular reports and items of particular interest would be provided to senior management. Similarly, reported case studies of successful IT innovation need to be circulated to build up a background awareness.

Management

The needs of the management and modelling sector are different. The population of non-professional developers needs an input of professional systems expertise. The IS response should consist of identifying and monitoring applications. Many of the efforts of non-professional developers are not cost effective and middle managers waste large amounts of their time developing computer applications, particularly programming spreadsheets and personal databases. These need to be evaluated early on and either put on a professional footing or killed off. Viable projects should be supported and managed like any other IS function. If programmers are needed they should be supplied; if project management techniques are missing these should be applied. Worthwhile applications will be resourced, the others will be monitored until they prove viable or are abandoned.

Professional services managers

The boundary between product champions and senior professional services sector managers is very blurred. A consistent trend is towards computer adoption in all professional services areas. Managers in personnel, marketing, finance consistently complain of poor service from the DP function. Much of this is due to the DP department's view of the users in this section. Users were typically minimally skilled in IT and had either only a vague idea of what they wanted or insisted that they wanted specific commercial applications and nothing else. In many cases the DP department was unwilling or unable to give support to users who had instigated computerised applications on their own initiative. Even where the user department was using in house applications, users generally felt that the level of support supplied was inadequate.

The appropriate responses for this sector include the provision of help desks to give users a first line of support for their packaged applications and to handle gaps in user knowledge. At higher level, larger organisations can provide Information Centres where professional managers can go for advice on purchasing hardware, software policy and IT options. User problems tend to be ill structured, set around complex procedures and outcomes tend to have high impact on staff working procedures. Where an in-house development is required, the most appropriate response in this sector appears to favour participative design techniques.

There is also a high degree of overlap in this sector with the provision of centralised database. Service systems applications tend to be 'information rich' and highly suitable to a database approach. The use of participative methodologies will include the use of rapid prototyping of service applications, the provision of fourth generation languages and report generators so data can be made available on a self service basis.

Transaction processing sector

The needs of the transaction processing sector more nearly accords the 'traditional' view of data processing and traditional methods are the best response. The number of users in this sector tends to relatively small, with well defined and limited data needs. The information needs of an invoice production system are well defined so do not required extensive prototyping, a payroll application does not bring up enough user interaction to merit

19

participative methods, and the output requirements of an inventory tracking system can be standardised.

These specifications are ideal for the application of 'hard' systems methodologies so the correct response is the adoption of structured systems analysis methods supported by CASE tools to provide a flexible working environment.

The challenge of the future

This chapter has tried to show that the work of the analyst and systems designer must be dictated by the objectives of the organisation and not by any particular technology or methodology. The analyst can expect to operate in an environment even more volatile than in the past. Developments in the Data Processing area of applications will see improved hardware, software, and methodologies. These will offer the opportunity to improve the efficiency of basic transaction processing.

Developments in MIS will include restructuring of databases, soft information applications, ways of turning vague requirements into workable solutions, and increased application of the intangible benefits of information technology.

The greatest challenge will come from applying IT in the SIS area. There is as yet no methodology for applying strategic thinking through the application of IT. There are many case studies to learn from but applications will continue to depend on the experience and flair of trained analysts and designers. However, the analyst must be a team player. Executive management will make the decisions on IS and IT. The primary concern on every application proposal will be to assess the impact on the organisation. The challenge will be to assess the importance of IT opportunities in business terms.

Analysts can expect to work in each of the three applications areas for many years to come. If they are to play their part in initiating, controlling and developing future applications they must learn the tools of their trade. That is what the remainder of this book sets out to teach.

Further reading

McFarlan, W. and McKenney, J. (1983) Corporate Information Systems Management. Irwin Inc. Homewood, Illinois.

Nolan, R. (1979) Managing the crisis in data processing,. Harvard Business Review, March/April pp 115-126.

Ward, J., Griffiths, P. and Whitemore, P. (1990) Strategic Planning for Information Systems. Wiley, Chichester.

Wiseman, C. (1988) Strategic Information Systems. Pub. Irwin, Homewood, Ill.

Chapter 2 Business analysis

The analyst's job

The systems analyst is a skilled worker whose principal function is to design and implement computer based solutions to business problems, normally involving the high speed processing of data and information. There are no laid down descriptions of precisely what a systems analyst should do and there are no formal qualifications which a person must have before they can call themselves an analyst. Originally the analyst's problems were those associated with high volume transaction processing such as calculating and printing out electricity bills or recording customer orders. Analysts then turned their attention to more complex problems such as inventory control and human resource management, gradually tackling more and more difficult applications until today there is virtually no area of business operations where the analyst's knowledge will not be applied.

Modern business computer systems, all of which are designed by systems analysts, include real time banking, personnel records, stock allocation, automatic reordering of goods, home shopping, word processing, emergency services despatch, management accounting, information systems and a wealth of other applications.

In different organisations there are different expectations of what an analyst will be responsible for. Rather than try to provide a list of activities which an analyst carries out it is easier to consider how an analyst gets involved in a common task such as converting an administrative process that is handled manually to one that is computerised.

Analysis and design task cycle

Except in very small companies, a systems analyst seldom works alone. Our analyst is more likely to be part of a systems team who share out the work between them, according to their own specialist skills and knowledge. The team is headed by a project leader who assumes overall responsibility for the project and who reports on progress directly to senior management or to a steering committee. The steering committee is made up of function managers and specialist advisors who dictate the general outlines or 'terms of reference' of a project and who monitor the progress made.

The task cycle usually begins when a manager in an organisation recognises that there is a degree of inefficiency in an operation and further recognises that there is a possibility that the application of a computer might be the way to solve the it.

The manager's problem must first be clearly described and precisely defined. It is then presented to the systems analyst for consideration. Not all problems can be solved by computerisation and so one of the first tasks of the analyst will be to advise the manager whether a computer solution is possible, or whether a different approach is called for.

If it looks as if the problem could be tackled by computer then the analyst carries out an initial study, a **feasibility study**, to determine whether using a computer would in fact be worth while. For example, if the value gained from installing a computer is less than the total cost of installing it, there would be no business case for it and a computerised solution would not be feasible.

During the feasibility study the analyst looks at the existing system to determine how and where it is going wrong. This is done by studying the work flows, talking to staff, questioning experienced workers etc., until the analyst has a clear idea of the difficulties. At this point the analyst will have formed an opinion as to whether the problem can be satisfactorily solved or not, and if so which of the range of possible solutions should be studied in more depth. A detailed account of how a feasibility study is done is given in Chapter 5.

When the feasibility study has been completed the analyst will formally present the findings of the study to the management, who will decide whether to continue or not. If the decision is to continue, in other words if the feasibility study has shown that a computerised solution will be feasible, the analyst does a much larger version of the feasibility study, a **full systems study.** This may take many months to complete and involves the analyst in the same work as for the feasibility study - fact finding, recording, analysing and summarising - but in greater depth.

Once the full systems study has been completed the analyst will be able to prepare a complete **systems specification,** a solution to the problem. This is a description of the proposed new computer system in great detail; it specifies what the system will do, how it will do it, the machinery needed, the programs which will be required, the time scale involved, and a list of the costs and benefits expected for the project.

If this is accepted by the management, the next step is to turn the proposed design into reality. The analyst gives the specification of what the program must do to the chief programmer, who is responsible for actually writing the

23

programs. The hardware specification is given to the chosen computer manufacturer who will supply the computer equipment needed. The analyst also ensures that accommodation is made ready for installation of the computer. Next, a check is made to ensure that the existing files and data are in a form suitable for easy changeover to the new system. The analyst must also make certain that all those likely to be in any way affected by the new system are kept fully informed as the project progresses.

When the programming team have completed their work the analyst has the responsibility of devising tests to check that the programs do what they are supposed to, both when run singly and when run in conjunction with other programs in the suite. A **program suite** is a number of programs, each performing different tasks, but which together can solve a particular problem. The speed of response of the system also has to be checked and all the hardware tested in position to ensure faultless running.

Simultaneously the analyst will have been supervising the preparation of documentation for the system and will have been supervising the conversion of the data files ready for changeover. Operator training, supervisor training and liaison with other affected departments will also be done as the project nears completion and changeover day approaches.

Once the system is changed over from old to new the analyst will supervise the initial few weeks running to ensure that the new system is performing up to specification, and deal with any of the inevitable small faults found. When the management is satisfied that the new system is running well the analyst's job is finished.

The analyst's environment

In many cases the design may be undertaken by an individual who is not a professional information systems worker at all, and just wants to solve one problem to satisfy their own needs. The situation for the analyst working in a small company or in a small data processing (DP) section is rather different from that applying in a large company as described above.

In many small companies one person might combine the job of analyst, programmer and even DP manager, so the idea of a whole team designing a new system (as happens in large companies) does not arise. This raises very great problems for systems design and implementation.

Where there are only one or two staff available for systems development there is often no ready access to technical expertise. In a larger organisation there will be a much larger pool of experience to draw from. In small companies, staff will have little opportunity to specialise and so will not have the same depth of detailed knowledge as their counterparts in larger companies.

When systems building staff have other DP responsibilities besides systems analysis, they will be unable to devote their full time attention to a particular problem. They will take much longer to arrive at a solution, which may possibly be a poorer one. It is likely that the system design (the solution proposed) will be much more affected by the short term factors and short term goals. With limited resources, the smaller company may impose financial constraints on the system designer as well.

A feature of small organisations is that they are generally much less formally managed than large ones. For the analyst this means that the problems may be ill defined, objectives may be unclear, and there may be no management guidelines available because busy managers cannot find the time to participate in the designing of the new system. This can be made worse by the fact that the management of many small companies is relatively unsophisticated as far as computers are concerned, with little or no knowledge of computing. This makes communicating ideas difficult and slows down decision making.

It frequently happens that a small company is computerising because of rapid growth. This often means that goals are not clearly defined, procedures adapt to changing situations in a haphazard way and company size and structure are in a constant state of change. This in turn means that there are fewer formal systems or well laid down procedures, so they become more difficult to analyse. Additionally, small businesses pose problems because they are often highly specialised businesses with highly specific problems for which few standard solutions are available.

The analyst's skills

From the descriptions given of the work of an analyst in both large and small companies, it should be apparent that a competent analyst is a highly trained person who needs mastery of a number of different fields.

The analyst must have:

- Technical knowledge of all hardware that is currently available and its performance characteristics

- Familiarity with the software and languages that the programmers will be using

- The ability to use established techniques in new and imaginative ways when creating a design

- A comprehensive knowledge of current business practice in a wide variety of industries

- The ability to communicate complex ideas to senior staff and top management, who may have little experience of these areas

- The self discipline needed to follow a methodical approach, but also enough flexibility to take advantage of unexpected opportunities

- The ability to interact successfully with staff at all levels when investigating an existing system, and to be able to deal with any misgivings or opposition arising in a constructive way

Because of the very wide experience required in the job, the position of systems analyst is usually a fairly senior one in the organisation. Most working analysts have either been programmers of long experience, or general managers or accountants who learned the fundamentals of data processing and combined this with a detailed knowledge of business and its processing needs.

Successful analysts have come from many other types of background, of course. The only fundamental characteristic shared by all is the ability to think clearly and logically about a problem and to be able to communicate clearly. This means being able to separate the general from the particular, and being able to recognise patterns occurring in a mass of detail, which may reveal a problem, or suggest a solution.

As well as the personal qualities which the analyst brings to the job, every analyst must also undertake training to develop further their knowledge and experience, and so their effectiveness. This may be informal, learn as you go training, or formal off site classroom based instruction. What ever the method, the analyst can expect to receive training in most of the following areas at some point in their career:

- Specific knowledge of the business process involved by working in a variety of business sectors, both computerised and non computerised

- Updates on computer technology, file design, storage, security, etc.

- Updates on new software, packages and languages, familiarisation with new methods and techniques

- Technical skills, such as. drawing flowcharts and data flow diagrams, and cost benefit analysis

26

- Presentation skills such as. report writing, documentation standards, and oral presentation skills

- Communication skills, such as interviewing techniques, questionnaire design, output design, political skills, interpersonal skills, and how to motivate and manage staff

The organisational framework

There are three main functional areas in any DP set up: systems administration, programming and operations.

Systems

The systems section is responsible for the design and implementation of new systems and the planned changes of existing systems. It is also responsible for the smooth running of the entire system and often offers sophisticated help desk facilities to end users and delivers regular training sessions. The section is normally relatively small in numbers but has highly qualified staff.

Systems administration includes data base administration and the communications and network administration. It is the responsibility of this section to produce an **application specification,** a detailed description of the actions that are to be performed by the computer, for each new application. This specification is handed over to the programming manager to be turned into a form which the computer can recognise, i.e. to be encoded in a particular language.

Programming

This section has the responsibility of turning the specification provided by the systems section into workable procedures which the computer can carry out. Programming is normally a team affair with a chief programmer who is in overall charge of the programming project, and who breaks the programming task down into manageable segments called **modules.** These modules are given to the programmers who convert them into a coded computer language and who eventually link all the program segments together into a complete working suite.

Strictly speaking, programming is the design of a series of steps, called an **algorithm,** which when carried out will arrive at a solution to a given problem. Translating those steps into a form the computer can understand is properly called **coding** (a much simpler task than design). The personnel in

27

the programming section therefore have a wide range of skill levels, from those very skilled who create the algorithms to those of a much more junior level who merely code the steps already given to them into a computer language, such as COBOL or BASIC, which the computer can understand.

Operations

This section employs the largest number of people in the DP department and is the section concerned with the day today running of the computer. Staff here are employed in three basic functions: data preparation, data control, and computer room duties.

Data preparation
Most data presented to the computer for processing is in a form which is not immediately suitable for use. It first has to be extracted, checked and converted into **machine sensible** form, a form in which it can be fed into the computer.

Traditionally, data arrived on paper documents and was then read by a human operator who entered the data on to punched cards using a special card punch machine. Because of the high risk of error in this process, due to fatigue or inattention, another operator was employed to check each card by re reading the original document and re keying the data, and so the job was very labour intensive, time consuming and expensive. Nowadays data is more likely to be transferred onto a floppy disk through a workstation keyboard, but the principle remains the same.

Auxiliary machine staff (also called ancillary staff) operate machines such as paper trimmers, envelope stuffers and other non input devices.

Data control
In the early days of computing all processing of data within an organisation was done with a central computer; all the work had to be taken to the computer site, processed there and then returned to the originating department. The importance of ensuring that all work was carried out in the correct sequence and that nothing was overlooked or submitted twice gave rise to the job of data control supervisor. Duties include ensuring that periodic data such as weekly workers' time sheets, or physical stock check figures, is received on time.

The data control supervisor also maintains a log of work sent to the Data Preparation section to ensure its safe and speedy return. Other duties include the batching of documents and maintenance of control accounts, batch totals, document counts, and the development of operating schedules to maximise computer throughput.

Computer room duties

Generally known as 'Operations', these cover a very wide range of activities. A computer operator is someone who actually works in day today contact with the computer. Operators get the machinery set up ready to run jobs, mount and remove tapes and disks, and respond to messages from the computer console. They also have to load and unload the printers, and periodically check the output print quality. Control and reordering of stationery and consumables, logging operations and job completion, and organising staff cover are also done by the operations section.

Operators are not just button pushers, however. They must be able to work closely with many people, including programmers, analysts and the client department staff. They are often able to correct erroneous data without referring back to the users. They need technical knowledge of the hardware and software so that they can fix minor malfunctions. They often also need to be able to explain problems succinctly to external experts, often over the telephone.

Increasingly, with the spread of distributed computing, operators are becoming involved with **data communications** and many have specialist knowledge in this area. Another common specialisation is **librarian**, who is responsible for the security of all stored data and programs.

The analyst as facilitator

A basic problem in any data processing situation is communication between the person owning a problem and the person with the ability to implement a solution. The communication gap is therefore between manager and programmer. The analyst's efforts should be directed towards getting a clear, direct understanding between them.

In order to do this, analysts use their skills in investigation and their experience of similar businesses to form a logical view of the problem and construct a generalised model for the manager to check and refine. As the model is discussed and examined, it moves closer and closer to what the manager requires, but is always guided by the analyst's technical knowledge of what is possible or feasible in the circumstances. At every step the data requirements, the files needed and the needs of any other users involved are added into the model.

Eventually the model contains a full specification of what is required to be done, virtually identical to how it would have looked if it had been produced by the analyst alone, but incorporating the manager's views fully, and in a clear, understandable format.

This model contains all the information needed to design the new system, and is produced in a standardised format familiar to the programmer. It can therefore be used unchanged as a specification for the proposed application and can be passed on straight to the programmer for coding and testing. By forming this intermediate step the manager is effectively able to communicate needs directly to the programmer.

In summary the problem is discussed between analyst and manager; the analyst seeks information for the model from the manager, from users and other sources; the manager and users agree the design with analysts; and the analyst finally agrees the design with the programmer. The analyst's role can therefore be seen as a bridge between the user, the manager and the programmer.

Conceptual approaches

For many people the analyst is seen as an expert who can go into any company, establish the cause of a problem, specify the best solution and then move on. This is far from the truth. In modern companies the problems are just too complex for this sort of approach to work. The analyst's role is better seen as that of a change agent rather than an infallible expert.

The person in a company who knows most about its problems and their possible solutions is not the analyst, who may have only a few weeks experience of that particular department's duties, but the managers and operators in day to day control. The analyst can take two approaches in this situation. Either the analyst can try to extract from the manager as much information as possible, as quickly as possible, in order to design the system. Or, better still, the analyst can help the manager and staff to design their own system and so get the full benefit of knowledge accumulated over a large number of years.

The modern approach to systems analysis favours this second approach. Analysts have developed a range of tools and methodologies to deal with the problem. The actual working of these is covered in later sections of this book but the philosophy behind them can easily be appreciated.

Integrative computing environments

The first computer applications were functionally oriented; each application was computerised to perform one main function only. If you wished to computerise the payment of wages then you developed a pay-roll application. If that was a success and it was decided to computerise the invoice production function then an order entry and invoicing application programme was developed. If later a stock control system was wanted then another separate series of programs was devised and written.

It was only once computer systems had matured and there were a lot of application programs running simultaneously that the error in this original approach became apparent. The functions of pay-roll and invoicing and stock control had traditionally been kept separate in the previous manual systems. However, treating them separately in computerised applications allowed errors to creep in since they really were very closely interlinked.

Consider the following example. The production of invoices, as goods are sold, will have the effect of reducing the quantity of free stock in a company's warehouse. This will very often also cause orders to be issued for more stock to be produced. This in turn will mean engaging workers on production of those goods. The goods will be added to stock as soon as they are finished and available for sale. In manufacturing industry workers are often paid according to the quantity of goods produced and so this production will be reflected directly in the earnings of the workers. This in turn has implications for the pay-roll. In this way there are often very complicated interactions within systems which must be taken into account. Errors arising in one area will inevitably affect the accuracy of processing in other areas. In an integrated computing environment programs will automatically update files to reflect the latest position

Designing systems piecemeal (the independent applications approach) leads to the danger of **suboptimisation.** This is where the objectives of the various subsystems are pursued at the expense of the organisation as a whole. A system can be designed with each of its parts operating at high efficiency but with overall performance relatively inefficient. For example the sales department of a company will want to be able to sell small lots of goods for immediate delivery on credit in order to maximise sales and income. However, this might only be possible by holding large stocks and providing extra finance. This is expensive and can in fact be counter productive. In this way optimising the sales manager's performance might lead to overall inefficiency.

Similarly the production manager might want to manufacture long runs of identical items because production costs are lower if large quantities are made. If this is done the stock holding costs go up which would affect profitability adversely and limit the variety of items available at any one time, which could in turn reduce sales.

Systems concept

Another concept which most analysts now accept is that of the systems approach to systems analysis. The systems approach to design can be defined as a way of investigating and designing which recognises that applications are interdependent sub systems embedded within a larger organisational, political and economic framework, and that no sub system should be developed in isolation. It focuses attention on the overall goals of the company at the outset and gives full consideration to the problems of fitting sub systems, both technical and human, smoothly into the overall organisational framework.

Design philosophies

Every analysis and design exercise uses a **methodology**, a series of steps leading to some desired outcome. The methodology itself depends on some basic assumptions, expressed as a design philosophy. These philosophies, or **paradigms**, may be clearly stated or may be hidden behind the detailed steps driving the methodology.

The paradigms held by analysts may be so fundamental to their way of thinking that they are not even recognised by the people themselves. For example, many analysts unconsciously uphold the idea of the 'technological imperative'. This states that technology means efficiency, and technology will inevitably replace other means of working. This common belief leads to the opinion, almost automatically, that anyone opposing the implementation of technology is being 'resistant' and should be over ruled. Other analysts take the opposite view, that technology must be subservient to people and only be introduced into an organisation as and when people feel comfortable with it. Every methodology contains one or more paradigm values. When deciding which design approach is appropriate the analyst needs to be aware of the paradigms implicit in each approach.

One way of bringing out the underlying paradigms is to build a matrix analysis, using the methodological basis as one axis and the degree of 'hardness' as the other axis. Application requirements can range from very detailed and highly structured to loosely defined, almost vague requests for

32

change. Strongly structured, well defined applications are termed 'hard' and are attacked with 'hard' methodologies. Applications where the user's procedures are difficult to define, such as selecting applicants for a job, or where there is no general agreement as to the causes of a problem, are known as 'soft'. Not because they are easy, but because there are so many non quantifiable elements in them and it is difficult to get a firm specification agreed.

There are two fundamental approaches to analysis. One approach, 'data flow' or 'process' oriented, sees organisations as made up of procedures or processes. These link up with each other in complex interactions but each has its own set information requirements. Another view thinks of organisations as containing 'stores' of data which can be called on to support particular processing procedures. The first view sees applications as organisations of data in restless motion and aims to hold the minimum amounts of data consistent with fuelling that movement. New applications cause new items of data to be added to the existing data. The 'stores of data' or database view tries to design ways of holding data such that all current applications can be supported and any future application can also be supported without altering the existing data stores. In practice no methodology is purely one or the other.

Combining these two spectrums provides a simple classification scheme to determine which methodology or combination of methodologies to use in particular circumstances.

Design methodologies

Some of the major methodologies that an analyst designer should have experience in are described below.

TACS

This stands for Tradition and Common Sense and is the methodology most used in practice. It is described in the chapter on the Systems Life Cycle. TACS is mostly a hard systems methodology but does have substantial potential for incorporating 'soft' aspects due to the iterative nature of the feasibility study. The use of the feasibility study section should ensure that adverse organisational reaction will not undermine the proposed changes later in the life cycle. The methodology is definitely in the hard area because it has very little in the way of participation in design by those directly affected.

Structured systems analysis

Structured systems analysis (SSA) suffers from the same defect. It allows for no real user participation or input other than as a source of data for design purposes. SSA is a much more formal version of TACS and so is shown further along the 'hard' axis. In most versions (there are several branded versions) the emphasis is on describing the activities of the organisation in data flow diagrams first and then determining the data model, so it is shown in the upper right quadrant of the diagram.

Information engineering

In its full version Information Engineering starts with detailed long term planning. A good description is found in Finkelstein, (1992).

The basis of the Information Engineering approach is that in every organisation different information is used at different levels. At the lowest level is **operational information** relating to transactions. This level is very well served by computer systems. At the next level up from this is **tactical information** which allows managers to monitor progress through reports and summaries generated from the operational data. Top management needs a higher level of information; this is known as **strategic information.** This cannot be derived directly from operational information. Every organisation has to interact with its environment: no company can afford to ignore the activities of its competitors or fail to anticipate future legislation for example. Strategic information has to be gathered from sources outside the organisation.

The organisation first has to identify its long term strategic goals and objectives. Once these have been defined the company then determines the ideal procedures it will need to allow it to achieve those goals. (The organisation's newly identified long term goals are unlikely to coincide exactly with its current goals, and so the ideal procedures will differ from the existing procedures.) Subgoals are then identified, the achievement of which will allow long term goals to be achieved, and so on. The analyst draws up a specification for the processes and procedures needed to support each subgoal, the decisions made within that procedure, the information needs of the procedure, the links to other planned procedures and so on until the future information needs of the whole organisation have been laid out. Each existing subsystem is then modified in turn until it matches the ideal subsystem within the overall design. Obviously if this is done correctly there will be no integration problems. In practice it is very hard to make this approach work successfully.

Information Engineering is strongly data model oriented. Many branded versions exist and all rely heavily on CASE (computer aided software engineering) tools. These automate the analysis and recording of the corporate

34

model and typically provide integrated tools for data flow diagrams (DFDs) and data analysis.

The database approach

Data modelling is the generic name for several related methodologies which produce a model of the company's information needs by considering its activities and recording the data items involved in each activity. The data model is the foundation for database design.

An organisation's activities can be conceptualised as consisting of 'clumps' of data circulating round the organisation through predefined channels. This data is always in motion and can be tracked from process to process where it undergoes various operations and transformations. An alternative conceptual view of an organisation's information needs regards corporate data as static. These are know repectively as the Process Based view and the Data Based view. These views give rise to two different but equivalent ways of producing a data model.

The process based approach

Transactions typically carry with them more data than is strictly necessary to process them. For instance, in a purchasing application where a customer orders a large quantity of goods which results in the need for a reorder there is no necessity to include the customer number on the reorder transaction. Similarly, in a pay-roll system although each worker will have a supervisor there is normally no need to include the supervisor's name on the weekly time sheets.

If this unnecessary detail can be safely eliminated, time in entering the transaction is saved, as is space for storing the transactions. The result is a compact efficient system which stores only essential data with no redundancy and allows easy access to all information relevant to the application.

The process based approach concentrates on one application at a time and asks the question 'What is the minimum data needed to support this decision, or to process this transaction?' Modelling data from in this way is know as 'bottom up' modelling.

Normalisation is classed as a 'bottom up' approach because it starts by locating every individual piece of data currently used in all the processes. The data model is then 'built up' by gathering the various elements together, and subjecting them to an analysis based on their relationships to each other. The result is efficient data storage structures which will hold all the data in the minimum of space. The normalised data model becomes the the basis for the database design.

Normalisation is normally used in an evolutionary approach where many separate applications are developed with a view to later integration. Typically a company uses the integrated, bottom up approach where it needs to computerise a series of transaction processing activities, for example invoice production and pay-roll calculation. Each activity is developed complete, with its own data stores, but in such a way that once other transaction based applications are finished, programs and data stores will be compatible, and higher level management information can be extracted from several application areas simultaneously by combining them. Sub systems are introduced as and when required, but always within the framework of the overall plan. This process can be repeated: as one application is implemented other applications can be introduced, maintaining compatibility all the time.

Data based view

An alternative conceptual view leads to a 'top down' method of data modelling called Data Analysis. Instead of tracking data moving from process to process, data stores are designed as independent objects. Groups of logically related data elements are held in these 'data stores' ready to serve any process which may require access to the data. In this conceptual view processes take data from a store, perform some sort of operation on it, and then return the amended data to the same or a different data store. If the data analysis is done properly then it is not necessary to know in advance what processes or programs will be required since the stores will be capable of supporting any future processing requirements. The methodology analyses organisational objects as either entities or relationships. An entity can be anything of interest to the organisation such as a customer or product. Entities are linked to each other by relationships. An invoice expresses a relationship between a customer and a product as it records the link created by one particular transaction. Data analysis takes each entity and identifies the data elements which logically need to be recorded. A customer for example must logically have some form of identifier, will have a name, an address,a credit limit and so on. An invoice must have a date, a value, a list of prices. These data elements can be determined independently of the actual processes. If you deal with customers and invoices then these data elements must exist. There is no need to rely on identifying the data elements currently used in the processes. The technique of data analysis applies a rigorous logic to the entities and relationships so that all relevant data elements are identified and all corporate processing rules can be supported. The advantage is that the analysis can start without first collecting all the data elements. Normalisation on the other hand cannot begin until all the data has been gathered.

The two approaches are really complementary. The final data model will be virtually identical whatever the initial modelling approach. In practice many analysts use one method to check on the other.

Information Engineering emphasises that any information system based only on an examination of internal transaction processing and functions will be unable to satisfy the requirements of all levels of management, no matter how well it is designed. Only by looking beyond the actual processing and considering the organisation's overall information requirements can you be sure of providing for all needs.

In addition, the fact that every organisation is inseparable from its environment means that it will be affected by, and have to react to, abrupt and unpredictable changes from the outside such as sudden changes in the requirements of its customers or changes in government legislation. The company can only react to changes in external forces on the basis of information available from within the organisation and since no one can know what changes will occur externally no one can say what information will or will not be required in future.

Soft systems analysis
The starting point of soft systems methodologies is that in every situation there is no one correct solution. In contrast, all the hard methodologies assume that there is a correct solution and set out to achieve it in their different ways.

The *Ethics methodology* is a way of formally assessing all the possible variations in changes in hardware configuration, software and the human element of information systems organisation. It is highly participative and does not assume the analyst will have the right answer or even any answer. Change only goes forward at the pace agreed with the staff involved and only to the extent that they agree with.

The *Checkland methodology* has a different focus. It adopts a soft systems approach to investigating the problem field. It is a rigorous methodology for questioning assumptions about the change situation, ensuring that the rights and perceptions of all participants are considered and of ensuring a good fit between the proposed solution and the organisational environment.

Prototyping

The philosophy of prototyping can be adapted to any methodology. In its ideal form an end user with no computing knowledge brings a business problem to a systems professional. The systems person will discuss the problem briefly and gain an outline of the problem. This is used to produce a crude solution using database tables to hold the main data elements with some rudimentary processing done in a fourth generation language. The results are offered to the user in matter of hours. The user can see the results and comment on them, suggest changes, try out the processing and point out mistakes. The analyst incorporates this feedback into the next version of the program, gradually improving it until it meets the user's needs completely.

Prototyping avoids the 'right answer, wrong problem' syndrome from the start. The methodology involves a great deal of interaction between user and analyst with emphasis on educating both. This enforces the soft element since the user is effectively designing a personal, custom made solution. The database and fourth generation language provide elements of process and data analysis approaches.

Exercises

1. It is said that modern businesses could not operate without computers. How true do you think this is? Make a list of all the different ways in which computers are used in the following businesses:

> A hotel group
> A bank
> A supermarket chain
> An airline

2. Why might an analyst's job in a small company might be more difficult than in a large company?

3. What would be the absolute minimum data required to

> Order a taxi from home
> Instruct a taxi driver in the street
> Reserve a theatre ticket by phone
> Arrange routine servicing for a car?

Further reading

Colter, M.A. (1984) A comparative examination of systems analysis techniques. MIS Quarterly March 1984

Finkelstein, C. (1992) Information Engineering: Strategic Systems Development. Pub Addison-Wesley, Wokingham, England.

Mahmood, M.O. (1987) Systems development methods: A comparative investigation. MIS Quarterly September 1987

Naumann, J.D. and Jenkins, A.M. (1982) Prototyping: the new paradigm for systems development. MIS Quarterly September 1982

Wood-Harper, A., Antill, L. and Avison, D. (1985) Information Systems Definition; The multiview approach. Blackwell Scientific Publications, Oxford.

Chapter 3 The system development cycle

Steps in developing systems

The commonest method of systems design is still some variation on the traditional systems life cycle. Probably no individual analyst follows every step exactly as specified here but most developers acknowledge that this is the model underlying their approach to design.

At first sight the systems development cycle (Figure 3.1) looks a little daunting. But careful inspection will reveal that it can be broken down into more manageable chunks by considering it as a four-stage operation where the main stages are:

- Identify problem (project selection and definition
- Logical analysis
- Physical design
- Physical implementation

We will look at each stage and determine its purpose, the documentation associated with that stage and the approximate time spent on each stage when developing a typical application.

Stage 1: Project selection and definition

The purpose of this stage is to identify any business procedures which might benefit from computerisation, examine each of these in turn from the point of view of current operating efficiency and to choose the one which promises the best return in productivity for a deeper and more comprehensive study.

Identify the problem
Normally the systems analyst is not directly involved in problem selection. Usually a problem will be brought to the systems analyst by a member of the general management and together they will assess its suitability for computerisation. If at first sight it looks as if a computer solution could usefully be applied to the problem, the analyst will ask the manager to draw up a detailed request known as the terms of reference.

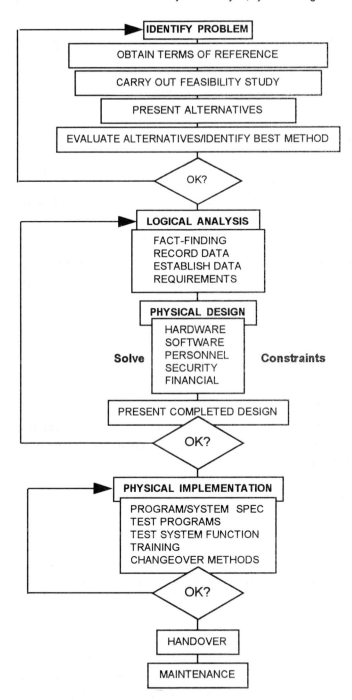

Figure 3.1 The systems development cycle

Obtain terms of reference

The terms of reference are needed by the analyst as formal approval for him to allocate the resources necessary to carry out a preliminary systems investigation. The terms of reference document also specifies clearly those areas of the business function which are to be included in the analyst's investigation and those which are to be left as they are. This preliminary investigation authorised by, and described in, the terms of reference is properly called a feasibility study.

Carry out feasibility study

As discussed earlier, the main purpose of the feasibility study is to investigate the proposed application described in the terms of reference in sufficient depth to be able to recommend to the general management, who usually have little knowledge of computing, whether it is worth continuing with the proposal or not.

The information resulting from the feasibility study is usually provided to the appropriate level of management in the form of a presentation. The analyst will describe the work done so far, and will publish a summary of the findings. At the end of the presentation the analyst will be expected to make a clear recommendation either to continue the project or to abandon it.

First management decision-point

Once management have listened to the presentation and studied the case made by the analyst, it is up to them to decide whether to continue with the proposed system or to abandon it altogether. Sometimes they may instruct the analyst to investigate a little deeper, or they may even revise the terms of reference and ask the analyst to begin a fresh feasibility study. If the decision is to press on with the proposed new system, then the analyst will proceed to the next stage.

Stage 2: Logical analysis

The purpose of the analysis phase is to produce a clear requirements specification showing what the newly designed or upgraded system is required to do in order to carry out its primary function efficiently and effectively. This is often called the logical analysis stage.

In order to produce a comprehensive specification the analyst must now embark on a lengthy and expensive full systems study. This is designed to give the analyst an in-depth appreciation of all aspects of the old system and to enable the analyst to determine the exact information processing needs of the application so that a logical model of the proposed system can be built.

Fact-finding methods
In order to carry out this investigation the analyst has a number of tools available to him which he will use as and where necessary. These include various flowcharts, decision tables, data-flow diagrams (see Chapter 6).

Recording the data
The full systems study is usually a major undertaking and very large quantities of data are generated by the analyst. In very large systems there will be a team of analysts whose work and findings must be carefully co-ordinated and recorded if duplication of effort is to be avoided and important data not lost in the sheer mass of data.

Analysing the data
A systematic approach to recording the data usually includes consideration of the sources of the data; as soon as a start is made on classifying the raw data then the analysing phase can begin. Very often the diagrams and charts used to record the data can also be used to analyse it and the work goes on in parallel. In other cases other types of data collected need separate analysis, for example the system's output documents. This analysis is continued until the analyst has a clear picture of all the data movements and data structures used in the application. This detailed knowledge is the foundation of the logical requirements specification used in the next phase.

Stage 3: Physical design

The purpose of the systems design stage is to develop a complete working system from the specification produced in the analysis stage. The physical design includes both the **hardware**, the computer equipment, and the **software**, the programs which cause the equipment to perform the specified functions and produce the required information output. This stage is often called the physical design stage.

Hardware
The exact hardware needs of the new system will be determined by the information collected in the previous phase and by estimating such things as file sizes, response times, input rates and output requirements. Depending on the particular application for which the system is intended, it may be necessary to order a new, fully-equipped computer hardware system if the organisation has none which is suitable; or it may only be necessary to purchase some additional processing power or storage capability if there is some existing hardware which can be added to; or there may be no need to increase the existing system at all.

Software

The analyst has the duty of designing all the programs needed to produce the exact output which the analysis stage specification requires. The analyst does not normally write the programs, but should have enough knowledge to know what it is possible to accomplish with standard software. The analyst also needs to specify in great detail the input and output layouts, as well as giving performance standards which the finished software must meet.

Personnel

The system design cannot be based solely on data needs and hardware efficiency considerations. Every successful system is a judicious blend of hardware, software and people. Due consideration must therefore be given to the effect that the proposed new system will have on existing staff. The designer must ensure that the personal and social needs of the staff who carry out day-today operations on the computer are looked after just as well as the needs of the ultimate users of the system are.

Security

All business procedures must have provisions built into them to guard against accidental disclosure and prevent unauthorised access to company information. The system designer must be aware of the security needs of the procedures which are to be computerised and must take care to include those needs in the new system. In addition, the fact that the new procedures are being run on a computer brings its own security problems and these too will have to be taken into account at the design phase.

Financial

Every new system must undergo a cost-benefit analysis to justify its continued development. As the detailed design phase proceeds it will be possible to make better and more detailed estimates of the final cost of the proposed system. As they become better defined, the analyst will be constantly evaluating the balance between the costs incurred and the ultimate benefits to be gained. Eventually this cost-benefit analysis will be presented to the management so that they can make an informed judgement on the continuation of the project.

There will always be more than one way of achieving the physical results which the specification requires. At the design phase the analyst will also be expected to investigate several different possible designs and to rank them according to the advantages, disadvantages and costs of each.

Completed design

The completed design will take the form of a large document, often running into hundreds of pages, in which the whole of the proposed new application is laid out in complete detail. It should be ready to be turned into a working system with the very minimum of further investigation needed.

The analyst's report this time will carry full details of the hardware needed, the recommended supplier, the programs to be written, the operating procedures and fully worked-out costs, as far as possible. It will also contain a realistic evaluation of the likely benefits to be gained in the first few years of the new system's operation.

Second management decision-point
The design phase is finalised by making a presentation to management, just as was done at the end of the feasibility study but the design phase presentation is of course very much more detailed and its recommendations will carry that much more weight. However, ultimate responsibility for continuing or abandoning the new project still lies with the management and not the analyst.

Stage 4: Implementation and maintenance

The purpose of the implementation stage is to turn the plans for the new system into a reality while ensuring a smooth, trouble-free changeover from the old system, and to ensure that all staff who will be directly affected by the changeover are properly trained in the new techniques.

The program specification
Once approval to go ahead and build the new system has been given the analyst and the chief programmer will get together and produce an implementation schedule for the software development process. The chief programmer will take responsibility for program completion and will normally sub-divide the total programming effort into smaller, more easily handled modules. These will be allocated to individual programmers who will actually write the lines of code in the chosen programming language.

System testing
While the programmers are getting on with the job of producing the working programs the analyst will be designing sets of test data which will be fed into the new programs to test their accuracy and efficiency. As each small module is tested and approved the completed modules will be linked together and then tested again to ensure correct interaction between the modules.

During the software development period the hardware will have been delivered. It too will be tested to ensure that its performance is up to expectations. The new programs will then be run several times on the new hardware with several different sets of test data until they can run without producing any errors, and at the correct speed of processing.

45

Eventually all the modules will have been tested individually, and in unison, and will have passed all the tests devised by the analyst. The programs are then ready to be tried out on real data.

Training

All this testing of course cannot be carried out without involving the systems personnel. They have to be trained to play their part in the testing and evaluation procedures of the new system. Training of other staff also has to start in this period. They must be ready when the time comes to change over to the new system.

The changeover procedure

Prior to the actual changeover a great deal of preliminary work will need to be done, one major part of which will be file conversion. It is unlikely that the records of the old system will either have the right contents or be in the right format for use in the new system so the analyst has to plan the conversion of the old records. In a large application with thousands of records this may take many months and so needs to be started well ahead of changeover.

Handover

Once the new system is ready for final testing it is usually run with real data from actual transactions at the same time that the old system is processing these same transactions. This process, called **parallel running**, allows a direct comparison of the results from the old system and the new so that any differences can easily be detected. It is normal for minor design changes to be made at this stage when the full system can be seen in operation. The process is continued until both the designers and the users of the new system are happy with the results.

When that time comes, the system is 'signed off' and responsibility for it passes from the systems analyst to the person who will supervise the day to day running of operations, usually the Data Processing Manager.

Maintenance

Every business works in an ever-changing environment. Every system, no matter how well designed, will eventually need to be altered to take account of changes in its operating environment. The process of making these minor alterations is called program maintenance. Individually such changes are small and infrequent, but over many years the cumulative effects of lots of small 'patches' will reduce the efficiency of the overall operation. As a result, at some point the performance of the system will be so bad that it becomes a candidate for a fresh analysis and redesign. And thus the whole cycle will begin again. This is known as the system life cycle (Figure 3.2).

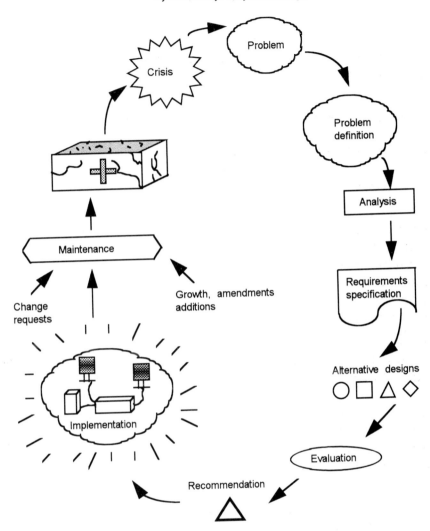

Figure 3.2 The system life cycle

Stage I outputs: project selection and definition

The primary output of this stage of the development life cycle is the feasibility report whose production signals the end of this phase. However, this is not the only documentation produced and most of the following would be found in any large project involving the application of systems analysis.

Problem definition
The problem definition document is drawn up by management. It will include:

Summary of problems being experienced

       Examples and evidence of poor performance
       Estimates of loss

Terms of reference

This is drawn up by management and the systems analyst. It will include:

       Primary objectives, system goals
       Boundaries and limits to investigation
       Constraints and resources available
       Preferred organisation and methodologies
       Minimum acceptable solution
       Optimum desired solution

Feasibility report

This is produced by the systems analyst. It includes:

       Restatement of the terms of reference
       Overview of investigation
       Summary of preliminary findings
       Summary of areas needing further investigation
       Outline design of several possible systems: cost-benefit rankings
       Recommended system: tentative hardware specification, project development plan, cost/benefit analysis
       Estimate of project completion time
       Estimate of resources required
       Assessment of risk factors

Feasibility evaluation report

This document is produced by management. Typically it includes:

       Report of discussions
       Requests for further information
       Preliminary budget allocation
       Staff secondment approval
       Approval/rejection recommendation

Stage 2 outputs: Logical system design specification

The primary output document will be a logical design specification from which the physical design can be built. In many applications the physical (hardware) and logical (software) specifications may be combined.

Responsibility for producing this document lies with the analyst although management and other non-computer department staff will be involved in providing the information upon which it is based. In addition the following may be produced:

Summaries and appendices of primary sources

> Interview transcripts
> Inspection results
> Staff notes
> Questionnaire results
> Document samples
> File utilisation analyses
> Procedure manuals
> Examples of source documents
> Document counts

Summaries and appendices of recording aids

> Graphs drawn from raw data, e.g. projected growth
> Procedure charts
> Gantt charts
> Flowcharts, flow process charts, etc.
> Document analysis grids

Detailed design documents

> Data-flow diagrams
> Logic flowcharts
> System flowcharts
> Data dictionary entries
> File contents listings
> File access requirements

Stage 3 outputs: *The physical design specification*

The physical design specification gives a complete description of the proposed new system and how it is to be built.

Hardware specification

> CPU (central processing unit) processors and speed
> Memory size
> Storage devices
> Printer specifications
> Data-capture equipment
> Communications equipment

Software specification

> Program descriptions
> System flowcharts
> Computer-fun flowcharts
> File and record layouts

Input and output data specification

> Document description and layout
> Input media
> Output media
> Controls and validation

Job specification

> Training schedules
> Operating procedures
> Changeover schedule

Final design evaluation

> Produced by management
> Contents:
> Report of discussions
> Requests for further information
> Confirmed budget allocation
> Personnel allocation
> Approval/rejection recommendation

Stage 4 outputs: implementation

The documents produced at the 4th stage will include the following:

Program specification

> Program documentation
> Program instructions
> Error messages
> Recovery procedures
> Security procedures

Detailed input and output

> Specimen documents
> Screen layouts

Operating instruction manuals

> Data preparation
> Operating
> User instructions
> Training manuals

File changeover

> List of affected files
> Changeover schedule
> Detailed transfer and checking procedures

Handover

> Test logs
> Acceptance document

Maintenance

> User change requests
> Management change authorisations

Time scales

Systems analysis is still a very inexact science and so it is difficult to state with certainty how long a project will take in total or how long will be spent on each of the individual stages. However, experience has shown that in any project the relative length of time spent on the component parts tends to be fairly constant, and the figures shown below can be taken as a reasonably accurate guide to current practice when using the traditional methodology.

Feasibility study: 5-10%
- Initial investigation

Analysis: 20-25%
- Finding, recording and
  analysing the data

Design: 20-25%
- Evaluating alternative strategies

Programming: 20-30%
- Coding and linking program
  modules

Implementation: 20-30%
- Testing, implementation and
  training

Further reading

Eliason, A. (1990) Systems Development: Analysis, Design and Implementation. Pub Scott, Foresman/Little, Brown. Glenview, Ill.

Flaaten, P., McCubbrey, D., O'Riordan, P. and Burgess, K.(1989) Foundations of Business Systems. Pub. The Dryden Press, Hinsdale, Ill.

Kendall, P. (1990) Introduction to Systems Analysis and Design: A structured approach. Pub Wm C. Brown, Dubuque IA.

Schultheis, R. and Sumner, M. (1992) Management information systems: The manager's view. Pub Irwin, Homewood, Ill.

Chapter 4 Project selection and definition

Suitability for computerisation

The systems life cycle starts with a problem definition. However, not all problems can or should be solved with a computer. In any business there will usually be more than one application which might benefit from computerisation. However, resources and time are always limited and it is not usually possible to do everything, so management has to choose which possible application to tackle first.

There are a number of criteria which can be applied to establish priorities. Depending on circumstances, management might choose to undertake the application which was

> Easiest
> Quickest
> Cheapest
> Most urgent
> Most profitable
> Most prestigious
> Most cost-effective
> Least disruptive

The correct choice of application will always depend on individual circumstances. It will often be a combination of two or more of the above, and is usually the result of compromise.

In general, the easiest areas for computerisation are procedures which have:

- Large number of similar transactions

- Very repetitive routines

- Defined and rigid formal procedures

- Well-defined interfaces with other systems

In general, applications which satisfy the four criteria given above will involve one or more of the following. They will:

- Require frequent access to stored information

- Require great accuracy in data processing

- Require high-speed data processing

- Require additional information processing in summary form for better quality decision-making

- Have rapidly expanding information to deal with

- Need a fast response to enquiries

- Are otherwise highly labour-intensive

- Involve complex mathematical or logical processes

Although the great majority of computerised applications fall into one or other of the categories listed above, you must always be careful to distinguish between the procedures that are easiest, and those which are most suitable for computerisation. For example, it would be very easy to computerise the procedures for paying out and balancing an office's petty cash book, but it is probably not worth doing and would be best left as a manual procedure.

Problems with computerisation

Just as there are factors which tend to make a system easy to computerise, there are also those which tend to make computerisation more difficult. The factors which make an application difficult to computerise are:

- Large data storage requirements, e.g. a picture library

- Very fast response needs, e.g. on airline bookings

- Very high security needs, e.g. banks

- Extensive communications needs, e.g. EDI (Electronic document interchange)

- Restrictive employment practices, e.g. newspapers, public utilities

- Unique systems, e.g. multicurrency payroll

- Severe environments, e.g. oil wells in very hot or cold areas

- Twenty-four hour availability, non-stop processing

Objectives of computer applications

Computer systems are never installed for their own sake, but always because the management has been persuaded that the benefits of installing and operating will outweigh their costs and the disruption which follows their introduction.

The benefits of computerised working can be in the form of savings, for example in reducing staff costs. They can be in greater efficiency, for example in more output per person. Or they can be unquantifiable benefits such as an improved image. Amongst the principal benefits and objectives usually quoted for the computerisation of business routines are:

- Reducing staff costs on routine data collection and processing

- Improving information flow

- Streamlined routines

- Integrating systems

- Improving cash flow by:

  faster order turnaround
  faster invoice production
  reduction in stockholdings
  better debtor control
  automatic discount collection
  elimination of duplication
  better credit checking
  bulk ordering and consequent discounts

- Production planning and scheduling

- Improved forecasting

- Improved accuracy and presentation of documents especially invoicing and ordering

- Real time control over machinery

- Improved design, Computer Aided Design (CAD)

- Remote working

Computer centre costs

The decision to change over to computerised operation involves a major financial outlay and the true cost of operations might come as a surprise even to experienced computer staff. The cost can be classified under two main headings, once-only costs and annual running costs.

Once-only costs

Hardware

   Time spent on selecting
   Purchase
   Delivery
   Site preparation
   Connection
   Time spent testing
   Scrapping of old equipment

Software

   Purchase or programming time
   Selection or evaluation
   Testing
   Loss through errors

Design

   Costs of systems analysts
   Manager's time
   Office space
   Secretarial support
   Consultant's fees

Implementation

   File changeover costs
   Data-checking costs
   Machine-time spent testing
   Staff orientation
   Staff training
   Redundancy pay
   Recruitment of new skills

Running costs

Accommodation

   Rent of premises or allocation of floor costs
   Cost of operating air-conditioning equipment

Hardware

   Depreciation on equipment or rental or lease charge
   Computer maintenance contract
   Communications lines and equipment hire

Staffing

> Data Processing Manager
> Secretarial support
> Programming staff
> Operators and supervisor
> Data preparation and input clerks
> Librarian or filing staff
> Training and education

Operations

> Input and output media and stationery
> File storage media
> Electricity
> Provision of standby equipment

Administration

> Stationery and telephone
> Insurance
> Travelling
> Recruitment

The exact size of the costs will, of course, vary from application to application but the general observation can be made that taking the whole lifetime of the system into account the largest single cost will be for staff salaries. These usually will amount to over half the total cost of the system, and usually represent the cost of programming and maintenance.

Even in small systems involving only microcomputers staff costs are still the greatest cost. Hardware is becoming cheaper each year and is taking a smaller share of project lifetime costs, now only representing about 15% of the total.

The disadvantages of computers

As is now widely appreciated, computers are not the answer to all business problems and often bring as many problems as they do solutions. Following a tried and tested methodology should produce a robust system and minimise errors. However, no methodology is perfect and even a well-designed and fully operational system is not free from problems.

Obsolescence

The rate of technological change is very fast. This often means that a solution which was installed only a few years ago with the latest hardware and software is now out of date and can be replaced with an equivalent system at a fraction of the cost. This has two consequences - the old equipment is virtually worthless (in terms of its asset value), and a competitor can buy the new, cheap system and enjoy a much lower cost structure which gives them a competitive advantage.

Disruption

Although a computer may be the most efficient way of carrying out a particular business process once it is installed, the process of changeoverr can be very disruptive to the normal business routine. Even when the new system is in place the other business functions which are affected by the new way of working may take many months or even years to settle down into the new pattern.

Complexity

Analysts have become better over the years and now are willing to tackle systems of any degree of complexity. As the systems they design become more complex, the chance that errors will creep into the system becomes greater. It also follows that the more complex the system the harder it is to *find* errors. Many systems contain known errors which cannot be traced because they only occur under a unique set of circumstances which only crop up once or twice a year and which the analysts have been unable to duplicate.

Illegibility

Business systems need human beings to operate them and the more information available to the people involved, the more the system will be able to cope with errors in the data. Computer data is held on magnetic media such as tape or disks and, unlike traditional books and ledgers, cannot be read directly. In order to access the information a knowledge of computing is required without which it is invisible.

Security

Computer files are very vulnerable to accidental or deliberate destruction. Magnetic media are very fragile and special steps have to be taken to ensure that duplicate copies are available at all times. This duplication, called **back-up,** costs a great deal in time and money.

Fraud

Because computer systems rely on a few specialist personnel and because the data is invisible to off-line inspection by auditors, there is a greater risk of successful fraud with a computerised system. It is fairly easy for a programmer to hide a fraudulent instruction inside a program because very few of the organisation's staff have the knowledge needed to detect it. Their task is also made easier by the assumption of most people that any instruction coming from the computer must be right.

Resistance

In many companies there is considerable resistance to the introduction of computers. This is usually based on a fear that people will lose their jobs. It can also arise from fear of the unknown, from a fear of feeling inadequate and unable to cope, and similar personal reasons. Many staff have these feeling but will often conceal them; they may behave by refusing to accept computers at all, refusing to cooperate, or even by sabotaging the system.

Vulnerability

Many large computer systems completely replace the old systems and have no backup in case of failure. Where all processing details are on computer files any faults arising in the file access routines will mean that the system will have to stop.

Reorganisation

When a computer system is installed it frequently becomes the very heart of the information-processing (or data processing) activities of a company and displaces one or more of what were previously key processes. These key processes usually evolve over many years and the organisational structure for their regulation and control grows with them. Introducing a computer system means that the existing structure will no longer be appropriate and that a new structure is needed. Because this affects every part of the company the restructuring often means a complete reassessment of the people dimension: the power relationships, status and politics within a company.

Staffing

In the computer industry skilled personnel are in short supply, and will probably continue to be for some years to come. A company introducing a computer will often have difficulty recruiting skilled staff and, owing to the very competitive rates of pay, may also have difficulty retaining them. This gives the computer staff a very powerful bargaining position and makes the company vulnerable to loss of staff. It may also mean that the company cannot carry out planned upgrading of its system due to staff shortages.

The terms of reference

All the factors discussed in this section, suitability for computerisation, ease of application, seriousness of problem, likely costs, possible drawbacks and potential benefits, should be considered by management when considering which application to choose.

Once they have chosen the application they want to go ahead with, the analyst is contacted and given the terms of reference.

The terms of reference for a particular project are in the form of a document issued by management specifying the terms under which the investigation of a particular procedure is to be done. This includes a statement of the scope of the investigation, the objectives, the constraints which apply and the resources available to the analyst in undertaking the task.

Scope

This refers to the limits beyond which the investigation is not allowed to pass. Every system is a part of a larger system, and every system has links to many others. The analyst must be clear as to how far to pursue inquiries-this is often not at all clear.

In investigating a stock control and warehousing system, for instance, the analyst may legitimately comment on the design and contents of the goods despatch notes. But is the layout of the warehouse his concern, or the type of goods stocked, or even the training of the drivers who have to fill in the forms? The terms of reference should make this clear.

Objectives

These are a clear statement of what the systems investigation aims to achieve. They should be expressed as specifically as possible such as:

'To reduce the current stock holding from sixty days of sales to not more than thirty days at any one time, with not more than one per cent of products out of stock longer than three days'

60

rather than in broader terms such as

'To improve the way the warehouse is run'

Constraints

These specify things the analyst may not do, or parts of the existing system which must not be changed. For example, the analyst may be required to retain an existing form because it is used extensively throughout the organisation and because any change would have unwanted repercussions in many non-related functions. There may also be constraints as the amount of time available, or that staffing levels are to remain unchanged.

Resources

These are the facilities available to the analyst. The statement of resources often details the staff who will be working with the analyst, or personnel whom the analyst can ask for assistance. It also often authorises the analyst to approach various managers as part of the fact-finding exercise.

Exercises

1. Choose one business system with which you are familiar and go through the list above, testing to see if your example could benefit from computerisation in that area. Can you think of any areas which have been left out? Can you make up a list of the one main benefit expected in each of the applications areas where computers are commonly applied?

2. All the disadvantages of computers mentioned in this chapter have been known about for a long time. Can you suggest solutions for each which might be effective, or if not, suggest why it should be that some of them appear to be unavoidable?

Further reading

Kendall, K. and Kendall, J. (1992) Systems analysis and design. Pub Prentice-Hall Englewood Cliffs, NJ.

Lucas, H. (1992) The analysis, design and implementation of information systems. Pub McGraw-Hill, NY.

Chapter 5 The feasibility study

The overall objective of a feasibility study is to assess the technical, social and economic viability of different approaches to improving the efficiency of a particular business operation. Its ultimate aim is to produce a factual and well-researched report which recommends to management a specific course of action. It could be described simply as a first look at a system with a view to establishing whether it can be computerised, and if so, how to go about it.

Conducting a feasibility study

The feasibility study comprises an initial investigation into how the present system works to determine broadly what programs, hardware and personnel will be required. After the investigation has been carried out several different possible approaches will be evaluated and an outline design produced for each. These designs are presented to management who after due consideration will then decide whether to go on with the application project or not.

The conduct of a feasibility study covers four main areas:

1. *Purpose.* Establishing firm objectives for the proposed new system

2. *Design.* Investigating the existing system and preparing outline designs for several alternative new solutions

3. *Appraisal.* Collecting data with which to evaluate the viability of the technical, social and financial aspects of each of the proposed solutions

4. *Proposal.* Presenting the results of the study

Purpose

The purpose of the feasibility study is implied in the terms of reference. In many applications the terms of reference are actually amended as the feasibility study progresses to reflect the increased information which becomes available following the initial investigation.

Design

The design process consists of investigating the problem and preparing applications.

Investigation

The investigation part of the feasibility study is meant to be an overview of the application requirements; not an in-depth evaluation, which is done in the next stage of the system life cycle. It is not possible to state exactly how rigorous the analysis should be in this stage, but the terms of reference will give an indication of how much time should be spent on the initial investigation of the existing system. This will determine the degree of detail which the analyst will need.

Each application is of course different, but some general guidelines can be given as to what the analyst will need to know as a minimum requirement.

- What are the required outputs of the system?

- What are the timing requirements? Are reports needed daily, weekly, monthly, or will information be needed immediately?

- What are the main inputs to the system? How are they presented - on forms, over the telephone, through a keyboard, by optical character recognition (OCR) or optical mark recognition (OMR)?

- What volumes of data will be handled? How many inputs, what frequency and size are the outputs? Does the volume vary significantly with the time of year, or the day of the week?

- What volume of data will have to be stored on the system? How much on-line information will have to be kept, what archival volumes are needed: last week's, up to a month, three months, two years of data?

- How many people will use the system? Will they be trained operators or casual users? How many will want access at any one time?

- What speed of response is wanted? What is the maximum wait that can be tolerated?

- Will the users be located at one site, or be scattered geographically and require extensive communications facilities?

- What is the anticipated life of the system? Will it expand in the future, and at what rate?

- What are the security requirements of the system? How many levels of password will be needed? What are the audit requirements?

- Is there an overall development plan to which this application must conform?

- Are there any overriding constraints which must be allowed for?

63

These questions, and many others, will generate a mass of data which will have to be recorded, assessed, checked, verified and classified. At some point the analyst will feel that enough information has been accumulated. He can then concentrate on the main task of designing a new system which will provide the specified outputs within the stated constraints. (The fact finding techniques used by analysts are discussed in Chapter 6).

Application

For any business problem there will always be more than one solution, and any competent analyst should be able to devise a range of possible designs covering a spectrum from almost completely manual at one end of the range, to almost completely automatic at the other.

The number of designs which are considered in depth will depend upon the particular application, but it is good practice to consider at least three. The list below shows some of the common alternatives available and illustrates the range of basic solutions which can be found for most proposed applications.

- Continue with the present system exactly as it is (usually because the cost of computerising would be too great, or because there is no computer system available which can do the job better).

- Design a better, but wholly manual, system

- Use a mixture of manual subsystems for the most part, giving flexibility, but share someone else's computer for time-critical parts of the application. Thus get the benefits of speed and accuracy without incurring the full costs of owning a computer

- Contract out most of the processing tasks to a computer bureau and use manual systems only for the preparation of input

- Use a batch-processing system centralised on one company-owned computer, or time-sharing on a third party's machine

- Develop a real-time on-line automatic solution based on an internally owned computer

- Buy ready-made software or commission a package to be specially tailored and run it on an internal centralised computer

- Distribute computing power by buying or developing applications software to run on personal computers in stand-alone mode

- Integrate personal computers by using a network to allow shared peripherals and data interchange

Appraisal

Each of the proposed system designs has to be evaluated to ensure that it is technically, socially and economically workable.

Technical feasibilityy

This evaluation is designed to answer the question 'Can the proposed solution be turned into a physical reality?' The ideal equipment requirement will be determined directly from the outline designs developed. These will specify minimum running speeds, rates of input, number of records to be stored, types of output envisaged, etc. These specifications can be checked against manufacturers' offerings quite easily.

Problems often arise where no one manufacturer can supply all the necessary hardware or software, and equipment from different suppliers has to be combined. There are frequently compatibility problems here and it may be that a promising solution will have to be abandoned because of a lack of comprehensive maintenance agreements or uncertainty as to the future operating efficiency.

Other potential problems which have to be considered are:

- Time required to implement the solution
- Types of computer configuration currently available
- Need for an availability of standby facilities
- Availability of specialist computer personnel
- State of computer know-how within the organisation
- Extent to which the hardware or software is untried
- Terms on which suppliers are willing to deal
- Compatibility problems with existing hardware or software
- Waiting time for the latest models
- Danger of equipment obsolescence

Social feasibility

This evaluation is designed to answer the question 'What impact will the proposed new system have on established working practices and will existing staff be adversely affected?' In the past, computer systems were imposed on staff by specialists working for outside organisations, with little or no consultation with the people most affected by the change. Today this approach is recognised as counter-productive. If a system is to be successful

65

the personnel working with it must feel they are a valuable part of it and so should be consulted and their views taken into account during the design phase.

Each proposed design should be evaluated from the point of view of its social implications. If there is too much disruption, or if workers are to be displaced, there is bound to be a degree of hostility. On the other hand, introducing a new system can be an opportunity for enriching jobs and making work more enjoyable. Some of the factors to consider are:

- The impact of any compulsory redundancies

- The degree of retraining needed

- The extent of any de-skilling

- The attitude of trades unions

- Past experience of new technology in the organisation

- The education level of existing staff

- Opportunities to create more meaningful work

- Ability to improve the working environment

- Problems arising from regrading and salary differentials

- Integration of new staff taken on for the project

Financial feasibility

This is designed to ensure that the costs of any proposed solution do not exceed the benefits. In order to do this the analyst will draw up two lists, one listing every item of expense expected and another listing every benefit which should result from this design.

These listings will of necessity be very inexact, but some attempt must be made so that potential designs can be ranked in order of suitability and unsuitable candidates eliminated at an early stage.

Proposal

The last major activity of the feasibility study is the presentation of the results to management. This is mainly done through submission of the final report.

Most analysts, however, also prefer to give a spoken presentation at which they can expand on any items not fully developed in the report or answer queries from the potential users.

This will usually mean the preparation of summary documents, tables of costs (to allow direct comparison between different possible solutions), overhead projection foils and various other visual aids.

The analyst can expect to be questioned closely about possible designs not recommended for development, about the basis of costings, the assumptions underlying estimates of benefits, degrees of risk etc. The presentation will usually finish with a restatement of the recommended solution and a proposed plan of action.

Stages of a feasibility study

The principal stages of a feasibility study are

1   Determine the problem

2   Determine the scope, i.e. the terms of reference

3   Analyse and chart the existing system in detail looking for:

   weaknesses

   inefficiencies

   wasted resources

   duplication of effort

   misdirection

4   Consider methods of rationalising the existing system

5   Consider alternative approaches to existing solution

6   For each possible strategy produce:

   a schedule of costs

   a schedule of potential benefits

   an estimate of risk and uncertainty factors

   a cost-benefit analysis

7   Present alternatives to the Board/Steering Committee

8   Produce a recommendation

For each of these stages a report is produced. In many cases the reports of more than one stage will be combined and so it is not possible to give a definitive listing of the outputs from a feasibility study. In general these will be at least:

- Problem definition (or user request)

- Restatement of project scope (or amended Terms of Reference)

- Analysis of existing procedures

- Evaluation of major operational problems

- Alternative design proposals

- Detailed cost-benefit analyses for each proposed design

- The analyst's recommendation

- The completed bound feasibility report

Contents of the feasibility report

This is the document which finalises the feasibility study. It should contain:

Introduction

Nature of the problem
Extent of the area considered

Present system

Outline description
Cost of continued operation
Evaluation of problems

New system requirements

Essential items
Desirable features
Idealised attributes

Evaluation of proposed alternative systems

Description
Cost-benefit analysis for each of:
     technical social
     financial aspects
High-level system flowcharts
Outline processing steps
Tentative equipment specification

File requirements
Input transactions
Master files
Output reports

Implementation plan

Stages
Resources
Time-scales

Recommendations

Advantages of the chosen design over others

Appendices (where appropriate)

Supporting data
Manufacturers' technical specifications
Detail of investigations data

Practical conduct of a feasibility study

A typical study: Fortune Securities Ltd

Fortune Securities is the venture capital arm of a large British company with major manufacturing interests in the UK and abroad. The main company has long had extensive interests in food processing and owns several large factories which have a substantial share of the market in their sector.

The group recently went on the acquisition trail with a view to guaranteeing a larger share of the retail market for their products. This was done by putting together fairly rapidly a retail group called U-Buy. The shops now incorporated into this group were mainly small chains or sometimes larger individual stores, mostly situated in the outskirts of towns. Most of the shops sell only food and the normal lines associated with groceries, i.e. cleaning materials, tights, small hardware items, batteries etc. Some of the larger ones also sell clothing.

As well as the shops, the main company has transferred control of two large wholesale warehouse units which it owns. These both trade as fully independent companies at the moment and supply all sectors of the grocery trade with a whole range of goods and are in no way tied to the output of the group to which they belong. It is envisaged that these two warehouses will continue with their current business but will also act as central distribution depots for the U-Buy group.

69

The main company also has a majority share holding in a nation-wide transport company. This company will serve as the physical distribution network for the U-Buy group, but will not be a part of the group, nor will it be under the control of the U-Buy directors.

The retail outlets which now comprise the U-Buy group are very varied in size and turnover. Some of them were old-established family firms which had not moved with the times. Some were modern well-managed chains with very go-ahead attitudes.

A few of these small chains already have some computer equipment installed, others in the new group have no experience at all.

The management of Fortune Securities think that it might be worth considering setting up a central buying facility to serve the whole group, and to have it linked in to an automatic stock reordering system.

The requirements

The board of directors of Fortune Securities want you to produce a report outlining how you would set about conducting an initial feasibility study. This should include a timetable, an indication of the information you would want to collect and how you propose to gather it, some initial ideas of possible hardware layouts and mention of any factors which should be given particularly close attention. It is expected that the feasibility study would be finished within four weeks.

The proposed feasibility study

In general any report prepared in this section will cover the following areas:

1   A problem definition

2   Analysis of existing system

3   Systems performance requirements

4   Alternatives considered

5   Proposals for further investigation

6   Recommendations

1. Problem definition

In this particular case there is no real need to ask for a problem definition as, although this is a start-up company, it is firmly rooted in a low technology industry and the information needs of a buying office can be clearly defined in advance. The terms of reference would best be established by negotiation.

Terms of reference
The systems analyst cannot begin a feasibility study until the overall aims and objectives have been clarified. In the case of Fortune Securities, little explicit information is given as to the aims; so in this report it has been assumed that the normal requirements of a buying office will apply.

It is felt that in an organisation such as U-Buy the general objective of a central buying office will be to try to secure the keenest prices possible from suppliers by co-ordinating orders to secure bulk discounts. Additionally, there will be subsidiary objectives. These will include the desire to build up expertise in purchasing by specialising, to reduce the costs of holding stocks by co-ordinating deliveries, and in longer term the buying staff may well also want to organise sales promotions by arranging supplies of specially packaged goods or by 'own branding' of products.

In the absence of stated objectives this report is based on the analyst's research into how other companies in the retail field operate under the basic assumption that the U-Buy operations will be broadly similar to those in the industry generally.

Objectives
In every feasibility study there will be some functions whose inclusion is considered absolutely essential while there are others, classified as desirable but not essential, which can be left out.

For the purposes of this report it will be assumed that the primary objectives of the proposed new computer system are to:

- Minimise the price paid for supplies to the shops
- Maximise the sales through the shops
- Minimise the stockholding needed
- Reduce unit buying costs
- Aid buyers' decision-making
- Streamline routines
- Develop a common stockholding policy
- Co-ordinate the activities of sales, deliveries and stockholding

In addition, the following subsidiary objectives are seen by the management as being highly desirable and appropriate to consider in conjunction with the main objectives:

- Automatic discount collection

71

- Improved forecasting
- Improved production planning
- Eliminate duplicated effort
- Ensure faster order processing
- Better cash control

Scope

The extent and duration of the feasibility study will depend to a large extent on the scope of the project and in particular on the boundaries of the system. The case study states that the primary requirements are to establish a central buying office and to set up an automatic reordering system. Creating the central office will not be the direct responsibility of the systems analyst as it would involve too many policy decisions and would probably be better handled by a project leader from general management. But the analyst would of course be deeply involved in determining the data processing requirements of the new office set up.

For the purposes of this report it is assumed that the analysis is to concentrate on the procurement of stock, the integration of the wholesalers into the U-Buy stockholding system and the provision of accurate and efficient transportation schedules.

No attempt will be made to influence the product availability from the holding company's factories, the design of products or outlets, the internal organisation of the warehousing companies or the working of the transportation company.

Constraints

It is assumed, for the purpose of this report, that there are no more constraints than are normally met on a project such as this. It is also noted that in a situation such as described in the case there are often problems with staff, whose attitudes to change is not always favourable especially after a company take-over.

Management should bear this in mind when considering the contents of this report as difficulties might arise in practice which could invalidate many of the timings and recommendations of this report.

It is assumed that the overall constraint is to produce a cost-effective system which can work within the established practices of the company and which is acceptable to the majority of those involved. It is also recognised that the

Resources

The proposals developed in this report for the conduct of the feasibility study are based on the analyst being given sufficient authority to carry out the investigations without undue difficulty.

It is assumed that there will be sufficient clerical assistance provided, and that some sort of office accommodation will be found for the feasibility study staff.

It is recognised that the feasibility study project will operate under the normal financial rules of the company and that a budget will be agreed with the finance office before commencement.

2: Analysis of the existing system

As this is a new application in a newly formed trading group there is no existing system. But the data handling requirements for the proposed system will be exactly the same as in any standard buying office arrangement. The main problem here will be gathering detailed information on which to base the outline design of the proposed new system.

Analysis

The object of the analysis in this case is determining the minimum information needed to allow the design of a suitable solution to begin. Once this detailed information is known, various designs can be evaluated for their suitability and some sort of cost-benefit ranking of them can be established for further discussion and refinement.

Unfortunately, analysts will not know what information is needed until they have a particular system design in mind, and cannot know what designs are worth considering until they have a certain amount of preliminary information. In situations like this there is a great danger that the analyst will spend precious time gathering information of all kinds without being able to tell in advance whether it will be useful in the long run.

In order to get round this problem, and in an effort to break the whole system down into smaller and more manageable units, a rough diagram was drawn up showing the way that the data will have to flow within the proposed new system. It was on the basis of this data analysis exercise that the fact-finding schedule was designed.

An examination of the Fortune Securities case shows that the entire system, however the final design comes out, essentially consists of three major subsystems:

73

- a data capture system for reporting retail sales
- a corporate reporting system for providing information to the buying office
- some kind of automatic stock replenishment system for the central warehouses

The relationships between the three sub-systems are shown in Figure 5.1. Each subsystem operates in a different physical location and so the analysis can be conveniently centred on these locations.

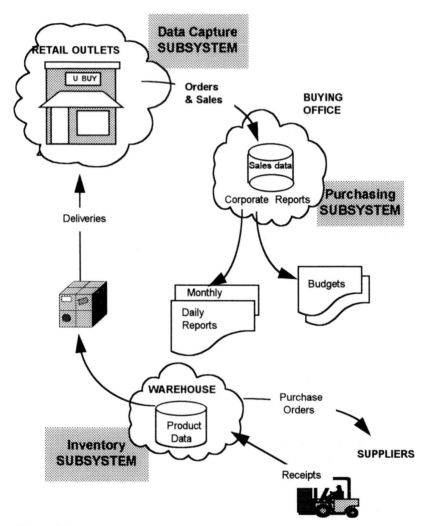

Figure 5.1

The analyst will have to gather information about the following.

The data capture subsystem

> The shops
> How many retail outlets are there?
> Where are they located?
> What size are they?
> How much turnover they generate?
> The staff
> How many are they?
> What training and experience do they have?
> What is their attitude to the new group and to computerisation?
> The systems
> What are the procedures used at present?
> How difficult will they be to change?
> What will be the cost of abolishing them?
> What computer experience is there?
> What information-recording equipment do they have?
> What computer equipment is in place?
> The stock
> How many items are carried?
> What particular items are sold?
> Any local specialisations?
> What is the age and composition of stocks held?

The storage subsystem output

> What precisely do the buyers need?
> What information:
> In what form
> At what intervals
> With what accuracy how speedily?

The storage subsystem input

> How many records will be kept?
> How much data do they contain?
> In what form?
> How often will it be accessed?
> What security will be needed?
> The interfaces
> What other systems will use the stored data?

The stock control subsystem

The stock

> How many different items are stored?
> What is the locations of all items?
> Any special needs of particular products? What is the minimum order quantity? What is the time taken to deliver?
> What is the average rate of sale?

The systems

> What are the procedures used at present? How difficult will they be to change?
> What will be the cost of abolishing them? What computer experience is there?
> What stock-holding systems are there? What computer equipment is in place?

The carriers

> How many deliveries can be made per week? What is a typical load?
> What restrictions will apply to particular areas? Any special terms applicable?
> The suppliers
> What is the number of different suppliers?
> What are ordering details needed?
> What products are supplied?
> What are the prices?
> What are the delivery terms

Outline timetable

As there will only be four weeks available for the conduct of the feasibility study a sensible arrangement might be for the analyst to allocate one week to each of the major subsystems and one week to collate the data and arrive at a recommendation.

Week I

- Interview a sample of shop managers
- Inspect a typical shop's storage area
- Despatch questionnaires to most shops to gauge opinions
- Read the records relating to shops to establish sizes etc.
- Determine shop staff and customer attitudes
- Contact the carriers

Week 2

- Interview the head buyer
- Interview the remaining buying staff in detail
- Inspect past records, if any
- Analyse the data requirements
- Determine file sizes etc.

Week 3

- Interview the managers of both warehouses
- Inspect their purchasing systems in detail
- Discuss possible options with affected staff
- Inspect the physical storage conditions
- Talk to suppliers about any proposed changes

Week 4

- Assemble data and collate and classify
- Draft out feasibility report
- Draw up outline systems designs
- Prepare cost-benefit schedules
- Finalise the feasibility report
- Make recommendations
- Present the feasibility report to management

3: Systems performance requirements

These are determined in the light of the information obtained in the analysis section and are constantly reassessed as more becomes known about the exact needs of the new system. Each of the users affected by the new system will have to be consulted to ensure that the performance of the system will match their operational requirements.

The feasibility study will have to determine, as far as possible, the sizes of files, the number and frequency of accesses, the minimum acceptable response times and similar information. Determining this information will be done in parallel with the investigations of the analysis phase.

4: Alternatives considered

It would be inappropriate to try to set out a number of alternative systems in detail within a report covering the plan for carrying out a feasibility study, but allowance for some general design considerations should assist the data gathering stage by focusing attention on particular information needs. This section will therefore outline some possible configurations very briefly.

Configuration 1: An on-line, centralised system

This would involve the use of a central mini-computer located at one of the warehouses. Every shop would have a point-of-sale terminal which would update the stock files in real time as sales were made. The buying office staff would have on-line access to the files, and reports would be available on demand. Goods would be automatically despatched to the shops when stocks fell to a predetermined level. Stock replenishment in the warehouse would be automatically generated by orders for the factory issued whenever warehouse stock holdings fell below a predetermined level. Receipts from suppliers would be keyed in by warehouse staff and stock records would also be available to them on demand.

Configuration 2: A distributed system.

This would involve every shop having a microcomputer-based sales terminal with the ability to capture sales data and store it until the end of the day, perhaps on a floppy disk. Each shop would then send their floppy disks to a central computer at the warehouse which would read the sales data and create a file showing the total sales for the U-Buy group. This data would be copied to the buying office in various formats every day. The central computer would then update a master stock file and calculate the replacement quantities for the shops and arrange for the despatch. The warehouse would then arrange for regular updating runs on the warehouse stock file to place purchase orders on suppliers.

Configuration 3. A decentralised system.

Each shop would have its own micro-computer and also keep track of its own stock situation. When the shop manager chose to make an order it would be produced, printed out and faxed to the central warehouse. A copy would go to the buying office who would enter the sales data into their own local computer system. The warehouse would fill the order from its stocks and use its own stock replenishment system independently, which might or might not be computerised.

Within even these three alternatives there are multiple possibilities involving say, bar codes or OCR (optical character recognition) in the data capture phase and nightly downloading to a warehouse minicomputer with batch reports for the buying office. Obviously the information arising from the investigation will determine whether any one alternative is viable or not.

5: *Proposals for further investigation*

Changeover

It is assumed that the new group will have a common stock-holding policy so there will inevitably be a problem of old stock in some shops which will not be replaced when it is sold, and in the meantime is not on the approved products file.

In order to clean the old stocks file it may be advisable to set up a list of approved products which the new group will all have available for stocking and to leave all other products held in the various shops off the stock file and allow the items to be sold out in due course until there are none left. Alternatively it may be better to transfer all non-standard stock to one or two shops in the group and use these to clear out the old goods by continuous sales promotions.

Staffing

The success of any computerisation project depends heavily on the goodwill of the personnel involved. The company would be well advised to build into the system a mechanism to allow full consultation to be made with staff at all levels so that a feeling of participation is encouraged. It is proposed that after the feasibility study is presented but before any design commitment is made there should be a company wide consultative exercise.

6: *Recommendations*

It is the recommendation of this report that the feasibility study be allowed to go ahead as outlined above. The proposed application appears suitable for computerisation and the time-scale allowed for the feasibility study appears adequate.

Exercises

1. Try writing some feasibility study objectives. What would be a suitable objective for

> A bus company
> A grocer's shop
> A hospital
> The police service?

2. Consider each of the basic design forms in turn and try to determine which would be most suitable for:

A cinema booking system
A police station
A library
A restaurant

3. Can you make a list of the possible social factors which would have to be considered if it was proposed to completely automate all the functions of:

A library
Cashiers in a bank

Further reading

Eliason, A. (1990) Systems Development: Analysis, Design and Implementation. Pub Scott, Foresman/Little, Brown. Glenview, Ill.

Flaaten, P., McCubbrey, D., O'Riordan, P. and Burgess, K.(1989) Foundations of Business Systems. Pub. The Dryden Press, Hinsdale, Ill.

Kendall, P. (1990) Introduction to Systems Analysis and Design: A structured approach. Pub Wm C. Brown, Dubuque IA.

Schultheis, R. and Sumner, M. (1992) Management information systems: The manager's view. Pub Irwin, Homewood, Ill.

Chapter 6 Fact finding techniques

There are a variety of fact finding techniques available to the systems analyst. They include interviewing, observation, record inspection and questionnaires. They each have their strengths and weaknesses and the right technique to use will depend on the particular situation. The analyst will normally use the techniques in combination to ensure the accuracy of the data collected.

When fact finding, the analyst should find out exactly:

- Who does what
- Where it is done
- In what manner
- At what time
- In what order
- Why it is done that way

Interviewing

Interviewing is probably the single most useful tool of the systems analyst because of the many different uses to which it can be put. Interviewing does not just mean a formal face-to-face confrontation over a desk - it is often done over the telephone, informally at the person's place of work, or in the home. In fact any opportunity for a structured conversation can be turned into an interview by the analyst. The only real requirements are that the meeting should be prearranged and under the control of the analyst.

Every interview conducted by an analyst must have a clearly defined objective. This principal objective will determine how and where and when the interview will take place. In most interviews there will also be subsidiary objectives to pursue and so the analyst must be alert to the possibility of useful information relating to these arising during the course of the interview, and should avoid over-managing it.

The purpose of interviews

Interviews serve four main purposes: data collection, verification, influencing opinions, and participation.

Data collection
Primarily concerned with finding out the basic data relating to some activity of interest to the analyst, data collection interviews can produce large

amounts of high quality data in a relative short time. They can be used to gather information not only about hard data but also about feelings, opinions, attitudes and so on.

Verification

Data previously gathered from other sources will be checked for accuracy, validity and relevance and to ensure that it is up to date. Interviews are an excellent way of cross-checking that information is accurate in a non-provocative manner.

Influencing opinion

Since the interview is usually a face-to-face meeting in circumstances largely under the analyst's control, the analyst can use the opportunity to discover the interviewee's views on the new system. If these views are largely negative the analyst can counter the points raised there and then, possibly dispelling any misunderstanding which might cause difficulties if allowed to remain until a later stage. Interviews are often held primarily as a means of giving out information, rather than gathering it in, particularly when the objective is to overcome resistance to change.

Participation

The interview is a good way of encouraging contributions to the design of a new system. Used this way there are two benefits. First, interviewees are usually pleased to have their opinions taken into account and so feel that they are participating in the new system. Second, the person being interviewed will often be an experienced member of staff with a deep knowledge of the workings of the system and may be able to suggest solutions or lines of enquiry which the analyst may have overlooked.

Planning an interview

Interviewing is the most important of the techniques available to the analyst because it is a flexible and powerful analysis tool when used properly. However, interviewing is an art which can easily go wrong and to do it well requires both training and practice.

The conduct of an interview involves three phases. The analyst has to be quite sure of the reasons for the interview and plan it carefully. The analyst must be constantly aware of the interviewee's reactions while the interview is under way and must consolidate the interview records immediately after it.

There is no magic formula for successful interviewing but a good interviewer will observe the majority of the following :

1. Interviews must be prepared in advance

The primary objective of the interview must be clear to the analyst before it begins. Do your homework:

- Prepare specific questions

- Prepare an interview guide for yourself. Go through the documentation, record inspection etc. Build up a picture of the application. Identify questions, missing pieces and contradictions. This will produce an initial outline of the interview

- Define the purpose of the interview before you start

- Draw up a check list of points to be covered. This will be your interview plan.

- Know what the your target does in the organisation. Understand the work of the department

- Send out advance information to the interviewee

The analyst must also ensure that the interviewee does not get the impression of dealing with someone with very little knowledge and who asks obvious questions which could easily have been checked beforehand. Items such as the interviewee's superior's name, or the job responsibilities of the interviewee should all be checked by the analyst before the interview, not during it.

Interviews are not the place to get detailed knowledge of a complex operation. If you need that sort of information write to the person and ask them for a detailed specification. They are then free to do it in their own time and to ensure any diagrams or sample documents are included.

2: Make an appointment

All interviews must be prearranged. The analyst cannot simply rely on chance meetings or drop in unexpectedly to a manager's office.

Interviews cannot be approached casually. Making an appointment ensures the interviewee is prepared and available and allows the interviewee to gather any materials that may be needed during the interview.

Managers are generally busy people and will tend not be very receptive to some outsider who comes round asking obvious questions at their busiest moments.

3: Interview the right person

Interview at the right level. Find out who can best answer the questions? Start with the organisation chart. Ask the functional manager. This will normally point you towards the right person. It is also politically a good move as it legitimates the interviewer in the eyes of the interviewee.

4: Choose the right venue

The obvious place to hold an interview is at the person's office or work area, but this is frequently unsuitable. It may be too noisy, lacking in privacy or subject to disruption. The manager may also be unable to give sufficient attention to the interview when in familiar surroundings and distracted by frequent interruptions. A quiet office somewhere else may be more suitable.

5: Observe good manners

The interviewee is giving up valuable time to the interviewer and the interviewer is normally regarded as an outsider intruding on the home territory of the interviewee. This means that relations must be treated delicately right from the start and the analyst must behave as a guest of the interviewee.

- Identify and introduce yourself

- Explain why you are doing the interview

- Try to establish some rapport

- Remember you are invading their territory

- Don't be late

6: Use appropriate language and style

Avoid using your jargon. Ensure that you understand their jargon. Dress appropriately.

7: Don't interrupt

If the interviewee tends to wander wait for a convenient moment to gently push them back on course.

8: Avoid Yes/No questions

Use 'open' questions which cannot be answered with a 'yes', 'no' or a single fact, e.g. 'Could you outline the steps of the billing system for me briefly?' Do not used 'closed' questions that can be answered with a simple 'yes' or 'no' like 'Is the first step in the billing system is the receipt of an order?'

Only once you are sure you have the main picture do you deal with specific details, checking facts with closed questions.

9. Don't express your own opinion.

During the interaction you will be asked what you think of this or that. Try to give a non committal answer. Many interviewees will try to mould their answers to what they see as your preferences.

84

Do not argue with the interviewee or impose your ideas on them. An interview is not a contest. Don't put the interviewee on trial or contradict them.

10. Work to build rapport
Give lots of feedback during the interview. Encourage the subject to open up by statements like 'You must be the expert in this area.'

11. Try to distinguish between fact and opinion
People will tell you what they want you to hear. Opinions are often stated as facts.

12. Distinguish between need and desire

13. Manage your time properly
Do not run over the agreed time without permission. Don't end up being asked to leave. Watch for signs that the interviewee wants to close it. Better to leave with a good impression and come back later.

At the end, thank the subject and offer to send a copy of the notes you write up. Ask if you can come back in case there are any follow up questions which become apparent later. If there has not been time to cover all the items then a further appointment should be made.

14. Check the information obtained
Before going on to another area summarise the discussion with something like 'Let's see if I understand this correctly...'.

Even when people are co-operative they can make mistakes of fact or miss out vital information or exceptional items which may later prove to be of major importance. Try to find some way of checking what you have been told.

People also frequently only tell you what they want you to know. They will hold back on some information and misinform you about other things where the truth might reflect badly on them: for example a typist may inflate the number of letters produced in an average day.

15. Confirm the data collected
Transcribe your notes as soon as possible after the interview while it is still fresh in your mind. Ensure that you add the full details of the time, date, place and subject name etc.

16. Try to be objective
Make sure you actually listen to the answers. Many interviewers only hear what they want to hear. Interviewers often only notice data which support their preconceived ideas. Don't be so keen on getting the next question in that you miss what is being said in reply to this one.

17: Taking notes

It is best to take some notes during the interview, but these should not be excessive. If you are writing too much you will miss what the interviewee is saying. (Remember that most of the detail should have been collected in writing previously). A good idea is leave space in your interview plan for you to write the answers in.

Do not tape record the interview without permission.

Transcribing an interview takes about four to six times as long as the interview itself.

18: Be flexible to a degree

Use your interview plan and question list as a guide only. Be prepared to find items you had not planned on dealing with.

Following up interviews

Immediately after the interview the analyst should review all the information gathered and write an interview report as a permanent record. A copy of this should be sent to the interviewee so that any inaccuracies can be dealt with.

The analyst will often want to arrange another interview as soon as possible with another member of staff in order to verify the information arising from the first one or may use a different data collection technique to check what has been learned.

Advantages of interviewing

- It is a useful way of verifying information obtained from other sources

- It may produce information from knowledgeable people that is not otherwise available

- It breaks down barriers and enlists support for future work by establishing personal relationships

- It starts dialogue between designer and affected/interested parties

- It shows interest in those likely to be affected by change and enlists their support.

Disadvantages of interviewing

- It can produce over-reliance on hearsay and 'soft' information.

- There is a danger of 'leading' the interviewee

- The interviewer may only hear what he wants to hear

- Stereotyping of interviewees can influence what the interviewer believes are the 'facts'

- Bias, prejudice and other psychological 'noise' can hinder fact-gathering

- Information obtained during an interview must be verified from other sources.

Questionnaires

Questionnaires are an obvious method of fact-finding when gathering information for considering a computer application, but they are very difficult to use properly and very easy to get wrong. Because of this they should only be used with great care, and in the right circumstances.

Questionnaires are best used when:

- there are a great many potential data providers and therefore the size of sample is too large for individual interviews

- only a limited amount of information is required, preferably of the 'yes/no' or 'how many' type

- information is required from a large number of individuals who are spread over a large geographical area or on scattered sites making interviewing impracticable

- preliminary data is required which will form the basis for follow-up interviews

- information is required very cheaply

- information is required very quickly

- it is necessary to verify information acquired by other methods

- there are no alternative means

Designing a questionnaire

As previously stated the design of questionnaires is a specialised field and the analyst should always approach the subject with some caution.

The overall design will of course depend on the information that the analyst needs to collect. It should therefore be obvious that the first requirement is a clear understanding of the object of the questionnaire and how the questionnaire is expected to achieve that object.

The analyst should decide what information is needed and carefully frame questions which will elicit it. Each question should be checked with colleagues, or with an expert if possible, to eliminate any ambiguities.

Once a set of questions has been assembled the analyst should try them out on a small sample of the target audience to test their acceptability and should check the effectiveness of the questionnaire by follow-up interviews. In this way the analyst can ensure that the information received is the information required. Only when the questionnaire is fully tested should it be sent to the whole target audience.

Remember that the information you receive is limited to written responses to prearranged questions.

There are two basic types of questions, open questions and closed questions.

Closed response questions. These are questions of the how many, how long type where the respondent is asked to produce a simple factual answer very often by choosing the appropriate response from a list of possible answers.

Open response questions. These are questions where a space is left for the respondent to write in an answer in their own words. They can write just a word or two or several paragraphs.

Questionnaires are normally best suited to collecting data where the responses are answers to closed questions as this makes them easier to analyse.

Making questionnaires work

Use a facilitator to help respondents

The accuracy of the responses and the speed of the responses can be greatly enhanced by using trained or semi-trained 'interviewers' to administer the questionnaires. Many people are functionally illiterate. In street interviews it is remarkable how few people can read the survey forms due to bad eyesight.

Send a covering letter

The response rate will be much higher if a covering letter is sent out with the questionnaire explaining what the data is for, how it will be used and what will happen to the results.

You should also assure the respondent that the information will not be used for purposes other than that agreed to in advance. It is usual to impose a deadline to encourage people to do something about it straight away.

Always send a follow up letter to non responders

The only practical way to improve the response rate is to send a follow up letter or to make a phone call chasing up the missing forms. This should be built in to your survey plan. The response rate will be depend upon

- sponsorship of the questionnaire
- attractiveness and clarity of format
- length of the questionnaire
- nature of the covering letter
- ease of filling it out
- ease of sending it back
- any inducements to reply
- nature of the people receiving it

Advantages of questionnaires

Cost effective
In the right circumstances the use of questionnaires can be highly cost effective. The production and printing can be very cheap to do. It is economical of the analyst's time. It requires less skill to administer than interviewing. Large amounts of high quality data can be gathered quickly and cheaply.

Confidentiality
Respondents often feel more comfortable with questionnaires since they can take their time, and think about the responses. Many respondents will also feel less inhibited by the presence of an interviewer and may answer questions more freely if they know that the responses are anonymous.

Large numbers of respondents
They can be used where the numbers involved would be too great for interviewing.

Geographical location
It may be necessary to collect data from people who are scattered at work sites over a large area, or who work at peculiar times.

Can be highly mechanised
The results of questionnaires can easily be made into a computer sensible form if it is properly designed. OCR and OMR are very popular forms of data

capture. It is even possible to use an on-line VDU to display the questions and capture the responses for immediate processing. This can be used by placing the display in a public place such as an airport and inviting the public to fill in the questionnaire.

Uniformity

Questionnaires are basically standard questions administered in a standard manner with standard instructions for completion. The gives a high degree of uniformity to the responses and allows the use of statistical methods in assessing the data. This degree of uniformity is seldom available in interview situations. It also allows one unique advantage, it allows you to administer before and after tests so that the effectiveness of the delivered system can be judged objectively.

Free from interviewer bias

There is usually minimal interaction between the person setting the questionnaire and the person filling it in so the problems of interviewers hearing what they want to hear is eliminated. This is where open ended responses are particularly valuable.

Verification

They are good means of verifying data obtained by other methods.

There may no other practical way to reach people.

You can reach chief executives who may not be available in person. You can get data from people who speak a different language.

Surveys by telephone

These somewhere in between face to face interviews and questionnaires. They involve mostly predetermined questions but also allow the interview to gauge the accuracy and reliability of the data through verbal clues. They also allow the interviewer to explain questions if necessary.

Disadvantages:

The design of telephone surveys is difficult

Facts obtained from questionnaires are likely to be less accurate than those from interviews. This is because during an interview the subject has the chance to explain exactly what is meant or ask for clarification of a question.

Questions are often ambiguous. Questionnaires have to be designed with great care because they are always subject to misinterpretation and even with the greatest care the questions can be ambiguous. The average intelligence of the general public is low when it comes to answering questions in surveys.

It is easy to antagonise people with them There is a risk of getting shallow replies because people are not interested or have too little time to fill them in

Their use usually does not permit face-to-face communication, so clarification and follow-up of points made can be cumbersome

There is a constant danger that people will only tell you what they think you want to know

Analysis of results may take time and prove costly

There is normally a poor response rate The low percentage response rate may give an unrepresentative sample

There is nearly always a slow response rate

The reliability of the data is often untestable

Record inspection

In some instances the analyst will be designing and implementing a totally new system. If so there will be no previous data to guide the study. If the application concerns an already operational manual system, or an existing but inefficient computer system, there will be existing documentation. This can often serve as a starting point for the investigation and can provide a wealth of high-quality data at virtually no cost.

Types of record

Most organisations have developed extensive written records to guide their activities and the problem for the analyst is often one of having too much data available, rather than too little. The exact source of this information will vary from application to application but will include some or all of the following:

Organisation charts	Office handbooks
Procedure manuals	System outlines
Job descriptions	Computer-run charts
Forms used	Computer procedure
Input documents and their	specification
control records	Previous investigation
Files kept and control totals	summaries
Reports produced	All forms of accounting
Training aids	records

Use of records

Stored data can be either primary or secondary sources. Primary data includes items such as products stocked and the quantities held. Secondary data can be extracted with a little processing, for example the average stock levels can be calculated, or the number of days debtors take to pay.

Stored data can also be much more accurate than data from other sources. If you want to know how many letters a typist produces on average per day, the way to find it is to count the number of copy letters in the file, instead of asking the typist who will probably exaggerate the true figure. Seasonal variances are also easier to spot from long-term records rather than from unreliable memories. Stored data can include the following

Quantities
Number of products stocked
Number of staff in departments
Number of undelivered orders

Times
Average time to prepare a report
Average time to extract a debtor's statement
Average time to prepare a quotation

Variances
Percentage of staff absenteeism
Wastage of materials
Waiting time for parts from stores
Average storage times of stocks
Errors in clerical procedures

Loadings
Number of orders handled per shift
Number of orders received per shift
Proportion of idle time of staff

The principal advantage of stored records as a source of information for the analyst is that the data is formalised and standardised and so needs very little interpretation or verification.

It should also be largely free from bias. Records showing the movements of stock can be relied upon to provide an accurate picture of the efficiency of suppliers in keeping to delivery deadlines. The same information obtained by interviewing stock clerks would be less reliable.

Advantages of stored data sources

They are useful where the system is already supported by much documentation, particularly where this is formalised and standardised.

They establish quantitative information-volumes, frequencies, trends, ratios.

They can be a short cut to fact gathering.

They do not depend on extensive staff co-operation.

They usually provide reliable data.

They can be used to check the accuracy of opinions about future trends and projected sales by verifying the base figures given.

The task can be delegated to relatively inexperienced staff.

For some purposes they can be the cheapest method.

Disadvantages of stored data sources

All documents eventually become out of date and therefore of limited use.

The analyst needs to use documents selectively, otherwise using them could be very time consuming.

They produce background information only.

Documents may only provide an 'official' version of events.

They can only really be used as a support to other methods.

They do not give the complete picture.

Data is not always in an immediately usable form.

They cannot give information on attitudes and opinions.

They can be very expensive in terms of analyst's time

They completely omit the informal information systems which exist in every organisation.

Exercise

Suppose you were asked to computerise the admissions procedures for a local college.

What documents would you ask to see to help you in your task?

Observation

Observation is probably the most difficult of the skills of the analyst. It can be very time-consuming and often causes friction when staff are aware of being observed. However, it can be a very valuable technique when properly used.

At its most basic this simply watching staff go about their routine tasks. Only observation gives the analyst first-hand experience of the system in operation. No other method can provide direct, independent corroboration of actual work methods.

The technique usually means that the analyst takes up an unobtrusive position in the relevant department or office and watches the activities of the staff for long enough to gain an accurate impression of work methods. Unless observation is carefully handled, people will resent being 'spied' upon, and may completely change their normal behaviour patterns while they think they are under observation.

The analyst may have to spend a very long time in position, or return several times, before being satisfied that the events observed are representative and not part of an abnormally busy or quiet period.

Observation is particularly useful for confirming or denying interviewees' statements about conditions within their office or department, particularly:

>   the volume of work carried out
>   the pressure staff are under
>   interruptions to work
>   'non-work' activities going on
>   staff attitudes, especially relations with supervisors
>   actual working conditions (noise, heat, surroundings)
>   bottlenecks and wastage
>   the normal pace of working
>   actual, as opposed to required, work methods
>   the layout of the office or department
>   informal communications channels
>   the relations between different departments
>   informal data stores

The main techniques of observation

The practice of observation, except at a very elementary level, is not for the novice. At this level of study you are only expected to be able to describe some of the main techniques. You would not be expected to know how to carry out the operations or how they are used in business applications.

The principal methods in common use are:

Activity sampling
Time surveys
Job synthesis or time synthesis
Time and motion study
Work study
Work measurement
Reperformance
Various forms of clerical work measurement.

Advantages of observation

First-hand knowledge is gained.

It exposes the informal information system.

It gives accurate information.

It demonstrates actual conditions.

It can show variation in workloads occurring during short periods.

Disadvantages of observation

It is very expensive in analyst's time.

Overall it is time-consuming; this holds up system development and can be expensive.

Unless handled very carefully it can easily antagonise staff.

Staff may change their behaviour under observation, so the analyst may only see a system modified for the outside observer's benefit.

There is a need to check the results derived from observations by discussion with people directly involved in the conditions observed.

Selecting the appropriate technique

In every investigation the analyst will have to use one or more of the four fact-finding techniques: interviewing, questionnaires, record inspection and observation. The correct mix of techniques will depend on the exact circumstances and on what the analyst is trying to achieve. An example may make this clearer.

A typical analyst's brief: Fashion Footwear

Figure 6.1 shows the organisational structure of Fashion Footwear Ltd. The company is a national retail group with seventy shops located throughout the country.

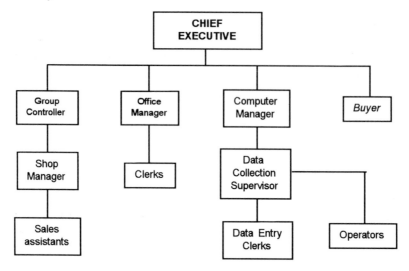

Figure 6.1

The shops sell a whole range of footwear from high fashion to workmen's boots. You have been employed by the management as an analyst to investigate their problems in order to propose a solution. You are briefed as follows.

> Each shop is staffed by a shop manager or manageress, and an average of four full-time assistants, usually with an additional two part-time Saturday assistants. The shops submit a daily report of sales to Head Office in Manchester. They also submit reports on any complaints about defective shoes. These reports are checked by head office staff. The complaints are destined for the Fashion Footwear buyer and the sales data is passed on to the data preparation staff before being processed by the computer.

> There are ten data preparation staff under the control of a supervisor. Day-to-day computer operations are run by three operators working under the data processing manager.

There is discontent at the shops because of incorrect and late processing of reports resulting in the shops not having adequate supplies of their fastest selling lines. There is also a growing dissatisfaction amongst both staff and customers about the handling of complaints. Staff notice that styles which have generated a lot of complaints are still being sent out from the warehouse and customers get no acknowledgement of their complaints for weeks.

The requirements

As an analyst you need to produce an overall plan for fact-finding indicating the method proposed for each different member of staff and for each group of personnel. You will also have to detail the fact finding study proposed for:

> The shop managers and shop assistants
> The head office clerical staff
> The data preparation staff

The solution for Fashion Footwear

The plan for fact-finding

The first thing that the analyst needs to do in this instance is to identify the problem precisely. It would be a mistake to assume that it is exactly as stated in the management brief above.

Real-world situations are always complex and the perceptions of the various staff cannot be relied upon to provide an accurate picture. For example, the statement that 'the staff notice styles which generated a lot of complaints are still being sent out' cannot be accepted by the analyst at face value. The statement appears to be based on memory which is generally unreliable. A lot of complaints to one person may be a few in someone else's judgement. The complaints may be restricted to just one shop, or even to just one batch of shoes. What is needed is hard data.

There are two aspects to this brief. One concerns the routine handling of stock requests, the other the more sensitive matter of the complaints procedure. One approach worth exploring might be to treat each separately.

For the complaints procedure perhaps the best approach would be for the analyst to set up a monitoring scheme. The first step would be to let all the staff in the group know that something was being done, and then to try to identify two typical shops and use them as monitoring centres. Here, the analyst uses the two shops as test outlets. With the co-operation of the two managers, every complaint is carefully logged by well-trained staff and the log periodically passed on to the analyst. The analyst then follows the progress of each complaint as it goes through the system.

The advantage of this approach is that after a relatively short time, say a week or two, the analyst would begin to get incontrovertible factual data on which to base a more detailed study.

The apparent problem of the sales returns is less straightforward. Probably the best approach would be to undertake some inspection of the records held in the two shops used to monitor the complaints. The objective of the record inspection is to get an accurate assessment of the average time taken to replenish stock sold and to ascertain the degree of discrepancy, if any, between items sold and items replaced.

By setting up the monitoring operation and assessing the results after a few weeks the analyst will soon be in a position to tell whether the charges of the shop staff are justified or not, and so identify the true extent of the problem and then proceed to investigate its causes.

Investigations with the shop manager and sales staff
From the brief details given in the question it is fairly obvious that it will be necessary at some point to interview some or all of the shop staff. With a large number of shops it is clearly impractical to interview every member of staff or even every manager.

The analyst would probably be best advised to set up an extensive in-depth interview with each of the two managers of the monitored branches, and with one or two of the full-time staff, as well as one of the part-timers. The arrangements for this would be fairly simple.

The interviews would aim to discover how well staff are trained, the pressures they work under and their understanding of the function of the reports.

From these interviews the analyst would be able to get a fair idea of the shop staff's point of view. As only two shops had been studied, the analyst would then produce a questionnaire to be sent out to some or all of the other shops to confirm or refute the impressions gained from the initial interviews.

The analyst would also want to carry out some direct observation of the shop staff at work, both in dealing with customers' complaints and to see how they actually went about completing the sales returns and complaints forms.

Investigations with the Head Office clerical staff
Very few details are available from the brief as to how head office clerical staff go about their tasks. The analyst would want to find out exactly what

their day-today routines are, and what problems arise in carrying out the procedures relating to sales returns and complaint forms.

The analyst would want to first set up an appointment with the office manager to appraise him of the situation and to get an overall impression of the section's work from a fairly brief interview.

The analyst would then want to meet the clerical staff at their place of work and observe them in the performance of their duties. This would primarily be in order to allow the analyst to trace the progress of the forms as they are checked and passed on to the data-processing section. This set of observations would allow the analyst to identify any blockages or delays, and to establish the care with which the forms are filled in by the individual shops. The analyst would use this opportunity to encourage the airing of any grievances which the staff in this section might have. It may also be possible at this point to gather any ideas the DP staff might have on how to improve the situation.

Investigations with the data preparation staff
The fact-finding study for this group of workers would be very similar to that for the Head Office clerks. An initial and brief meeting with the section head would be followed by a detailed evaluation of the working practices of the data entry staff.

This detailed study would try to assess the quality of the data presented for input, the exact times taken for work to be progressed through the system, any unnecessary delays in processing and the accuracy with which the operators do their work.

The study would depend very heavily on the observation of working practices but would also take informal interviews and record inspection into account.

Exercises

1. Design two questionnaires for Fashion Footwear, one for the shop manager, the other for the assistants, and comment on any differences between them.

2. Prepare an interview plan for the following proposed applications:

> A computerised ingredient-purchasing system for a canteen or restaurant
> A lending library's loan procedures
> A cost-control system for use in a garage or workshop

2. It is proposed to introduce micro-computers into parts of your organisation and the management want to know where the need is greatest and what the main benefits will be from installing the new equipment.

a) Design a suitable questionnaire for this situation.

b) What difficulties do you foresee arising from the installation of this equipment?

Further Reading

Davis, G. and Olson, M. (1985) Management Information Systems, conceptual foundations, structures and development. Pub McGraw-Hill, NY.

Eliason, A. (1990) Systems Development: Analysis, Design and Implementation. Pub Scott, Foresman/Little, Brown. Glenview, Ill.

Kendall, P. (1990) Introduction to Systems Analysis and Design: A structured approach. Pub Wm C. Brown, Dubuque IA.

Lucas, H. (1992) The analysis, design and implementation of information systems. Pub McGraw-Hill, NY.

Chapter 7 Charting techniques

Systems analysts have developed many different techniques to help in the process of analysing existing systems and the design of new systems. Many claims have been made for the superiority of one particular system but in practice no one system or technique will always be best. A good analyst will use different techniques at different times or on different stages of the job.

Advantages of the various techniques

There are three main techniques which every analyst should be familiar with:

- flowcharts
- document analysis
- decision tables

In addition there are a large number of less used techniques which every analyst should know of, without necessarily being skilled in their use, and which can be called on whenever a particular situation warrants it.

Flowcharts

Fowcharts are a means of showing the sequence of steps in a procedure in diagrammatic form **(logic flowcharts)**; alternatively they can be used to clarify the relationships between various parts of a system **(system flowcharts)**.

There are many different sets of flowcharts symbols, each of which answers a particular need, but all systems can be reduced to only five main symbols, the NCC standard symbols (see Figure 7. 1).

Advantages of flowcharts

Communication.
Flowcharts give a good visual representation of even very complex procedures. This makes them ideal for communicating the logic of a system to personnel at all levels. One picture is worth a thousand words.

Documentation
Flowcharts also provide a means of documentation useful in case analysts or programmers leave the firm. It also happens that the passage of time can obscure the logic behind a particular method, or there may be changes in the

101

operating procedures or in the system itself. Such changes can be easily shown on a flowchart.

Accuracy
In a complex procedure the problem can be tackled accurately, as a team effort by using flowcharts. This method has proved very effective in reducing the number of errors in program writing.

Analysis
Writing out the logic of a system as a flowchart is always of great help in understanding a system. By charting the many possible routes the programmer should be able to find a practical way of solving the problem.

Clarity
Flowcharts help the programmer get an overall view of the logic involved. This often leads to a realisation of poor structure and allows the programmer to refine and improve the program.

Visual impact
Presenting ideas in the form a flowchart may stimulate more interest in people associated with the project than a written report would.

Disadvantages of flowcharts

Complex logic
Where the logic is very convoluted the flowchart quickly becomes very complex and tends to obscure instead of clarifying.

Causality
The link between an action and the conditions which give rise to that action is not always apparent in a large flowchart.

Maintenance
For anything more than the very simplest of amendments it is usually necessary to redraw the entire section affected. This can be very time-consuming.

Reproduction
Flowchart symbols cannot be entered directly from a keyboard. It is not possible to store flowcharts in a standard word processor along with the descriptive text of the system under development.

Size
As systems grow in size so does the flowchart and they can easily become too large for convenience, or face the danger of being split over many pages.

Decisions
Flowcharts are not really suitable for systems containing large numbers of decisions. Such logic is much better displayed using a decision table.

Detail
Flowcharts offer no simple way of treating different levels of detail. Sometimes important features can be obscured where they are mixed in with logic of lesser importance.

Decision tables

Decision tables are used to analyse a problem in a related but different way from that of flowcharts. In general anything which can be described by a flowchart can also be incorporated into a decision table. Although there are no fixed rules, decision tables are usually preferred when the number of possible outcomes or conditions rise above ten or so. There are two types of decision table: **limited entry** and **extended entry.** Only limited entry decision tables are dealt with here.

The objective in preparing a decision table is first to ensure that all conditions and their associated actions are included and second, to ensure that all the rules of the procedure are both logical and clearly understandable. There must be no ambiguity whatsoever as this would defeat the whole point of the method.

Advantages of decision tables

Completeness
Simple mathematical techniques can ensure that every possibility is covered in the table. Similarly, they can ensure that every combination is unique and not duplicated.

Structure
Unlike flowcharts, the layout and format of decision tables is standard for all applications. This makes training and communication with non-specialists easier.

Reproduction
The table can be typed on an ordinary typewriter, so reproduction is simple.

Causation
There is a clear and direct link between actions and the conditions which lead to those action. This link allows the logic of a system to be followed easily and ensures that every eventuality is dealt with.

103

Compact size
A decision table is usually much more compact than an equivalent flowchart.

Clarity
Because of their standardised layout and compactness, decision tables in many cases are more acceptable in documentation which is aimed at casual users.

Maintenance
Decision tables are easily amended and maintained.

Analysis
When drawing up a decision table the analyst can arrange for the alternative actions to be grouped thus making analysis easier.

Design
Decision tables are an integral part of structured systems analysis and are extensively used in advanced analysis and design methodologies.

Disadvantages of decision tables

Sequencing
Decision tables give no indication of the sequence to be followed in evaluating the various conditions met.

Size
Where there are a large number of different actions the table can become excessively large, particularly with limited entry tables.

Clarity
To people unused to decision tables, a simple system with relatively straightforward logic might be better understood as a flowchart.

Document analysis

Most office systems are largely designed around the reception, origination, processing and filing of forms. Many offices are no more than paperwork production lines. This means that any attempt to design improved systems for office functions must inevitably concentrate on the forms in use.

Document analysis largely consists of carefully recording the information held on forms and then transcribing this on to grid charts. The grid charts are designed to reveal unnecessary duplication of data, data being collected and not used, and any unnecessary forms.

Advantages of document analysis

Rationalisation
Document analysis can almost always result in reduction of detail and elimination of duplicated documents.

Costs
A reduction in the number of forms in use and in the amount of data to be entered on them will normally lead to a reduction in the labour of forms processing, and ultimately to a reduction in costs.

File design
The careful examination of every document's information content will allow the analyst to build up a data dictionary for the whole system. This will give an insight into the files needed and serve as a basis for data modelling.

Verification
Document analysis can be performed independently of the main analysis as a way of checking that file contents have been correctly specified. An analyst will often want to ensure that day-today processing needs have not changed significantly from those specified in the early stages of a large project.

Analysis
Since the movement of forms and their data contents are central to many types of data processing systems, carrying out an initial document analysis exercise can be a good starting point for further investigation.

Disadvantages of document analysis

Time
To be done properly document analysis needs great care and so can be very time consuming.

Skills
Many clerical systems are of considerable complexity and it is often necessary to hire an experienced analyst to carry out document analysis successfully.

Logic flowcharts

Systems analysis is a relatively new discipline. It grew out of Organisation and Methods (O & M). When O & M specialists began turning their attention to the analysis and design of new computer systems they naturally used the tools and techniques with which they were familiar. Foremost amongst these were the various flowcharts techniques.

Although their techniques were very sophisticated, they soon had to be modified to deal with the special problems of computer logic. Each analyst developed his or her own way of accommodating the needs of computer logic by making modifications as and when needed. This rapidly led to a situation where the same flowcharts symbol could have many different meanings, depending on who had drawn the flowchart.

To overcome this problem the National Computer Centre (NCC) devised a reduced set of symbols to be used for expressing the logic of computer programs. These symbols are shown in Figure 7. 1.

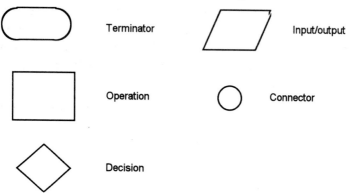

Figure 7.1 The NCC standard symbols

Interpretation of the symbols

Terminator
Terminators show entry and exit points from a program or sub-routine. All flowcharts must start and stop somewhere: the terminator shows where.

The word 'Start', 'Stop', or 'End' is written inside the terminator symbol as appropriate. A flowchart can have only one starting point, but may have more than one finishing point. You can see start and stop symbols in Figure 7.2.

Operation
This symbol is used to show any operation which does not involve moving data, storing data, or making a decision. This might be doing a calculation, resetting a value, or keeping count of a loop. Every operation box (also known as a process box) can have as many flow lines going into it as required, but never has more than one line leaving it.

Decision
Programs get their power from their ability to make decisions. However, computers have very limited reasoning powers and the only decisions they can

make are based on very simple questions which have a definite 'yes' or 'no' answer. These-are questions such as 'Is the customer's age greater than 18?' or 'Is this customer over the credit limit?'. Questions such as 'How old are you?' or 'How much is the credit limit?' cannot be answered by a 'Yes' or a 'No', and will have to be reworded before they can be used in a flowchart decision box.

No compound questions are allowed. A compound question is one which is really more than one question at a time. 'Is the order from a foreign company?' is really two questions: 'Is the customer based overseas?' and 'Is the customer a company, as opposed to a private individual?'.

Consider the question 'Is the applicant a woman over 30?'. If the reply is 'No', you could not be sure whether this means that the woman is actually under 30, or whether the applicant is in fact a man! The question must be rephrased to ask first 'Is the applicant female?'. Only then can it be established whether the applicant is over 30 or not.

A decision box can have only one input but must always have two outputs ('yes' and 'no').

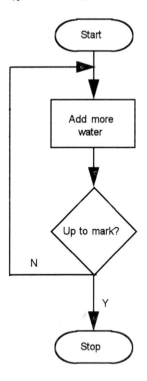

Figure 7.2

Loops

Decisions are frequently combined with operations to produce loops. Computer programs almost always contain loops. Consider the following instruction for making tea: 'Pour cold water into the kettle until it reaches the maximum mark'. This can be flowcharted as shown in Figure 7.2.

The logic of the program flows down the line from the start terminator symbol to the operation box 'Add more water', then continues to the decision diamond 'Up to mark?'. If the water level is not up to the maximum mark then the answer is 'No' and the program follows the *N* branch up the line to join the logic flow back into the operation box 'Add more water'. Eventually, having gone round the loop enough times the water level will be up to the mark and the answer will be 'Yes'. When that happens the program logic follows the *Y* line and the program stops.

Loops can go either forward or backwards. You can have loops within loops (**nested loops**). In order to avoid confusion the convention is that, as far as possible, the control lines of loops go clockwise. Forward loops go down the right hand side, backward loops go up the left hand side.

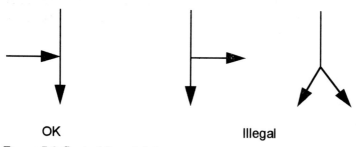

OK   Illegal

Figure 7.3 Control lines joining

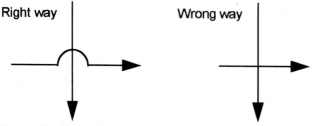

Figure 7.4 Control lines crossing

Control lines

All the symbols of a flowchart are linked by lines which show the flow of control. In general the flow should be from top to bottom and from left to right. Control lines may join at any point but may not diverge (Figure 7.3).

Lines can be shown crossing if necessary, using a hoop (Figure 7.4). In general, crossed flowlines should be avoided as they tend to make the flowchart more difficult to follow. Flowcharts should always be drawn with the lines parallel to the edges of the page and never at an angle.

Input/output

This symbol (see Figure 7.1) is used for any action which requires data to be moved. For example, input could be data being read from a file, such as a customer record; output might be data sent to a printer to make a hard copy of the customer record. This is also the symbol used to indicate the display of data on a VDU screen.

Off-page connectors

Flowcharts rapidly grow much larger than can be comfortably fitted onto a single page. A connector circle (see Figure 7.1) is used to link separate parts of a flowchart together. One connector is used to terminate a flowline on one page and another picks up the flowline on another page. They are identified by a reference, usually the page number.

It is not good practice to use connectors to link different parts of a flowchart which is all on the same page. Any number of flowlines can meet at a connector.

Rules of flowcharts

1   Always use a template

2   Use only the standard NCC symbols

3   Each chart should be clearly labelled with the title, author and date

4   Charts should be designed to be read from top to bottom, and left to right

5   The whole chart should be drawn at the same level of detail

6   Every flowchart must have one and only one starting point, and have at least one finishing point

7   Entry and exit points must be marked with terminator symbols

8   Control lines should have arrow heads on them whenever this makes the direction of flow clearer, but not otherwise

9   Avoid flowlines crossing wherever possible

10   All loops should go clockwise

11   Every decision box must have one input and two outputs

12   Questions in decision boxes must not be compound

13   The centres of symbols should be aligned vertically

14   A process box (operation), can have only one exit

15   A terminator can have many inputs, but only one output.

Analysing procedure descriptions

Drawing good flowcharts is largely a matter of practice. After a very short time you will be able to recognise what sort of flowchart will be needed just from reading the description of a procedure, called a **procedure narrative.**

The way to do this is to analyse the procedure description and separate out the operations, transfers of data and decisions. Decision situations can be further analysed to locate the various conditions and the corresponding actions.

As you read through the following description you should aim to first identify the decision situations. The key words to look for are 'if' and 'when'. Mark out the decisions by drawing a rectangle round any conditions in the text. Then underline any operations mentioned. Finally, look for keywords such as 'read', 'display' or 'print' which signify some input or output activity. Draw a ring round these in the text. You then have the basis for the flowchart. In practice it is normal to try out two or three rough attempts before producing the finished, final flowchart.

Example

Consider the following example. A clerk in a sales office takes the first order from the top of the pile. Then he calculates the value of the order by multiplying price by quantity for the first item mentioned on the order. If there is more than one item he does the same calculation for each item and adds the item total to the order total. When all the items on the order have been dealt with he writes out the order total and the job is complete.

We will work through this example in order to illustrate the principles involved. The first step is to identify inputs, outputs and decisions and processes. Circle the words 'takes' (a movement of data from the pile into the procedure), and 'writes' (a clear indication of output). The operations are not quite so easy to spot but it should be clear that there are two operations here: a price times quantity calculation, and an accumulation of the item totals calculation. The decision stage is quite obvious and you should have boxed in the condition 'When all the items' which is a statement which triggers some action. Now look at Figure 7.5 and see if you can find the similarities between your marked text and the finished flowchart.

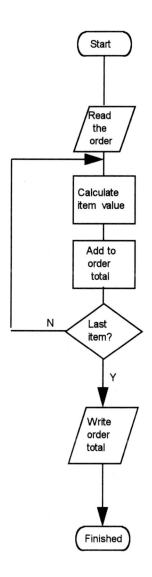

Figure 7.5 Order processing flowchart

Exercises

A few more examples will help you consolidate these ideas. For the two examples given below first go through the text and mark up the operations, data transfers and decisions as before and then compare your analysis with the finished flowcharts.

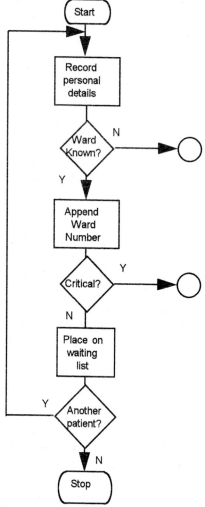

Figure 7.6 Casualty department flowchart

Exercise 1

An admissions nurse in a hospital casualty department records in the casualty register the personal details of all patients arriving for treatment. If the nurse is unsure of the treatment needed by each new arrival and is therefore unable

112

to establish the correct ward to which the patient should be sent, she hands over the patient to an orderly who takes over all responsibility from then on. Where there is no problem with the diagnosis the nurse then adds the ward number to the register. If the patient appears critically ill the nurse will summon a doctor immediately who then removes the patient to the appropriate ward. Patients who are not critical have their names added to a waiting list. The nurse then carries on with the next patient, if there is one.

The completed flowchart is shown in Figure 7.6.

In this flowchart the operations symbols could have been replaced by input output boxes if it was felt that this was more of a data exchange, i.e. a transfer, than an operation. This illustrates the point that there are often several correct ways of flowcharts the same procedure, depending on the assumptions made by the flowcharter.

The connector symbols are used here to signify that the patient passes into another system; in a commercial flowchart the correct page for the remainder of the procedure would be inserted in the circle.

Exercise 2
A wages clerk extracts the details from the next time card in his or her in-tray. From this the number of hours that the employee has worked in the previous week is established. Gross pay is then calculated by the clerk; once this figure is established the clerk can then work out the correct amount of income tax due. Workers with more than two years' service are in the pension scheme for which a deduction of 2% from their gross pay is made. The pay clerk can then calculate the net pay figure, and issues a completed payslip before carrying on with the next employee's time card.

The completed flowchart is shown in Figure 7.7.

By now you should feel comfortable about recognising the stages in a flowchart after analysing procedure descriptions. The next stage is to construct a flowchart for yourself. This will be done in two stages. You will first be asked to select the symbol appropriate to a particular descriptive phrase, and then to put these symbols into the correct order, so producing a finished flowchart. After working through the next three exercises you should be able to go on to the next stage, which is constructing a flowchart just from reading the procedure description.

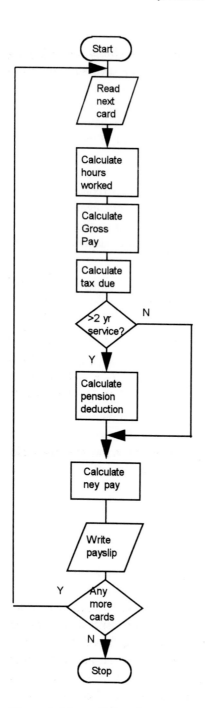

Figure 7.7 Payroll flowchart

Exercise 3

Suppose someone wanted to post a letter. This might involve the following steps (the phrases describing the various stages in the process have been arranged according to length, not logic):

A   Fold the letter
B   Post the letter
C   Sign the letter
D   Write the letter
E   Seal the envelope
F   Address the envelope
G   Put the letter in the envelope
H   Stick on a first class stamp if urgent
I   Stick on a second class stamp if not urgent

To write a flowchart for all the stages in posting a letter you must do three things. First, put the steps in the correct order, then identify the correct symbol to use and finally arrange the symbols into a well-drawn flowchart.

Arrange these steps into their logical order, select the appropriate symbol for each step, and draw up a flowchart according to the rules given earlier. Compare your answer with Figure 7.8. Your answer may differ slightly from Figure 7.8, for instance in the sequence of filling and addressing the envelope, but should be broadly similar to it.

Exercise 4

The following steps can be incorporated into a flowchart describing the tasks carried out by an operator at the check-out of Mason's Micromart.

A   Last item?
B   Display purchases total
C   Another customer waiting?
D   Read the price on the item
E   Reset register total to zero
F   Add the price to the running total

Arrange these steps into their logical order, select the appropriate symbol for each step, and draw up a flowchart according to the rules given earlier. Compare your answer with Figure 7.9. Once again your answer may differ slightly from that illustrated, in that an operation symbol can be used instead of an input/output symbol depending on the assumptions you have made, but the sequence should be the same and you should have remembered to add the start and finish terminators. Notice how nesting occurs when you have two loops, one inside the other.

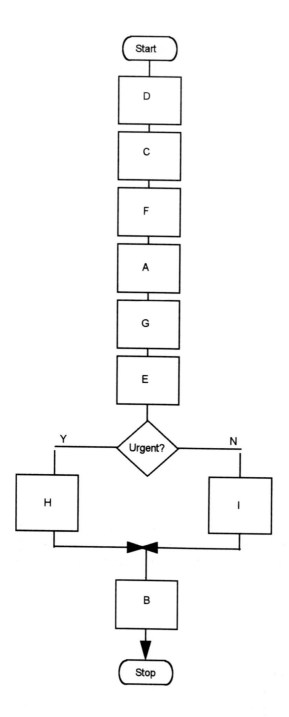

Figure 7.8 Flowchart for posting a letter

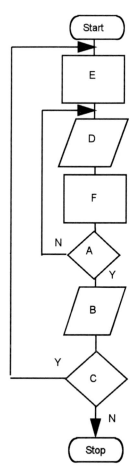

Figure 7.9 Mason's Micromart: checkout flowchart

Exercise 5
The service centre of Hatter Heating Engineers allocates call-out jobs for servicing heating equipment they have installed to the maintenance staff using the following instructions (guarantee work gets priority treatment). Compare your solution with Figure 7.10.

A   Any more requests?
B   Put on priority list
C   Fill in service register
D   Add name to waiting list
E   Is the equipment our brand?
F   Accept next service request
G   Model still under guarantee?
H   Allocate engineer to priority job

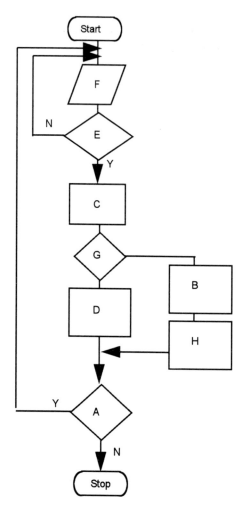

Figure 7.10 Hatter Heating Engineers: maintenance flowchart

You should now be ready to tackle the real thing: producing flowcharts direct from a procedure description. Flowcharts are largely a matter of practice. Try as many examples as possible and examine critically any complete flowcharts you come across. A wide variety of flowcharts conventions are currently in use, many of which do not conform to the general rules given here.

Exercise 6

Pelissier Photography Services charge for developing films on the basis of the type of film sent in for processing. For black and white films a basic processing and printing charge of £3.99 applies, unless the customer has specified a matt finish, in which case there is an additional charge of 75p per film. The cost of colour film processing depends on whether the film is disc or not. Disc costs £4.99 to process and print, other types are charged at £5.25 per film. There is a 50p postal charge for each film (Figure 7.11).

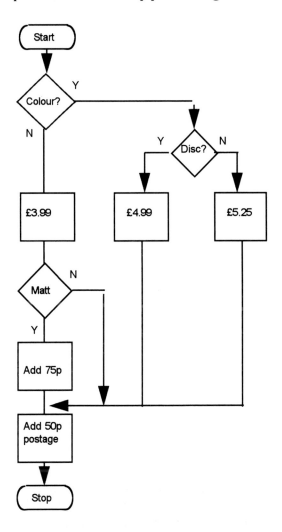

Figure 7.11 Pelissier Photography Services: processing charges flowchart

Exercise 7

The stock control section of Alfred Waller Motors Ltd are very proud of the fact that they very seldom run out of spare parts, no matter how hard to get they may be. They are able to maintain this level of service by always following their stock reordering procedure correctly. They reorder stock once a week without fail.

To reorder stock, the chief clerk goes through each stock record card. If stock level is greater than the reorder level, the card is replaced without further action. If below the reorder level the clerk calculates the quantity required.

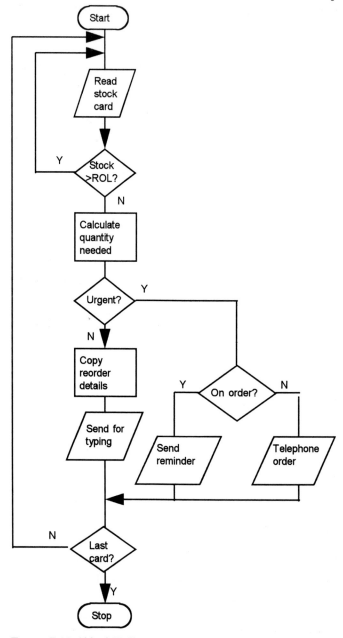

Figure 7.12 Alfred Waller Motors: parts department flowchart

If the order is not urgent the clerk writes out the part number and the quantity to order, and passes this on to be typed. If the order is urgent the clerk checks to see if there is already an outstanding order for that particular part. If there is, the clerk sends a reminder; if not, he or she telephones the supplier straight away. (see Figure 7.12)

Exercise 8

Jeremy Green runs a computer supplies company in the north of England and always applies the same rules for calculating delivery charges. These are that there is no charge for deliveries in Cleveland if the order is over £100 and no charge for orders over £250 outside the Cleveland area. Otherwise orders in Cleveland are charged at a flat rate £2.50 for orders valued at £50 or more and at 5% of value for smaller orders. Deliveries outside Cleveland, other than those mentioned above, are charged at £5 for orders valued at £100 or more; otherwise at 5% of value (see Figure 7.13).

Rules for checking flowcharts

1   Use only the prescribed symbol set

2   Logic flow should be mainly from top to bottom and mainly left to right

4   Begin with a terminator symbol and end with a terminator symbol

6   Only given terms may be used

7   Each given term should be used at least once

8   Each term may be abbreviated

9   Each term should be associated with its appropriate symbol

10   Each term should be written inside its appropriate symbol

11   Every decision-box should have one entry and two exits

12   Flows from a decision-box should be labelled either Y or N

13   A process box can have only one exit

14   A process box can have any number of inputs

15   All loops should move in a clockwise direction

16   Flowlines should be shown with arrows

17   Flowlines should diverge only via a process or decision box

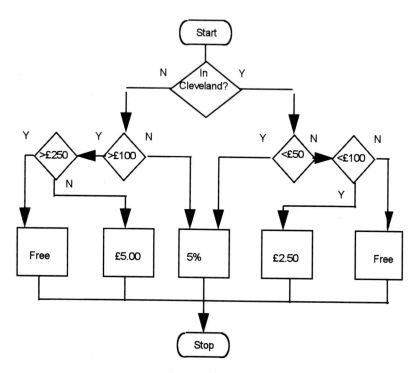

Figure 7.13 JSG Computer Consumables Ltd: order value flowchart

System flowcharts

Flowcharts can be constructed for every level of detail ranging from very low-level logic charts with a mass of detail, written with programmers in mind, to very high-level computer procedure charts with much less detail, written for managers who need only a rough overview of how a system operates. In between these two extremes there is a whole spectrum of flow-charting techniques, each designed to serve a different purpose.

One of the commonest of these charting techniques describes the relationship between the input, output and processing functions of a particular computer

122

system. It emphasises the logical view of the processing function, describing the actions which the system must perform, but not the hardware which will carry out those actions.

Unfortunately there is quite a lot of confusion as to what these various intermediate charts should be called. They are variously called system run charts, program run charts, system flowcharts, system charts, procedure charts and system process charts. There are many other names for them. In the text which follows this type of chart will be called a system runchart.

System runchart symbols

As was the case with logic flowcharts, the NCC has drawn up a standard set of symbols which should be used in the construction of system flowcharts. The standard symbols are shown in Figure 7.14.

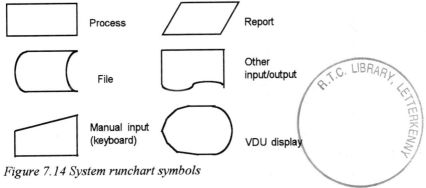

Figure 7.14 System runchart symbols

Process
The process symbol is used to indicate any processing of data, that is, any action which transforms data from one state to another, such as sorting, validating, updating or storing. In system runcharting, the process box generally summarises the effect of the relevant program and is labelled accordingly; sometimes it contains the actual name of the program. The process symbol serves very nearly the same purpose as the operation symbol does in logic flowcharts.

File
This is the symbol used to show any store of data. Only one storage symbol is used, no matter what type of physical storage media are involved. Master files must be clearly identified and treated separately from transaction files. Some common types of flowchart that you may come across use more than one symbol for storage, for example to show magnetic tape or disk drives. Those flowcharts are designed to emphasise the physical organisation of the system,

123

in other words, how the processing is organised. The flowcharts in this section, system runcharts, are designed to reveal the logic of the system. This emphasises what processing must be done, and is less concerned with precisely how this is achieved.

Manual input

This symbol represents a computer keyboard seen from the side. The commonest form of data input to a computer system is still by manual key depressions, which is why this form of input has its own symbol.

Report

A report is any printed output delivered by a computer system. This means that a report could be anything from the description of last week's sales broken down by product, a listing of customer's names and addresses, or even a pay cheque.

Other input/output

Originally computer installations almost exclusively used keyboards for input and printers for output. In modern data processing there is a wide variety of other, newer, input and output methods, far too many to have their own symbols. But they are all represented by this one symbol. The symbol is generally referred to as the 'I/O' (input/output) symbol. Typical I/O methodologies include: OCR (optical character recognition), OMR (optical mark recognition), and bar codes for input; plotters; and COM (computer output on microfilm) and paper tape for output.

Display

Because of the increasing importance of on-line interrogation facilities, and because the information potential of on-line access differs significantly from that of printed information (hard copy), this type of output, a VDU (visual display unit), has been allocated its own symbol. It is often combined with the report symbol to show that the information is available both as hard copy (computer printout) and as soft copy (on-line VDU screen display).

Flowlines

The relationship between each symbol is shown by flowlines. These always have an arrowhead on them to indicate the direction of data flow and to give an overall impression of the order of processing. As before, charts are designed to be read primarily from top to bottom and from left to right.

Labelling

Every symbol must be labelled, except keyboard input and VDU output where labelling is optional. Report symbols should have the report name or the subject written inside the symbol. Similarly, the actual input/output method must be written inside the I/O symbol whenever it is used.

Processes should be labelled according to the following scheme:

the first word should be a verb, such as 'sort', 'match' 'validate', 'update', etc.

the second word should be a descriptive adjective such as 'unsorted', 'invalid', 'validated', 'allocated'

the final word should be a noun such as 'record', 'file' or 'transaction', for example.

File labels should describe the contents of the file such as 'product', 'customer', 'order', plus some qualifying adjective such as 'unsorted', 'valid', 'matched' or 'rejected', for instance.

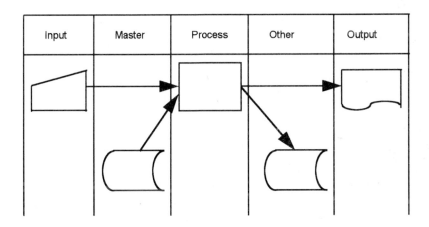

Figure 7.15 General layout of system runchart

System runchart layout

The general layout of a system runchart is fixed, and there must be no deviation from it. The framework is shown in Figure 7.15 with some symbols drawn in to make its purpose clearer.

The first column, labelled 'Input', is used only for the keyboard symbol or the I/O symbol. The second column always holds the system master files and nothing else. The middle column always shows the processes (programs) involved. The 'other' column is for any files which are not master files. These will include work files, reference files, and of course transaction files. If there are no files other than transaction files in this column then it can be labelled as 'transaction', instead of 'other'. The final column shows the system outputs. Three symbols can appear here: the VDU, report and I/O symbols.

This framework is used extensively in commercial data processing to describe the processing activities in a system, but although the symbols are always shown in their correct positions, the framework is often omitted altogether. After a little practice, reading the runcharts this way becomes quite natural and the framework is not missed at all.

Using the symbols

As an example of the use of system flowcharting consider the following description of a credit card company's processing system:

'Every day we receive payments from customers, we call them cardholders, and vouchers from the retailers which end up as charges to the cardholders. We take the payment records, put them into batches of fifty, and enter them in at a VDU terminal. A program stores all the records in one large transaction file, and for security purposes we produce a batch summary sheet for each batch. We do the same thing for the vouchers.

At the end of the day we take the voucher file and the payments file and sort them into the same order as the cardholder master file. We then use this sorted cardholder charges file, and the sorted payments file to update the cardholder master file, and we produce a new version of the master file which then shows the most up-to-date position. As part of the master file update two reports are produced, one showing the total of the payments for the day, the other totalling the day's charges.'

The finished flowchart of the credit card company's processing is shown in Figure 7.16. Most of the flowchart should be self explanatory once you have read the description, but some comments may be helpful at this point.

The subsystems for creating the batches of payments and charges are shown separately because they are operated as separate programs. The dotted lines help to make it clear which parts of the processing are done several times a day, depending on the number of batches, and which parts are done only once a day.

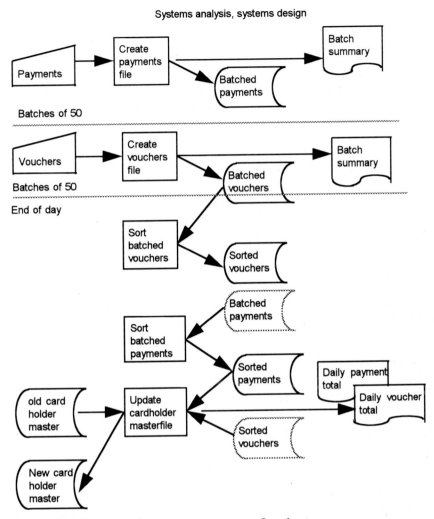

Figure 7.16 Credit card company: processing flowchart

The vouchers transaction file is shown joined to the sort procedure even though this means that the control flowline crosses the batch process boundary. This is perfectly acceptable because the meaning is quite clear. The payments transaction file, on the other hand, cannot be shown connected directly to its sort program because the voucher sort procedure is in the way. It is a convention of flowcharting that system runcharts should not have any crossed lines.

The way to get round this problem is to show the transaction file again, in a more convenient position. In a large system runchart it might not be clear that the duplicated file had in fact come from elsewhere on the chart, so the duplicated file is shown with its symbol drawn dotted, as in the example.

The processing described is a classic 'updating by copying' routine and uses the 'old master, new master' type of file update. If it was required to show the cardholder master file being done by an 'update in place' routine, with disk instead of tape storage, then a single master file symbol would be shown, but the line from the process would have an arrowhead at both ends.

Principles of flowcharting

The following examples are given as further illustrations of how to use the symbols correctly in drawing up system flowcharts, largely by showing how not to use them.

Example
The runchart in Figure 7.17 is meant to show a transaction being matched against its corresponding master file and the record then being printed out. However, the flowchart has two major errors in it. The wrong symbol has been used for a storage device, and it is in the wrong place. A file can only ever be shown in the 'master' or 'other' columns, which are to the immediate right and left of the process symbol. Therefore, whether the misrepresented file is meant to be a master file or a transaction file, it is not in the correct position.

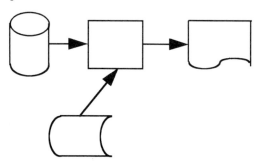

Figure 7.17 Incorrectly drawn flowchart

Example
The runchart in Figure 7.18 is meant to describe how a transaction is entered at a keyboard and then printed out on one list if it is correct and onto another list if it is incorrect. The runchart is wrong because it contravenes one of the rules of runcharting: Input must always go into a process; it cannot go directly into any other symbol. In this case it should be obvious that some sort of processing symbol should be included to distinguish between valid and invalid records: this cannot be done by a file alone. The decision as to which is valid is assumed to take place within the program. A system runchart never

shows decisions directly, the way you would in a logic flowchart. Notice that two outputs from one process is quite acceptable.

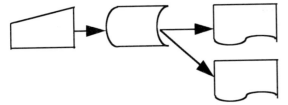

Figure 7.18 Incorrectly drawn flowchart

Example

The runchart in Figure 7.19 is trying to show information essential to a calculation being entered at a VDU; this is then checked for consistency, some data is called from a master file and the results of the calculation are sent to a graph plotter.

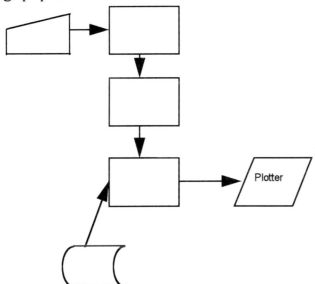

Figure 7.19 Incorrectly drawn flowchart

This runchart appears to be in order with all the right symbols in the right positions. However, the processes shown are wrong for this type of runchart. The basic rule is that no process ever connects directly to another process; it must be linked through a file. The logic of the runchart is still preserved if the three process boxes are combined into one, as they should be.

This runchart also illustrates another important point. Before data can be obtained from it, the master file must first be opened and the correct file located within it. But the arrow only shows data coming out of the file. This is another convention of system runcharting, that only the major flows of data are shown. The instruction to open the master file is not a major item and does not affect the overall logic of the system and so is not shown. Only the net effect of data flows are shown.

Example

Figure 7.20 shows data being input through an OCR reader, validated against a master file and stored in a transaction file. The transaction file is matched with the corresponding record in another file to produce a listing of the matched records. This flowchart is incorrectly drawn because it contravenes the rule that data may not pass directly from one file to another; it must go through an intermediate process. Inserting a process symbol, suitably labelled, between transaction and master file would make this chart correct.

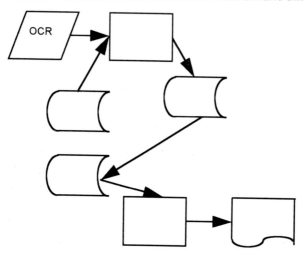

Figure 7.20 Incorrectly drawn flowchart

The rules of system flowcharting/runcharting

1. Use only the prescribed symbol set

2. Logic flow should be mainly top to bottom

3. Columns must be in the order of: Input, Master File, Process, Other files (or transaction), Output

4. All data flow lines must be arrowed to indicate flow direction

5. Arrowheads should show only the direction of net data flow

6. Updates in place are shown by a double arrowhead

130

7.   Every symbol must be clearly labelled

8.   Repetition or batching is shown by a dotted line and appropriate wording

9.   Input must always be to a process

10.   Output always comes from a process

11.   Files always get input from a process and send output through a process

12.   A process always has both input and output

13.   A process never connects directly to another process

14.   Decisions are never shown

Example

The following example is given as a final demonstration of the principles and practice of system runcharting. You should attempt it yourself before looking at the solution given in Figure 7.21.

R & S Maher Ltd's stock control procedure involves keying in all orders received in batches of twenty. As the day goes on each batch is added to a transaction file. A batch summary is printed out as each batch is completed.

At the end of the day orders received are sorted into customer number sequence. The sorted file is then validated against the customer master file with the object of producing two new transaction files. One contains all the orders which are within the customer credit limit (valid orders), the other contains the remainder, those orders which cannot be filled because the customer has gone over the credit limit. As part of the processing the customer is notified that the order has been rejected.

The valid orders are then sorted into product number order and a file is produced which is matched against the product master file to check the current stock level. Any item with a low stock is listed out for the buyer, any item which is almost out of stock is copied into a reorder file.

The reorder file is used in the final process to print purchase orders for suppliers. This process reads the current balance figure from the products master file and the supplier name and address from the supplier master file. Using the quantity ordered figure in the reorder file the program calculates the amount to order and prints this on the purchase order. At the same time that the program reads the supplier name and address details it updates the supplier file directly to show that an order has been issued.

131

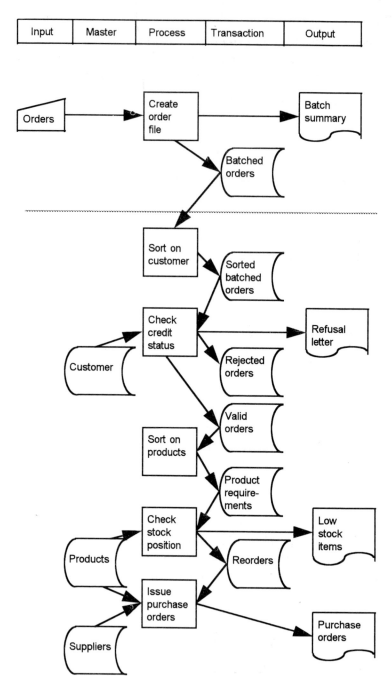

Figure 7.21 R & S Maher Ltd: stock control flowchart

Exercises

1. Which flowchart goes with which computer situation?
Figures 7.22 to 7.25 are designed to test your knowledge of flowcharting and your powers of reasoning. Each runchart represents one of the following:

A.   Give managers on-line access to updates files

B.   Create a transaction file with on-line validation

C.   Create a transaction file with off-line batch validation

D.   Update a master file where the system uses tape files only

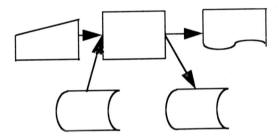

Figure 7.22 Self test flowchart

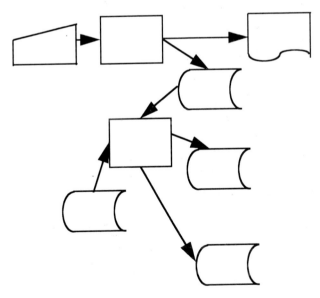

Figure 7.23 Self test flowchart

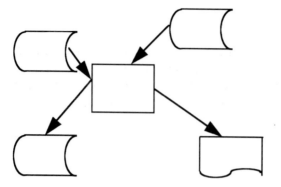

Figure 7.24 Self test flowchart

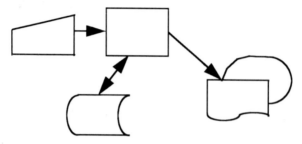

Figure 7.25 Self test flowchart

2. *Whangarei Pharmaceuticals*

A manager has told you: 'Orders are input as soon as they are received from the reps. We type them all in regardless of where they come from but they have to be sorted into sales territories before they can be processed any further. Then they are sorted into product order so that they can be checked against the sales contract master file. Any products which are not available for that territory are listed out as error items, products which are no longer made are written into a transaction file. We do this every day until Friday when we run the weekly order processing program.

This procedure first of all merges all the daily transaction files into one weekly file. The weekly file is sorted into customer order within area order and a confirmation of the order is printed in two copies taking the shipment details from the customer file. When that job is done the file is sorted into product order and a master listing of all the ingredients needed to make this weeks orders is produced by running the products against the manufacturing description file. As well as being printed out the total ingredients needed are recorded in a master file which is later used to send purchase orders to suppliers.'

Draw a system runchart; How could this procedure be improved?

Decision tables

Decision tables are used to analyse a problem in a related but different way from that of flowcharts. In general anything which can be described by a flowchart can also be incorporated into a decision table. Many different types of decision tables have been developed, but for the examination you are only required to use the limited entry type described here.

The aims in preparing a decision table are:

1   To ensure that all conditions and their associated actions are properly considered

2   To ensure that all the rules as stated are both logical and clearly understandable

3   To ensure that any areas of ambiguity are identified and resolved

Constructing a simple decision table

Decision tables are arranged in four parts as shown below (Figure 7.26).

Conditions	Rules
Actions	Outcomes

Figure 7.26 Arrangement of decision tables

The best way to show how decision tables are drawn up is to take a simple example. Suppose you are the green-keeper at Wimbledon. To do your job properly you are given a set of rules to follow:

> 'If the grass is too long you cut it; if there are weeds you apply a weedkiller'.

This description of the problem is called a **procedure narrative**. In this case we have two conditions: the grass either is or is not too long, and weeds are either present or they are not. There are also two actions which can be taken, cut the grass or apply weedkiller. The logic of this situation can be expressed very neatly in a decision table (Figure 7.27).

You start by drawing two crossed lines, then write all the conditions in the top left section in the form of simple questions with only 'yes' or 'no' answers, and then list all the possible actions in the bottom left section.

Grass too long?	
Any weeds showing?	
Cut the grass	
Apply a weedkiller	

Figure 7.27

Now you have to work out all the possibilities and decide what the correct action would be for each different case.

In this example if the grass is too long the correct action is to cut it, and if there are weeds, to apply weedkiller. This information can be entered in the table by putting a 'Y' (for yes) in the upper right section opposite the condition it applies to, and an 'X' in the lower right section opposite the correct action to be taken. Use a separate column for each one (Figure 7.28).

Grass too long?	Y	
Any weeds showing?		Y
Cut the grass	X	
Apply a weedkiller		X

Figure 7.28

What happens if when you look at the lawn the grass is too long and there are also weeds present? That is clearly another possibility and the correct answer is of course that you must both cut the grass and apply weedkiller. This is shown by putting a 'Y' opposite the first condition and another 'Y' opposite the second condition, but in the same column, and putting 'X's opposite both of the actions in the bottom section (Figure 7.29).

Grass too long?	Y		Y	
Any weeds showing?		Y	Y	
Cut the grass	X		X	
Apply a weedkiller		Y	X	X

Figure 7.29

There is still another possibility to consider. What happens if the grass is not too long and there are no weeds? This is also a possibility and has to be allowed for. What will the correct action be? In this case it will

136

presumably be to get out the deck chair, relax and wait for something to grow - but whatever the correct answer it is not yet included in our list of actions. Since you are a hard-working type, we'll say that the correct action is to get on with the next job.

This possibility is shown in the table by first adding the missing action to the list of actions, putting an 'N' (for no) opposite each condition in the upper section and entering an 'X' opposite the action in the lower section (Figure 7.30).

Grass too long?	Y	Y	N
Any weeds showing?		Y Y	N
Cut the grass	X	X	
Apply a weedkiller		X X	
Go on to next job			X

Figure 7.30

Finally, to tidy up the table we remove any possible ambiguity by entering 'N's in the two blank spaces in the upper right section to show that the conditions applying in column one and column two are quite different from those in column three (Figure 7.31).

Grass too long?	Y	N Y	N
Any weeds showing?	N	Y Y	N
Cut the grass	X	X	
Apply a weedkiller		X X	
Go on to next job			X

Figure 7.31

The decision table is now complete.

Building more complex decision tables

Decision tables are not always so simple. Consider the following procedure narrative for calculating the insurance premium for a car driver.

> 'Young drivers, anyone under 25 that is, are the most likely to be involved in an accident; the riskiest cars are sports cars and any driver with a licence endorsement is twice as likely to have a claim as one with a clean licence - so we set our premiums accordingly.'

A young sports-car driver with a clean licence will be charged 30% over the standard rate; older sports-car drivers with a clean licence get charged 10% over. If you've got endorsements and want to drive a sports car older drivers are charged 20% over and young drivers are just refused - we won't cover them at all.

A young saloon-car driver (saloon cars are cars that are not sports cars) with an endorsed licence pays 20% extra and an older saloon-car driver with a clean licence pay no surcharge on the standard car. All other cases pay a 10% surcharge'.

The way to draw up the decision table is the same as in the first example. First draw two crossed lines and write all the conditions in the top left section and all the actions in the lower left section. In more complex procedure narratives, separating out the basic conditions and actions from the text can sometimes be difficult and it often helps to underline the conditions and circle round the various actions with a pencil to make them stand out clearly.

Another problem can be wording the conditions as questions with only yes/no answers. You cannot use a question such as 'Age?', since a Y or N response is meaningless but a question such as 'Less than 25?' is fine since all drivers are indisputably either "under 25" or "25 or over" at the time of application. Similarly the question 'Young driver?' would be acceptable provided an exact definition of what is meant by 'young' was easily available.

You must not ask compound questions such as 'Young sports-car driver?' or 'Older driver with clean licence?'. These questions have yes/no answers but they combine two questions within one. The first example should be phrased as 'Young driver?' followed by 'Sports car?'; the second as 'Young driver?' followed by 'Clean licence?'.

Once the conditions have been identified and the questions formulated fill in the table as far as you can with the information from the procedure narrative. The second paragraph gives you details for sports cars and lets you fill in four **rules** (each column of a decision table is called a rule) (Figure 7.32).

The order of the questions is not important, so you could ask about age first and then the type of car if you wanted to.

The next paragraph of the procedure narrative gives details of charges for saloon cars (consider anything not a sports car as a saloon car). This time the information is not so easy to get at. Two rules and actions can be filled in right away, but how many 'other cases' are there?

Fortunately, with a correctly constructed decision table you can always tell how many rules there should be and can therefore identify any missing ones. In this case there are two rules missing and the total number should be eight rules.

Sports car?	Y	Y	Y	Y
Young driver?	Y	N	N	Y
Clean licence?	Y	Y	N	N
30% surcharge	X			
10% surcharge		X		
20% surcharge			X	
Cover refused				X

Figure 7.32

Permutation rule
The number of rules required is always two raised to the power of the number of conditions, i.e.

2 x 2 = 4 (2 to the power of 2) 2 conditions

2 x 2 x 2 = 8 (2 to the power of 3) 3 conditions

2 x 2 x 2 x 2 = 16 (2 to the power of 4) 4 conditions

and so on. The partly completed table now looks like this, with two rules still missing (Figure 7.33).

Sports car?	Y	Y	Y	Y	N	N
Young driver?	Y	N	N	Y	Y	N
Clean licence?	Y	Y	N	N	N	Y
30% surcharge	X					
10% surcharge		X				
20% surcharge			X	X		
Cover refused				X		
No surcharge					X	

Figure 7.33

139

After a bit of juggling you will find that that the only other possibilities not covered are NNN and NYY. The completed decision table is shown in Figure 7.34:

Sports car?	Y	Y	Y	Y	N	N	N	N
Young driver?	Y	N	N	Y	Y	N	N	Y
Clean licence?	Y	Y	N	N	N	Y	N	Y
30% surcharge	X							
10% surcharge		X					X	X
20% surcharge			X		X			
Cover refused				X				
No surcharge						X		

Figure 7.34

Principles of design

Standardising the rules
A general way of tackling problems is by standardising. Once you've done a few decision tables you will find it easier to determine the number of rules needed from the number of conditions found and lay the rules out in a fixed order first, instead of in the order they happen to be in the procedure narrative. This ensures that in a large table you do not miss any or put in duplicate rules.

The easiest method is to find the number of rules using the number of conditions. This will always be an even number. In the first row of the rule section write half the entries as 'Y' and the second half as 'N'. Then move down to the second row and under the 'Y's write half of that number as 'Y's and rest as 'N's. Under the 'N's in the row above again put in half 'Y's and half 'N's. Continue in this way until you are down to alternate Y's and N's (see Figure 7.35).

Two conditions

Condition 1	YYNN	then	Condition 1	YYNN
Condition 2			Condition 2	YNYN

Three conditions

Condition 1	YYYYNNNN	Condition 1	YYYYNNNN	Condition 1	YYYYNNNN
Condition 2		Condition 2	YYNNYYNN	Condition 2	YYNNYYNN
Condition 3		Condition 3		Condition 3	YNYNYNYN

Figure 7.35

140

Standardising the actions

Reading and constructing decision tables is usually made easier if you arrange the actions into some sort of logical order, rather than as you find them. Combining standard rules and ordered actions produces a neater table as shown below.

Sports car?	Y	Y	Y	Y	N	N	N	N
Young driver?	Y	N	N	Y	Y	N	N	Y
Clean licence?	Y	Y	N	N	N	Y	N	Y
No surcharge						X		
10% surcharge			X		X			X
20% surcharge				X		X		
30% surcharge	X							
Cover refused		X						

Figure 7.36

Standardising the conditions

In the insurance premium example, changing the order of the conditions makes no difference but in other examples a lot of time and effort can be saved by imposing some sort of order. This is particularly true when varying quantities or values affect the outcome.

The Everitt Employment bureau operates the following procedure:

'Every applicant for office typing work has to take our speed and competence test. Any one getting 25% or less is not registered, no matter what they have said on their application form.

Applicants who get between 25% and 50% are still not very welcome and we only put on our branch provisional list if they have a City and Guilds Certificate and have had at least two years' relevant experience.

People over 50% up to 75% are a better prospect. If they have 2 years experience or if they have the certificate we put them on the provisional list but if they don't have either then we won't register them at all.

Anyone doing over 75% goes straight onto our city-wide circulation sheet unless they don't have the relevant experience and they don't have the certificate. Those applicants only go on the provisional list'.

The conditions for the test in this example can be reduced from four, requiring 16 rules, to three, needing only eight, by suitably arranging the order. The obvious way to arrange the scores is:

0-25%
26-50%
51-75%
76-100%

but a better way is in descending order which eliminates the need to ask 'Is it over 25%, then is it over 50%? etc. and allows the introduction of the **dash rule**. The dash replaces a yes/no question where it would be superfluous as here, where if someone scores over 75%, you don't have to ask if they've scored over 50% (Figure 7.37):

Score over 75%?	YNYY
over 50%?	- YNN
over 25%?	- - YN

Figure 7.37

Adding in the conditions about experience and qualifications and using the dash rule there too, produces a final decision table (Figure 7.38):

Score over 75%?	YYY	NNNN	NNN	N
over 50%?	- - -	YYYY	NNN	N
over 25%?	- - -	- - - -	YYY	N
2 yrs experience?	YNN	YYNN	YYN	-
C & G certificate?	- YN	YNYN	YN -	-
City register	XX	?		
Provisional	X	?XX	X	
Reject		? X	XX	X

Figure 7.38

In this example the decision table has demonstrated one of its main advantages, that of finding any ambiguities present in the narrative. It is not precisely clear from the narrative what happens when there is a score over 50% with both experience and qualifications - the analyst would go back to the source and seek clarification.

Notice that without ordering the conditions there would be six conditions requiring sixty-four rules (2 to the power of 6), but with ordering and the dash rule the final table is actually very compact (and in fact could be reduced even further by the more refined techniques used in extended entry decision tables. These are beyond the scope of this level of study).

Rules for drawing up decision tables

1   Underline all the conditions in the procedure narrative

2   Circle or use dash underlining to identify all actions in the narrative

3   Express the conditions as yes/no questions

4   List the actions as instructions in the action stub

5   Calculate the number of possibilities from the number of conditions

6   Fill in the Y/N combinations using the 'rule of halving'

7   Select the appropriate action under each rule

8   Use only X's in the 'outcomes' section

9   Use the dash rule where appropriate

Example

Citycentre Couriers operate a motor-cycle courier service for computer media, mostly in central London. For a standard item the charge is £4.00 anywhere in the city centre, or £8.00 for the outer suburbs. Each item is guaranteed collected and delivered that day, but usually within four hours. However, when the sender wants the item picked up and delivered immediately, say within 20 minutes, an express rate of £8.00 applies in the city. In all cases if the item is of a financial nature, for instance to and from a bank, a 10% security surcharge applies (usually this is paid in cash to the cycle rider).

A limited-entry decision table for the example could be as in Figure 7.39:

| Standard delivery? | YYYY NNNN |
| City delivery? | YYNN YYNN |
Financial item?	YNYN YNYN
Charge £4.00	XX ??
Charge £8.00	XX XX
Add 10% surcharge	X X X

Figure 7.39

The solution you might have arrived at could be a little different depending on the assumptions you made. The decision table was constructed on the basis that there were three conditions:

• Delivery can be standard or express

• Item can be financial or non-financial

• Area can be city or suburbs

It was assumed that the 10% surcharge paid to the driver was incidental, did not affect the logic of the decision table, and so does not appear. The 10% surcharge is shown in the action stub just as an instruction, but it

143

could be shown as 'add 40p' and 'add 4.40' and so on, if preferred. Any of these methods is acceptable.

The last two rules have no actions associated with them. This is because the question does not state explicitly what happens when there is a request for an express delivery outside the city. You might well have decided that there are no such deliveries, or that they are charged at £8.00, or some other figure applies. As long as you have stated your assumption clearly, your answer will be acceptable.

Document analysis grids

Document analysis is a simple technique which uses a grid to clarify the relationship between the various documents used in a department, and to identify the information carried by them. This grid is simply a matrix with the names of the documents written down one side, and the various items of information used listed along the top. A simple example is shown in Figure 7.40.

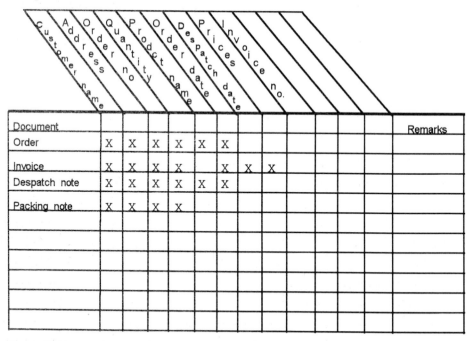

Document	Customer name	Address	Order date	Quantity	Product no	Order ref	Despatch date	Price each	Invoice no.						Remarks
Order	X	X	X	X	X	X									
Invoice	X	X	X	X		X	X	X							
Despatch note	X	X	X	X	X	X									
Packing note	X	X	X	X											

Figure 7.40 A simple document analysis grid

Data items

Forms consist of two parts: the heading (e.g. 'order form') and the entries (the information which the form contains). Internal documents start with

144

just a framework and have all their entries inserted during processing. External documents arrive with some entries already made, although additional entries are often added. For example on an order form, which is an external document, typical entries might be customer name, customer address, quantity ordered and order date. Other entries which could be added once the order had been received might be prices, delivery date, and the corresponding invoice number for cross-referencing purposes. The general name for all types of information entries is **data item**.

The same data items typically appear on several different documents; for example; the customer name will be on the order, the advice note, the packing note and on the invoice. It may be unavoidable, but this duplication is often the source of mistakes. It is also very time-consuming if the same data items have to be copied many times onto different documents and files.

An analyst will often use a document analysis grid to try to highlight duplicated data items. The type of grid shown in Figure 7.40 is typical of the sort of analysis produced. This grid shows a number of data items and the documents on which each of them appears. Where a data item is present on a document a cross is entered in the appropriate square.

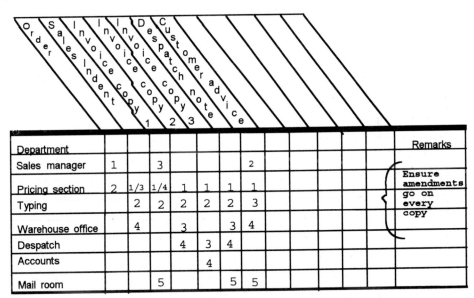

Key: sequence of document routing is 1,2,3 etc

Figure 7.41 Document grid

The grid pattern is essential to this form of document analysis, but there are two variations that are possible. Grids can be used to show how forms are routed through departments or processes within the system; these are called **document/department charts**.

Alternatively, a grid can be used to record the flow of information as one particular form or set of forms passes through a data processing activity; this form of grid is called a **document/data item grid chart**.

Document/department grids

An example of a document/departmental grid chart is shown in Figure 7.41. This shows the sequence in which various documents progress from office to office within a sales order procedure.

The construction of the chart is quite simple. The analyst merely has to identify all the documents in use and follow each through all the stages of its processing. As each document is traced the analyst fills in the order of movement by recording the sequence number in the appropriate box. For instance, consider the third document shown in the list along the top side of the grid. This is the top copy of a multipart invoice set and is described on the grid as 'invoice copy 1'. This is shown as originating from the pricing section, going to be typed, then going to the sales manager for checking, then returning to the pricing office (for any amendments), and finally going to the mail room, from where it will be posted to the customer. Similarly, the two other parts of the invoice set can be traced in sequence from department to department.

Document/data item grid chart

This type of grid chart is simply a refinement of the X-chart shown in Figure 7.40. Instead of only indicating the presence of a data item, the chart can be made to show its origin as well. There are only a very limited number of ways in which data items can arise. They can be present when the form arrives (input), or be the result of an interaction between two or more existing data items. Alternatively, a data item can be created internally as the result of data processing activities, for example the next invoice number, be copied from a document (transfer), or be read from an existing file (maintained) without changing the contents of the file. It is also often useful to record when and where data items leave the system (output).

146

It is customary to use one letter to denote the particular source of each data item in a document/data item grid. Unfortunately various notation schemes are in use and none is standard. One common notation is know as ITOM, input, transfer, output and maintained. Figure 7.42 shows a typical completed document/data item grid chart, with explanatory notes.

DATA ITEMS

Document	Customer name	Customer no.	Address	Order no.	Qty ordered	Product Order	Product Ordered	Price	Despatch	Invoice no.	Qty Despatched	Remarks
Order	I		I	I	I	I		T	T			Rec'd by post
Invoice	O	O	O	O		O	O	O	O	O		
Despatch note		T	T	T		T		O	T	T		Copy of invoice date added by hand
Customer file		M	M									Add customer number
Inventory										M		
Product file						M	M					Check current prices

I Item is on document as it enters system
O Item is on document when it leaves system
T Transfer item: entered on a document not from thje master file and does not leave system
M Item from a master record

Figure 7.42 Data document grid

Rules for drawing grid charts
The grid chart must be drawn up following rules of established practice which include:

1 The chart must be drawn as a grid

2 Every document mentioned should be present on the chart

3 In the case of a document/department chart:

   every department must be listed on the chart
   the routing of every document must be shown

4   In the case of a document/data item chart: all data items must be listed on the chart and the chart must show when a data item appears on a document

5   Each chart must have a key to the symbols used

6   Explanatory notes should be used where needed

7   Various layouts are acceptable but they must follow the logic strictly, be without unnecessary redundancy; and be as compact as possible

String diagrams

Figure 7.43 shows a typical string diagram. This example traces out the path which is followed by an order received in a sales office. String diagrams are constructed by first drawing a plan of the office or department being investigated. Then a line is drawn tracing the movements of the document within the office area as it passes from process to process. The same technique can be used to examine the movements of workers as they go about their duties.

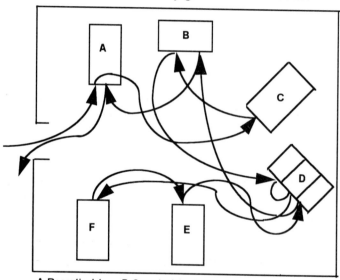

A Receptionist   B Copy typist   C Supervisor
D Filing cabinets E Stock clerk   F Pricing clerk

Figure 7.43 String diagram

The objective, of course, is to highlight any inefficiencies or unnecessary travelling. In the example given most of the travelling within the order-processing procedure could be eliminated. By rearranging the desks the order could be made to progress smoothly in a near circular route: In, round the department and then out again.

148

Flow process charts

Flow process charts are sometimes known as clerical procedure charts. They are used to examine in detail the exact sequence of events within a clerical task.

These are complex tools and their exact method of construction is beyond the scope of this book.

There is a whole family of flow process charts which use a wide variety of special symbols. The simplest use only the five symbols shown in Figure 7.44.

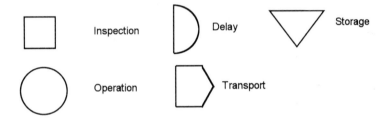

Figure 7.44 Process flow chart symbols

Knowing the meanings of these five symbols, you should be able to trace the process described in Figure 7.45 without much difficulty.

HIPO Charts

HIPO charts (hierarchy plus input-process-output) can describe a complete system. They consist of two parts: the **vertical table of contents** (VTOC), and the **functional diagrams**.

The functional diagrams are a pictorial way of representing the parts of a system, broken down into inputs, outputs and process descriptions. Figure 7.46 shows a high-level functional diagram. Standard flowchart symbols represent the input and output media used. By convention, the flow of control is shown by a solid arrow, the flow of data by a hollow arrow.

Functional diagrams can be expanded to show any level of detail required. Figure 7.47 shows an outline example of a more detailed functional diagram. Eventually every process in the system has its own functional diagram showing the appropriate level of detail. These are then arranged

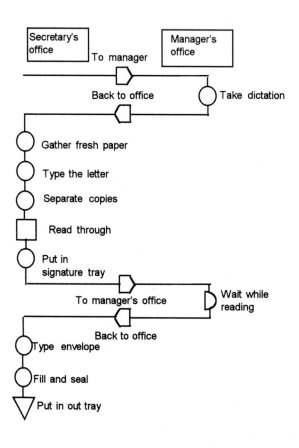

Secretary's office

Manager's office

To manager

Back to office — Take dictation

Gather fresh paper

Type the letter

Separate copies

Read through

Put in signature tray

To manager's office — Wait while reading

Back to office

Type envelope

Fill and seal

Put in out tray

Figure 7.45

into a simple-to-follow structure called a vertical table of contents (VTOC).

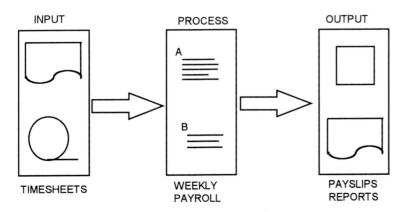

Figure 7.46 Simple functional diagram

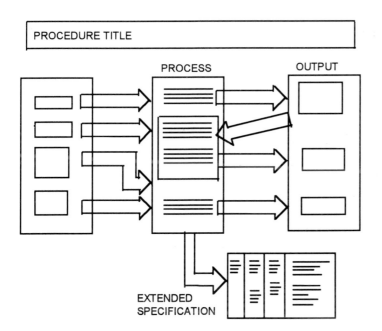

Figure 7.47 Detailed functional diagram

The VTOC is designed to show the relationship between each of the functional diagrams. The VTOC can be broken down into as many levels as required. Figure 7.48 shows a VTOC with three levels of detail. For each box in the VTOC there is one functional diagram.

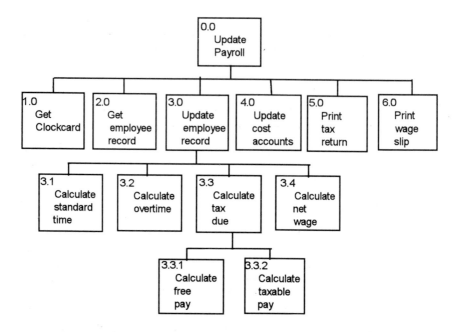

Figure 7.48 VTOC diagram

Chapter 8 Structured English

Why Structured English?

An analyst investigating a procedure with a view to computerising it normally has to rely on someone who is familiar with the detail of that procedure to explain its workings. The result is normally some sort of written explanation of the steps involved, with an indication of the order in which they are carried out, and instructions as to what to do if and when various exceptional events occur.

The trouble with this is that most people are not very good at expressing themselves in plain English anyway, and in addition when explaining something which is very familiar to them people tend to leave out things which they expect the reader to know already.

For example, could you explain to a neighbour's child how to make a cup of coffee in a letter? Something like:

> 'First fill the kettle and boil it. Put one teaspoonful of instant coffee in the cup and pour on the boiling water. Add sugar and milk to taste'.

This is a perfectly adequate explanation to someone already familiar with coffee making but of no use to someone who has never heard of the stuff. Practically every word of the 'explanation' is ambiguous or misleading.

What does 'fill the kettle and boil it' mean?

> What is a kettle? It has not been defined
> Fill it with what? This assumes previous knowledge
> How full? Up to the rim? - hidden assumption again
> Boil the kettle? Shouldn't that be the contents?
> Boil it for how long?
> What should I use? Electricity? Gas?

Inspection of the other lines should reveal that ordinary English is totally inadequate to define an everyday procedure concisely and unambiguously without going into excessive detail.

What is Structured English?

Structured English is used to explain the complex logic of data processing operations in a clear and simple manner. It consists of a series of command statements which are performed in the order predetermined by a control structure. When the procedure logic is written out in command statements, using Initial-Capitalisation to denote defined terms, UPPER CASE LETTERS to indicate control words and indentation as a guide to nested control structures.

STRUCTURED ENGLISH is built from
Command-Statements
      consisting of RESERVED words and Key-words
      INSIDE
      Control-Structures made From
          One or more of
              Sequence
              DO...
              Selection
              IF.... THEN... ELSE CASE OF...
              Iteration
              REPEAT.... UNTIL
              DO...WHILE
USING Indentation as a visual guide and UPPER CASE and Capitalisation to identify different categories of RESERVED Words.

Writing in Structured English

Each statement is made up from a limited range of reserved words and describes a single action. Statements can be executed singly, or as part of a larger group of statements which collectively define a data processing procedure.

Command statements

Command statements are normally in the form of an active verb followed by a simple action description, e.g.

    DO Something
    OPEN Customer-File
    GET Hours-Worked
    READ next record
    PRINT Credit-Limit

or an active verb followed by a compound action description e.g.

    ADD Hours-Worked TO Total-Hours

DIVIDE Total-Hours BY Records GIVING Average-Hours
MULTIPLY Hours-Worked BY Rate GIVING Gross-Pay
SET Lowest-Reading = Current-Value

You will have noticed that in the statements given as examples some words are in UPPER CASE, some in lower case and others have been Capitalised.

Reserved words

The words in UPPER CASE are RESERVED words, that is words which have a permanent fixed meaning and cannot be assigned any other meaning. Reserved words are always commands to do some action. Their use is very similar to that of reserved words in high level programming languages.

In programming languages the definition and conditions of use of a reserved word is fixed once and for all by the compiler writer. Reserved words cannot be used as variable names in any program, and their meaning and function is common across any number of different application programs written in that language.

In writing Structured English, analysts decide for themselves which action words will be designated as reserved words. They must also decide what the precise meaning of each reserved word will be, and how and in what circumstances it can be used. Normally the analyst bases the initial selection of reserved words on some language with which he is familiar, (very often COBOL, but any other will do), and adds more words as and when they are needed. Very quickly a private list is created and each analyst soon has a standardised set.

There are a few limitations but the analyst is largely free to choose any words he wants as reserved words. However, the list should be as short as possible and the meaning assigned should not be in conflict with the ordinary meaning of the word. The analyst also should avoid some words like 'handle', 'process' or 'deal with" as these are too vague, (and whenever the analyst feels a need to use such words it is a clear sign that the steps in the process are not clearly understood). Reserved words used in the control structure are always in upper case. The operators plus, minus, equals, greater than etc. are also treated as reserved words.

Key words

Since the list of reserved words is common to many Structured English descriptions there is no need to define these afresh each time they are used.

However, there is a category of reserved words which do need to be defined and whose use is restricted to one particular application. These words are the names given to data items, field names, variables, names of procedures, document descriptions, file names, labels assigned to groups of statements. These are collectively called Key-Words and are shown with a leading Capital Letter and the rest of the word in lower case letters. Where a Key-Word's name is longer than one word it is always hyphenated. The commonest form of Key-Word is the Data-Item. Data-Items are smallest 'units' of data and cannot usefully be further subdivided.

Every Data-Item used in a structured English description is entered into an alphabetical list. Opposite each entry full details of the meaning, usage and possible values which the Data Item can take are recorded along with any other relevant information which might prove useful. This listing and the data recorded about the Data Items is called a Data Dictionary.

Using a Data Dictionary avoids many of the problems encountered in our coffee making problem, e.g.

> FILL the Kettle WITH Water
> BOIL the Water

is now unambiguous. FILL... WITH.. and BOIL are both reserved words with predefined meanings. The Data-Item named Water is defined once in the Data Dictionary as is the Data Item named Kettle, including the information about where it is kept and how it is operated.

Lower case words

Words which are not Key-Words or Reserved words are shown in lower case and are normally added to command statements in order to make the meaning clearer or to make the Structured English sound less like dictation by a robot. In the example above the lower case 'the' was put in to make the command statement read better. It contributes nothing to the logic and takes nothing away from the logic of the process. Any lower case text introduced into a piece of structured English should have this property. That is, removing the lower case words should leave the logic completely unchanged.

Levels of Structured English

The objective of Structured English is clarity and whenever possible compound actions should be reduced to simple actions e.g.

> MULTIPLY Qty BY Price INCREASING Current-Balance and File-total with Result

is not correct and is better expressed as

> MULTIPLY Qty BY Price GIVING Result
> INCREASE Current-Balance BY Result
> INCREASE File-Total BY Result

or perhaps by

> MULTIPLY Qty BY Price GIVING Result
> ADD Result TO Current-Balance
> ADD Result TO File-Total

or even by

> Result = Qty Price
> Current-Balance = Current-Balance + Result
> File-Total = File-Total + Result

All of these last three examples are correct because they accurately express the logic of the procedure in a compact unambiguous form. The one that you choose to use depends upon who you expect will be reading and using the finished product.

You might be showing the Structured English to a manager who previously supplied the process logic in another form and you want to check the accuracy of the logic used. Or you may wish to incorporate the Structured English into a training manual for use by newly hired clerks who have to do the job manually. Alternatively you may be satisfied that the logic is correct and the purpose of the structured English is to allow a programmer to use the results of your investigation to produce a working program.

In each case the degree to which the finished product departs from normal written English and descends almost to programming statements is determined by the level of knowledge of the target reader and not by the content of the procedure. It is possible to write Structured English only a little removed from ordinary business language and if it is to be shown to people with little computer awareness then that is how you should write it. It will be longer and more wordy and less elegant but that is the price the analyst must pay if the reader is to understand the logic without being put off by unfamiliar formats.

Equally, when you are using structured English to communicate with people familiar with programming you can safely eliminate most of the words and write statements very close to programming statements. This is known as pseudo-code, structured English that is very near source code, but expressing a generalised logic and conforming to no particular programming language.

Basic control structures

Statements which are to be executed more than once are set within a controlling framework which determines exactly how and when each statement is to be used. Although structures may become very elaborate the framework must always conform exactly to the strict rules governing permitted sequences of execution. Only three basic control elements are allowed and every legal framework is built up from various combinations of these.

The three basic control structures and their subdivisions are

Sequence
    In-line Order
    Out-of-line Order
Decision
    IF... THEN...ELSE
    CASE OF...
Iteration
    DO WHILE...
    REPEAT UNTIL....

Just one thing after another

When using command statements the assumption is always that statements will be used in the order in which they are met e.g.

    READ Hours-Worked
    READ Hourly-Rate
    CALCULATE Gross-Pay
    ADD Gross-Pay TO Gross-To-Date

would be executed in order from top to bottom of the list.

This top to bottom ordering, in programming terms called 'in-line' order, is sometimes varied when dealing with large procedures. We can take advantage of the fact that many command statements fall naturally into groups which perform one specific function. For example the four statements quoted above could be referred to collectively as 'Update-Gross-To-Date', and writing 'PERFORM Update-Gross-To-Date' would have the same effect as the original in-line order.

158

Giving a unique name to each function and grouping function names together as high level control groups is a convenient way to make long Structured English descriptions easier to read and understand. For example

'Each consultant's time sheet is first checked to see if it has been properly authorised. Then you have to make sure that the consultant has written on their number and that the hours claimed are not unreasonable. Every consultant also has to quote the job number allocated to them when they started. They often miss these out or misquote them. Next you look up the appropriate hourly rate for that person and work out the gross pay, net pay and tax payable for this claim. Once you've done that you add these figures to the year to date figures on the consultant's card.'

can easily be seen to consist of three procedures, i.e., check the time sheet, calculate the payment, and write up the appropriate card.

This can be expressed in Structured English as

```
BEGIN
    PERFORM        Check-Time-Sheet
    PERFORM        Calculate-Net-Pay
    PERFORM        Update-Consultant-Record
END
Check-Time-Sheet
        CHECK Authority-to-Charge
        VALIDATE Consultant-Number
        VALIDATE Hours-Claimed
        VALIDATE Job-Codes
Calculate-Net-Pay
        READ Payrate
        CALCULATE Gross-Pay
        CALCULATE Tax-Payable
        CALCULATE Net-Pay
Update-Consultant-Card
        LOCATE Consultant-Card
        ADD Gross-Pay TO Pay-To-Date
        ADD Tax-Payable TO Tax-to-Date
        ADD Net-Pay TO Pay-To-Date
```

The command statement 'CALCULATE Gross-Pay' could itself also lead to a further series of lower level command statements in ever increasing detail. In this way even very complex procedures can be 'levelled' so that only the level of detail necessary for the target audience has to be shown and a hierarchy of levels can be designed to serve different purposes, It means that where a function is used more than once in an application the details do not have to be recorded since they will be entered under the appropriate Key-Word in the Data Dictionary.

Decisions, decisions

The simplest control structure is the decision branch which chooses which one of two or more alternative command statements should be executed.

The basic format is

```
IF Condition-One applies
        THEN DO Action-A
ELSE (Condition-I does not apply)
        DO Action-B
ENDIF
```

Notice that the IF... ELSE... ENDIF are lined up vertically, and the THEN and any consequent command statements are indented to show clearly which command statements are affected. Also note that there should normally be an explanation in brackets after the ELSE to show which condition is being negated. The explanation can be omitted in simple cases but if in doubt put it in.

Sometimes there will be no 'ELSE' part to the decision. For example, IF you like your coffee white, then add milk. Otherwise don't. In this case you may include the ELSE section or not as you think right, but you must have the ENDIF.

The basic format can be expanded by making Action-A itself a decision

```
IF Condition-I
        THEN
IF Condition-2
        THEN Action-C
ELSE (Not Condition-2)
        Action-D
ENDIF
ELSE (Not Condition-1)
        Action-B
ENDIF.
```

160

Note how this example has the IF..ELSE..ENDIF lined up correctly in both decisions and how the explanation in brackets greatly aids comprehension as the control structure gets more complicated.

A more involved example will show how these rules apply.

> A shipping company's tariffs are calculated according to the following rules. All cargoes are surcharged according to whether they are containerised or loose, the goods are fragile or not, and whether there are cranes available at the port of discharge or the goods will have to be lightered.

> Containerised loads classed as non fragile are surcharged $15 per ton if lightered, otherwise only $5. Fragile loads are much riskier (even if containerised), so cost $10 when not lightered and $25 when they are. Loose cargoes are $25 per ton when non fragile and discharged by crane, but $35 if lightered. Fragile loose goods are very risky so get surcharged by $40, and any other cargo pays the top rate of $50 per ton.

In order to produce a procedure summary in Structured English we must first

> a) identify all the possible actions and express them in the form of correctly worded command statements

> b) identify the control structure governing the order of the command statements.

An examination of this procedure narrative shows a mixture of actions and conditions which have to be separated out. In this example the actions are all straightforward and can easily be put into command statements.

The next step is to determine the control structure by listing out all the conditions, or underlining them as we did with decision tables. At first sight there appears to be large number of conditions but a moment's thought will quickly reduce these to three - Containerised/Loose, Fragile/Not fragile, Lightered/Not lightered. These conditions are all independent variables, i.e. each of them can occur with any combination of the others, and they completely determine the actions to be taken.

In order to write Structured English it only remains to combine the command statements with the control structure according to the conventions of Structured English and Indentation.

BEGIN
IF Containerised

```
        THEN
                IF Not-Fragile
                THEN
                        IF Lightered
                                THEN Surcharge $15
                        ELSE (Not-Lightered
                                Surcharge $5
                        ENDIF
                ELSE (goods are Fragile)
                        IF Lightered
                                THEN Surcharge $25
                        ELSE (Not-Lightered)
                                Surcharge LIO
                        ENDIF
                ENDIF
ELSE (Not-Containerised)
        IF Not-Fragile
                THEN
                        IF Lightered
                                THEN Surcharge $35
                        ELSE (Not-Lightered
                                Surcharge $25
                        ENDIF
                ELSE (goods are Fragile)
                        IF Lightered
                                THEN Surcharge $50
                        ELSE (Not-Lightered)
                                Surcharge $40
                        ENDIF
                ENDIF
ENDIF
END.
```

A case in point

Consider the following procedure narrative

'When typing up the Invoice you have to allow the correct discount. Only established customers qualify for any discount and not all of those. Our discount threshold is $250, anything below that doesn't qualify. Invoices up to $500 get a discount of 2% on the total

162

amount: over that slightly different rules apply. Amounts up to $2500 attract the normal discount up to $500 and then an additional 1% on the amount over that. For larger orders still, the amount over $2500 qualifies for another I%'

In this procedure we can identify one decision construct - the customer status - and then a separate series of actions resulting from various conditions.

These conditions have the property that they are not dependent on each other and cannot occur together, e.g. an invoice cannot be both under $500 and over $500. When these conditions are seen you should always consider using the Case Construct instead of If-Then-Else. This can be used as follows

```
BEGIN
        IF Customer-Status is Established
        THEN SELECT CASE
                CASE 1: Invoice-Value is less than $250
                                Discount is Nil
                CASE 2: Invoice-Value is greater than $250
                                AND less than $500
                                        Discount is 2% of Invoice-Value
                CASE 3: Invoice-Value is greater than $500
                                AND less than $2500
                                        Discount is 2% of $500
                                        PLUS 3% of Invoice-Value MINUS
                                        $500
                CASE 4: Invoice-Value is greater than $2500
                                Discount is 2% of $500
                                PLUS 3% of Invoice-Value MINUS $500
                                PLUS 4% of Invoice-Value MINUS $2500
        ELSE (Customer-Status is NOT Established)
                Discount is NIL
END
```

(In this example some of the words have been expanded to aid clarity, e.g. 'is greater than', 'less than' could be replaced by the arrow-head symbols, 'is 2%' is equivalent to '= 2%')

Repetition commands

WHILE... ENDWHILE
The first repetition control mechanism is the WHILE command. This surrounds a block of command statements and ensures that they continue to

be executed as long as some controlling condition which is true at the moment continues to be true.

For example, returning to our coffee making exercise:

> WHILE Water-Level NOT = Maximum
> > ADD Water TO Kettle
>
> ENDWHILE

In plain English as long as the water level is below the maximum fill mark keep going round the loop and add more water. The ENDWHILE is there to show the limit of the while loop, i.e. how many command statements are included in the repetition.

Similarly, the BOIL instruction could be restated as

> WHILE Water-Temp less than 100C
> > APPLY Heat TO Water
>
> ENDWHILE

In general,

> WHILE some condition remains true
> > DO Something
> > DO Something-Else
>
> ENDWHILE

The WHILE and ENDWHILE commands must be lined up and the command statements which they control should be indented.

WHILE... ENDWHILE commands may be nested to any level.

REPEAT... UNTIL

This control mechanism is an alternative to a while loop and serves exactly the same purpose, that is to continue executing some group of command statements over and over. But in this case the loop continues only until some controlling condition which is not true at the moment becomes true.

For example

> REPEAT
> ADD Water TO Kettle
> UNTIL Water-Level = Maximum

and

> REPEAT
> ADD Heat TO Water

164

UNTIL Water-Temp = 100C

are both equivalent in effect to the while loops demonstrated above. The choice of which control mechanism to use in a particular case is largely a matter of style and personal preference.

The REPEAT and UNTIL commands must be lined up and the command statements which they control should be indented. REPEAT..UNTIL commands may be nested to any level.

Exercises

1. Square root problem

One way to find the square root of a number is to take the number you are interested in and divide it in two. Multiply the result of this division by itself and if the answer is the same as the original number then you have found the root.

If the answer is greater than the number you started with then reduce the trial root by ten per cent and multiply it out again. If the answer is still bigger than the original number then continue to reduce it by another ten per cent until either you get exactly the same as the original number or the answer is smaller than the original.

Once you have a multiplication which is smaller than the original you begin to add to the trial number by one per cent and try multiplying again until the answer is greater than the original. As your result again gets larger than the original you start to reduce the trial number by one tenth of one percent and carry on in this way until either the exact root is found or an approximation is found which is close enough for your purpose.

Express this procedure in Structured English.

2. Reporting values from a file

A file contains a series of temperature readings in the range 0 to 212 terminating in a rogue value of 999. Use Structured English to express the logic required to open the file, read the values and report the highest and lowest temperatures found in the file.

Solutions

1. Square root problem

BEGIN
DIVIDE Original-Number by two GIVING Trial-Number
REPEAT
        MULTIPLY Trial-Number by itself GIVING Result
        (COMPARE Result with Original-Number)
      IF Result = Original-Number THEN Root is found ELSE (Result not
equal to Original-Number)
           IF Result less than Original-Number
           REDUCE Trial-Number BY Fraction
          ELSE (Result greater than Original-Number)
           INCREASE Trial-Number BY Fraction
ENDIF
ENDIF
UNTIL Root found OR Approximation close enough
END

Alternative solution

BEGIN
Trial-Number = Original-Number/2
IF Original-Number = Trial-Number Trial-Number
THEN Root = Trial-Number
ELSE (Original-Number <> Trial-Number Trial-Number)
      IF Original-Number < Trial-Number Trial-Number
          THEN Trial-Number = Trial-Number * 0.9
ENDIF

2. Reporting values from a file

BEGIN
OPEN Temp-File
SET Lowest-Reading to 212 SET Highest-Reading to 0
      REPEAT
      READ next Temp-Value
      IF Temp-Value NOT EQUAL to 999
      THEN
IF Temp-Value less than Lowest-Reading
THEN Lowest-Reading = Temp-Value

166

```
ELSE (Temp-Value is greater than Lowest-Reading)
ENDIF
IF Temp-Value greater than Highest-Reading
THEN Highest-Reading = Temp-Value
ELSE (Temp-Value is less than Highest-Reading)
ENDIF
        ELSE (Temp-Value = 999)
        CLOSE Temp-file
        ENDIF
UNTIL Temp-Value = 999
        DISPLAY Lowest-Reading
        DISPLAY Highest-Reading
END.
```

Recommended reading

De Marco, T. (1979) Structured Analysis and System Specification Pub Yourdon Press, NY.

 Gane, C. and Sarson, T. (1979) Structured Systems Analysis: Tools and Techniques Prentice-Hall Englewood Cliffs, NJ.

Parkin, A. (1987) Systems Analysis. Pub Edward Arnold, London.

Chapter 9 Physical design of new systems

Design methodology

When you are asked to design a computer system, where do you start? There is no standard approach to designing a new system. Anyone can use the tools of analysis to determine the data requirements of an application but moving from analysis to design is a major step. There is no method which will automatically derive a design from a specification. However every computer application has elements of input and output, processing and storage. If the analyst considers each of these in turn a basic systems outline can be determined which will satisfy the minimum requirements. From there the analyst can begin to experiment with different combinations of hardware and software and gradually establish an optimum design. However in the end the design is a product of the individual analyst's experience and skills, in much the same way that a building reflects the ability of the architect, and is not simply determined by its site and function.

Establishing a workable design methodology

The methodology typically used with the systems life cycle takes the required output as its starting point. For data to be produced that data must have been stored somewhere. So the next question to be considered is 'What files must exist to hold the data which is being output?' If data is being held in files, then that data must be maintained. What programs and processes are needed to update the data in the files? The answer to that question will show what data has to be captured to go into the files to produce the output.

At the end of this process the analyst will have a minimum data model describing the flow of data through the application. The analyst can then concentrate on finding the best hardware to suit the input and output requirements, and then design a file layout for each file required. In addition the analyst has to take into account operational requirements such as speed of response and give some thought to how and when the system will be implemented.

The process may go through many iterations but the end result should be an implementable design. If they are considered roughly in the order in which they are given, the following points should give the analyst some ideas on which a preliminary design might be based.

- What output is wanted?
- What files are needed?
- What input must create the files?
- What processing creates the files and output?
- What controls are required?
- What software is available, required?
- What hardware will support it?

Factors determining output

What will be the content of the output? What are the requirements for data, fields, files? The type and quantity of output required will determine the speed with which it is produced. For printed output printers range from very fast laser printers to slow but high quality daisy wheels. Output can be printed as text or diagrams, or displayed on a screen. The output type will depend on the use to which the information is put. Factual information which is constantly referred to and which changes only infrequently will best be output as hard copy, while fast moving information which must be constantly updated, such as stock exchange prices for example, is usually best displayed on a VDU screen.

Volume and complexity

What is the maximum and minimum number of data items involved and how much fluctuation is there between them? Closely related to the consideration of processing speed is the question of the volume of data to be handled, and the variation in physical inputs, processing requirements and output types. Low volumes of transactions can be just as difficult to deal with as large volumes. Large variations in the quantity of transactions at different times of the year can also cause difficulties.

Size

How big is the system going to be? The main processing requirements and the average volume of transactions and master records will dictate the appropriate scale of computerisation. For example the designer can choose between powerful mainframe computers for large throughputs, minicomputers which offer more moderate processing power at lower cost, and microcomputers which provide personal interaction and flexibility of use.

Users

What degree of support is required? This will affect the choice of data capture devices and data input method as well as determining the controls which need to be built into the system. The user profile expected will also have a large bearing on the style of user interface. Systems need accuracy and must avoid errors at all stages, but the degree of error protection needed will depend on the training level of the user. Systems which are used by relatively unskilled staff are probably best designed with all entries to the system through menus, which can be rigorously controlled. Where the system users are more skilled, more complex systems can be installed and the system design can allow more flexible inputs.

Files

What data must be stored in the system? The purpose of the system will determine the type of information to be output from the system. This output can only come as a result of program calculations or from data held in a file. The file contents can therefore be determined from an examination of the output and the file structure can be determined from a consideration of the speeds, volumes and output types needed. Batch applications will be suited to sequential files; real-time applications will need indexed or random access files.

Processing

How can the output be generated from the input? At this stage the designer can begin to think about the actual detailed processing, i.e. logic and programs which will transform raw data into useful information.

Controls

The decisions made about the type of processing operation will largely determine the controls to be applied. For example, if a batch solution is feasible then the appropriate control accounts, document counts, hash totals etc., will be designed. If the system is to be real-time then controls and validation techniques suitable to on line working must be developed. In either case audit controls should be built in at an early stage.

Hardware and software

What type of processing is required? Not every application needs a fast turnaround; a balance can always be struck between high speed, high cost processing and low speed, low cost processing. Some applications are naturally suited to batch processing. This usually results in relatively long periods between file updates but is very efficient in processing terms. Other applications, such as airline ticketing or on-line banking, require rapid real-time responses, i.e. virtually instantaneous file updates. Systems like these need more expensive hardware, which is not only usually more complex than the simpler equipment suitable for batch processing, but also less efficient in processing terms. The programming and testing of high response systems is also a major factor in design.

In essence then, the output required has implications for the file design which impacts on the input processes which in turn determines the hardware characteristics and the software needed to make it all work.

Output design

The main considerations in output design

The primary consideration in the design of all output must be the requirements of the ultimate user of the information. The major function of output is to convey information and so its layout and design needs careful consideration. However, the content of any particular form will depend on the specific information needs of the manager involved. Therefore the guidelines given below can only be very general and will have to be reinterpreted to suit particular circumstances.

Who is going to use the output?

Information must be carefully tailored to the needs of the target user. The choice of text, graphics, hard copy or screen display will be based on the task being done.

For example, a credit control clerk will want a detailed breakdown of debts and payments, but only of selected customers, while the credit supervisor will want the same information summarised and covering all the current debtors. The finance director, working at a higher level, will be more interested in the trends of unpaid invoices from last year to this.

The clerk may want the debtor information available on line so that associated data such as telephone numbers are easily available and the record always shows the current, up-to-date situation. The supervisor might prefer the data presented as hard copy perhaps, with a daily or weekly update. The director is unlikely to be interested in individual debtors, and would probably prefer data to be presented as a graph or bar chart comparing current with previous performance.

What should be reported?

A common fault of computer systems is that they deliver too much information. Managers should be supplied with just enough information to be able to carry out their job efficiently, and no more. In most cases this means applying the principle of **management by exception.**

For instance, in the credit control example used above, there would be no point in supplying the credit control clerk with details of all active customers. Only those who haven't paid on time, the exceptional ones, are of interest. The application of management by exception to all output will actually improve the information flow to those that need it as well as reducing the volume of print needed.

When should it be produced?

In general the faster the turnaround of data from transactions into information, the more expensive it is. Managers do not always require information as soon as it is available and the timing of output should conform with the manager's usage pattern. If the output has to be immediate, defined as under 4 seconds, then the output will have to be to a screen. If the output is required on demand but the user can wait up to 1 minute, then either a VDU or a fast printer would do the job. In a batch application with run periods of up to 1 month printed output would be acceptable.

In the credit control example, the clerk needs details of payments immediately they are received but the supervisor can probably wait for a week or so, and the director would be happy with monthly data.

The choice of the production cycle will nearly always be a compromise between operational needs and management control uses.

What format will be best?

There is a wide choice of output media and once again the final destination of the information will determine which to use. Data is not always produced solely for internal use. Output also goes to people and companies outside the organisation: invoices to customers, advice notes to suppliers, or letters to the public. Internal documents can be produced as cheaply as possible and may only need to be legible. Documents for external use such as word-processed letters might need to be of high quality to create a good impression, while invoices and advice notes only have to be clear and unambiguous.

The desired appearance will therefore dictate the choice of printer.

Obviously, on line data will require a VDU or personal computer to display output.

Where does the information go?

Re-input. Most of the data produced from a computer goes on a one way journey out of the system. Some of it, however, eventually finds its way back

172

in slightly different form. The system designer can take advantage of this and make use of **turnaround documents.** These are a form of output which carries information in both human readable and machine sensible form. Common examples are telephone bills, gas bills etc., which carry customer information out of the system printed in OCR characters which can be machine read when the document is returned with the accompanying payment.

Temporary. Very often output is only used as a means of storing data temporarily before it is used as input to one or more associated processes. In these cases the output format does not have to be human readable and can be output into purely machine readable format such as magnetic tape or disks.

Disposal. The disposal of used output should also be considered. The information provided to managers is often highly confidential and some thought must be given to its ultimate destination. If this data is produced as hard copy then there will be the problem of disposing of it securely, so it might be better to make sensitive data available on line only.

Storage. The storage of output for archival purposes can also be a problem. Hard copy is very bulky and takes up a lot of room. It may be better to provide output in a form which is easily stored, such as microfilm, if very large quantities are produced.

How much will it cost? All peripheral devices are expensive, and many of the output options given above are only feasible if there is sufficient output to make the equipment cost-effective. There will normally have to be very large quantities for computer output on microfilm (COM) to be viable for example, while MICR is normally an expensive option too. All forms of good quality graphics equipment tends to be expensive and so although it may be the best form of output companies may have to do without it because low rates of usage do not make it worthwhile.

Output media

A wide variety of output media is available to the system designer and the analyst should be familiar with those shown below.

Visual display unit (VDU)

Features:

> Dual purpose, versatile TV-like device
> Keyboard for input, display for output
> Allows interactive operations
> Can display text or pictures

Advantages:

    Can have other devices attached such as light pens, mice
    Full colour options are usually available
    Entirely silent in use
    Can be converted to touch terminals
    Allows full on line instant updating

Disadvantages:

    All output is ephemeral, i.e. temporarily displayed
    Relatively expensive
    Keyboard skills may be needed to use

Uses:

    Interactive applications such as file enquiries, database operations
    Nowadays virtually universal in DP

Line printer (also called drum, chain, band printers)

Features:

    High volume, low quality impact printer
    Prints a whole line at a time
    Uses preformed characters
    Speed of 20 to 50 lines per second

Advantages:

    Very cost effective for large runs
    Can print multi-part stationery
    Usually have a choice of type face

Disadvantages:

    Often requires extensive set-up times
    Only printing in black available
    Print quality is often poor
    Very large and bulky
    Handles continuous stationery only

Uses:

    Typical medium to large DP department
    General mixed outputs e.g. reports, invoices

Laser printer

Features:

> High volume, high quality printer
> Prints a complete page at time
> Speeds of up to 20,000 lines per minute

Advantages:

> High-speed output, with good quality
> Can print text, diagrams and photographs
> Can replace pre-printed stationary
> No restrictions on formats or layout
> Colour options available

Disadvantages:

> Expensive to buy
> Cannot use multi-part stationery

Uses:

> Large DP departments with constant high volumes.
> Medium volume application with mixed format requirements, e.g. advertising agencies

Matrix printer

Features:

> Widely used, relatively low speeds
> Prints one character at a time
> Characters are formed from a matrix of dots
> Speeds 30 to 250 cps
> Can produce graphics as well as text

Advantages:

> Can operate in draft or letter quality mode
> Can use multi-part stationery
> Different character sets are available
> Different sizes of characters can be produced
> Mixed sizes and fonts are available simultaneously
> Can print in different colours
> Can print bar codes
> Relatively cheap
> Often incorporated into other devices, e.g. tills

175

Disadvantages:

> Quality in draft mode can be rather poor
> Can be very noisy in use

Uses:

> General purpose low volume office work, e.g. a warehouse office
> Internal reports
> Program listings
> Intermediate drafts of general correspondence

File design

Files are at the centre of all commercial data processing activities and will be a major concern of the system analyst in the design phase. A **file** is simply a collection of records which are related in a way that is meaningful to the user.

Files serve three basic purposes. There are transaction files, master files and reference files. Master files and transaction files are closely related.

Master files

These are essentially collections of records holding semi-permanent information about the organisation's customers, products, sales, etc. or any other information of interest to the organisation. The purpose of a transaction file is to hold new data temporarily until it can be used to update one or more master files.

Master files hold data about entities. This is mostly static. An employee master record might show:

Employee number	Name	Job	Standard hours	Pay rate	Gross

Transaction files

These hold data elements relating to specific events, or transactions, which have happened in the real world, and which will affect the accuracy of the information which an organisation wishes to hold about its customers, products, sales etc.

Transaction files hold data arising from processes. They are used to update master files. A payroll transaction record might show:

Employee number	Hours worked	Week number

Reference files

These hold information of a permanent nature which is used in a number of different data processing operations and whose records are not regularly updated with information transferred from a transaction file. Examples of reference files are files holding current VAT rates, or selling prices.

A reference table for a company payroll might show:

Job type   Pay rate   Date altered

From the systems design point of view master files and transaction files are far and away the most important types of file. In a standard batch processing operation a transaction file on tape might be used to update a master file on tape, creating a new master file in the process. This is an efficient process when the hit rate is high and has the added advantage of leaving the two old tapes as security copies.

File organisations

The systems designer only needs to consider three basic types of file organisation: sequential, indexed sequential and random files.

Sequential files

These are collections of records which have been sorted into a useful sequence, such as customer names in alphabetical order, or products in ascending number order, and which can only be accessed in the same order in which they are stored.

Indexed sequential files

These are collections of records held in sequential format but have the advantage that they to not have to be accessed solely in the order in which they were recorded. Records can also be found and read directly, by consulting an index which records the position at which each individual record is held.

Random files

These are files where the individual records are not stored in any particular order, i.e. the location of one record is not in any way related to the location of the record which precedes it. These records are stored and accessed directly (in other words without making reference to any record except the one required for processing) by a variety of physical means. The exact method of storage can be postponed until later in the development cycle and does not need to be decided at the design stage.

177

Choice of file organisation

The choice of which file organisation is most appropriate will depend upon a number of interrelated factors, the most important of which are listed below.

The media available

Basically there are two types of media in common use in commercial data processing today. These are magnetic tapes and magnetic disks. Magnetic tapes only support serial access and can therefore only be used for sequential files. Disks can be used for both direct access files and sequential access files.

The acceptable response time

The main drawback of sequential files is that in order to locate one particular record it is necessary physically to pass over all the records which are located in front of the one wanted. This means that serial access files are slow, and cannot be used for applications which require fast responses, such as file enquiries where customers want to find out stock balances over the telephone.

The expected hit rate

The hit rate is the name given to the ratio between the number of records held in a file and the number of records which require to be changed by transactions. In some applications there is a high hit rate, for example in a payroll application there will be almost a 100% hit rate with virtually every record in the file being used each time the pay calculation program is run.

Other applications have a very low hit rate. For example, in a stock control application not every product stocked by a company will be needed every time a file is accessed. In extreme cases where a customer telephones to find out the current stock levels, for example, perhaps only one record out of the whole file will be accessed.

The importance of the hit rate lies in the fact that sequential file processing is cheaper than direct file processing. But it is only efficient if the number of records to be processed is a sufficiently high proportion of the file total, in other words, where the hit rate is high. If the hit rate is low then there is no advantage to sequential file organisation, and its slow speed of access becomes a major drawback.

The inherent flexibility of direct access devices such as disks is best exploited where an application sometimes has a high hit rate and sometimes a low hit rate. A stock control application with random enquires has a low hit rate most of the time but a very high hit rate whenever the company decides to examine all its records to see if more stock should be ordered. In this case the indexed sequential organisation is the best to use as it can handle individual enquiries efficiently through the index and the periodic stock checks by acting as a pure sequential file when needed.

The flexibility of access required

If the application is going to require access to data through a number of different fields for each record then a direct access device is the only feasible storage medium. In this case the most suitable file organisation would probably be indexed sequential as it can support multiple indexes based on a number of subsidiary keys.

The volatility of the file

If the number of records in the file changes very rapidly, or if the number and length of the fields within the records is subject to great changes then it may be necessary to opt for a random file organisation. Indexed sequential files become very inefficient if too many changes are made to the underlying sequence of records.

Frequency of updating

If the records in any particular file need to be updated very frequently, this would normally rule out the possibility of using sequential files as they work best under batch processing conditions. **Batch processing** allows transactions to be collected until sufficient have been accumulated to make it worth processing them.

This of course means that some time will elapse before the individual records can be processed. The frequency of updating required may not allow sufficient transactions to be accumulated.

Other factors

These other factors should also be considered:

> The maximum storage capacity needed
> Variable/fixed length fields
> Length of fields
> Output and input requirements and constraints
> Security requirements and standards
> Backup and recovery procedures
> Integrity and audit
> Costs per standard unit of stored data

Input design

What information must be captured? Where will it come from, and how much of it is there? Once the file contents and file organisation have been determined the designer will be able to assess what data must be presented to the program in order to produce the desired output. This in turn will influence the choice of input media which must be compatible with the speed and volume of transactions to be processed.

Often the designer will have no control over how the data is presented to the system. If it is presented on source documents originating outside the system there may be severe difficulties with its format. Hand-written orders will need extensive checking and keyboard entry while good quality printed documents may be suitable for high speed input technology such as OCR.

The main considerations for input design

Introduction of data into systems

Every system designer has to find a way to deal with information originating outside the processing system. At first sight the variety of input devices and input methods can seem bewildering but there are basically only four ways in which data can be introduced into a system.

1. The data is converted into machine sensible form by someone who reads the source documents and types in the relevant items using a keyboard .

2. Documents can be read directly by a machine. This converts information held in a human readable form into a machine readable form without the need for human intervention.

3. Data is entered into the system through a keyboard, but this is done interactively by the person using the system.

4. Data is presented in a form suited to the computer as a result of some other processing, that is, it arises as a by-product.

Each of these methods has its advantages and disadvantages. However, the designer will not always have a free choice. One or more of the following factors may influence the final design decision.

The processing style

What is the basic processing style? Is the system primarily batch oriented or real-time? In some applications input arrives periodically and is naturally batched, orders received through the post, for example. Some data entry is initiated by the user on demand and must respond in a set time, bank automatic teller machines are like this. In other circumstances the input device may have to interact with other processes continually. The speed of response needed increases the complexity of the input design.

Often the designer will be able to get the user to do the data input. Customers do their own data input when using a bank's ATM. Credit cards have magnetic stripes which hold data which can be read automatically in a shop.

Expected variations
To what extent will the input data vary in size and content? If the input is very variable there may a lot of wasted space or inefficient processing. For example will the space for input data on the source documents be of a fixed length? Suppose space is left for names and addresses: there will inevitably be wasted space if the system has to allow for the longest possible entry. How much variation is there in the volume of input over a given period? Are there peaks and troughs at regular intervals? Can the workloads be evened out?

Accuracy levels
What level of accuracy will be needed and how are errors to be detected and eliminated? Allied to this consideration is the type of verification envisaged. Is the system so sensitive that extensive checks have to be built into it, or will machine validation checks be enough?

Error handling
What will be an acceptable level of errors? How are discovered errors to be handled, corrected and re-input? How many will be encountered? Will special facilities be required? Are there any special security requirements? What controls will be needed to counteract loss of data, corruption, fraud etc.?

Data preparation
How much preparation will be needed? How difficult is it to convert the data, and will it have to be prelisted, summarised or sorted first?

The physical form
What are the print requirements and how will the data to be input be physically presented? What about the cost of associated stationery? Is there a need to make forms serve several purposes? Will the physical form of the input cause problems? How will the input be stored or disposed of once used?

The costs involved
What existing hardware is there? Can it be adapted or must it be replaced? What data capture methods are already available? How much would new equipment cost?

Selecting input devices

A full list of input devices would run into many pages: the list given below covers the minimum with which a competent analyst would be familiar.

Keyboards

Description:

> Devices similar to typewriters which allow data to be input by pressing various keys. One of the oldest input devices, keyboards are almost universally used, and are available in a wide variety of layouts for general purpose and special applications.

Advantages:

> Allows great flexibility of use
> No shortage of people with keyboarding skills to operate them
> Cheap and simple hardware

Disadvantages:

> All users need extensive training
> The standard QWERTY layout is very inefficient
> Data entry tends to be slow

Uses:

> The commonest form of data input
> All transcription entry is keyboard based
> A standard feature of VDUs and workstations

Kimball tags

Description:

> Small cardboard tags used in much the same way as miniature punched cards (see below). A newer version uses a small piece of magnetic tape glued onto the card to record the data rather than having holes punched in it.

Advantages:

> Allows easy and secure stock control
> Eliminates a great deal of detailed record keeping
> Cheap to use
> Wide acceptability

Disadvantages:

> Can only be prepared by special punches
> Not directly human readable
> Can only be used once

Uses:

Retail applications such as clothes shops

Used as 'seed tickets' in applications where many small or low value items are stored in bins, e.g. electrical components in a radio and TV repair depot, nuts and bolts in an engineering store. Can be combined with bar coding

Punched cards

Description:

An obsolete form of data entry and storage. Usually 80 or 96 characters per card. Characters are represented by combinations of holes

Advantages:

Robust, unaffected by dirt or magnetic fields
Cards can be amended individually

Disadvantages:

Rates of data capture are very slow
High error rates during punching
Nearly always need to be verified separately
Input rates very slow

Uses:

Formerly the standard form of computer storage Now only used in very specialised circumstances for new applications or in existing applications because, and while, existing hardware is still working and has yet to be replaced.

Magnetic ink character recognition (MICR)

Description:

Magnetic ink character recognition. Characters are printed in a very distinctive style using a special ink which contains minute fragments of iron and which is capable of holding a magnetic field. The shape of this magnetic field can be decoded by a special reader which converts it to a recognised character.

Advantages:

Eliminates the need for rekeying data

Widely used with turnaround documents
Offers a high degree of security

Disadvantages:

Uses expensive machinery
Needs a special ink

Uses:

Most common use is on bank cheques
Also used to record the numbers of postal orders
Mostly used in finance related applications

Bar codes

Description:

A sequence of bars and spaces printed in ordinary ink which is read for direct input into a computer using a 'wand' or 'light-pen'.

Advantages:

Cheap to produce
A fast method of input
Widely used and well established technology
Can be produced on a dot matrix printer

Disadvantages:

Needs special hardware to operate
Difficult to incorporate into some products
Many different standards in use

Uses:

Retail sales applications in supermarkets
Recording books in libraries
Catalogue parts and sales operations

Optical character recognition (OCR)

Description:

A flexible input method using machine readable characters in a variety of type styles, including normal output from typewriters.

Advantages:

Easily produced by a wide variety of devices

Portable readers are available
Very suitable for use with turnaround documents
Low error and rejections rates
Machine and human readable
No special inks are required

Disadvantages:

Difficult to deal with hand written documents
Can be difficult to print on some products
Cannot deal with different sized text easily
Requires a fairly good print quality

Uses:

Gas, electricity and telephone billing incorporating turnaround documents. Meter reading applications.

Mouse

Description:

An analogue input device used for pointing or as a cursor control which eliminates the need for keyboard skills

Advantages:

A natural and easily learned input method
Usually much faster than a keyboard for cursor control
Very user friendly and acceptable to first time users

Disadvantages:

No use for text input
Normally cannot completely replace a keyboard
For skilled operator mouse input may be slower than key stroke input

Uses:

Menu oriented applications intended relatively inexperienced uses.
Graphics applications
Computer aided design and Computer aided manufacture

Voice recognition

Description:

The operator speaks into a microphone and the wave forms of the sounds produced by the operator's voice are digitised. These are compared with stored wave forms with predetermined meanings and where a match is found the computer will act on it as if the input had come from keyboard.

Advantages:

No keyboarding skills needed
Very little preliminary training needed
Most people can speak faster than they write

Disadvantages:

Usually have to be tailored to one individual's voice, and must be reprogrammed if a different voice is to use the system
Normally only a limited vocabulary can be used
Very few robust systems are available right now

Uses:

Any application with hands busy, eyes busy, e.g. a technician using a microscope or where the physical environment is such that other methods would be inappropriate, e.g. fish packing in a processing factory.

Optical mark recognition (OMR)

Description:

Source documents are designed with pre-printed spaces for users to make a choice by inserting a mark by hand in the appropriate column. The mark can be sensed either by optical or electrical means.

Advantages:

Very easily learned and fast to fill in
Suitable for first time or relatively inexperienced users
Very low error rates once trained
Ideal for numeric type data capture

Disadvantages:

Not suitable for capturing text
Expensive for volatile data capture applications
Tedious to collect large amounts of data

Uses:

Typically used on questionnaires of all types
Multiple choice exam questions

Often combined with OCR in meter reading

Writing tablets

Description:

Allows the user to enter textual information into a laptop or notebook computer by 'writing' on a screen or tablet in the same way as they write on paper with a pen. In the office a similar technology, digitising tablets, lets the user enter images with an 'electronic pen'.

Advantages:

Very easily learned and fast to fill in
Suitable for first time or relatively inexperienced users
Ideal for low volume input on the move.

Disadvantages:

Accuracy of recognition can be a problem
Needs powerful hardware
Not suitable for bulk data entry

Uses:

People who need totally portable computing, e.g. salespeople .

Processing

Once the input, files and outputs have been determined the analyst will have achieved a logical data model. From this the programs needed can be identified. There will be programs which create the files, update the files with the input data and programs to produce the output. The programs will still have to be specified in complete detail but they will have been identified, along with the files that they operate on.

Design and system objectives

The overall objectives of new system will be unique to that system and will be found spelled out in detail in its terms of reference. However, these will not be the only objectives. Every system has an additional set of assumed objectives which, although unspecified, will largely govern the design of the new system.

The extent to which each of these general, unspecified objectives influence the final design will vary, so the final version of the new system will always involve some sort of compromise between conflicting objectives.

187

Reliability

Many firms would go out of business if their computer systems failed, so reliability must be a fundamental consideration. It is usually best to base a new system on hardware and software which has been tested and proven in use, rather than go for 'state of the art' equipment or unproved experimental techniques.

Reliability is also a function of the support available from supplying companies, so the company installing a new system needs to consider whether the prospective suppliers have the necessary maintenance staff, spares, and technical know-how available. Alternative equipment should also be available in case of complete breakdown.

Flexibility

No business is static, so a good system will allow for both growth and contraction of the transaction loads on the system. The system should be designed in such a way that it can be upgraded and enhanced without difficulty and that it can handle fluctuations of peak loads now and in the future. Wherever possible the new system should be modular and allow for future integration with other hardware and software.

Cost-effectiveness

Where a computer system is replacing a manual or mechanised system the capital and running costs of the new system must compare favourably with the costs of the old. When a new system is not directly comparable with a previous one it is still essential to ensure that all operational objectives are being met cost-effectively and that the system will provide an efficient return on capital.

Practicality

An efficient system is one which is easy to use and maintain. This means that the system designer will have taken the three Ss fully into account:

> specialisation
> standardisation
> simplification.

Security

Every system must be protected from accidental or deliberate loss of data or of processing capability. This means building in standby facilities for hardware and software and allowing for a certain degree of redundancy and duplication in the system. In order to safeguard data and the integrity of records control systems such as batch totalling, dumping and logging, and the provision of audit trails have to be included. Data must of course be protected in order to comply with the law and so proper provision must be made to guarantee confidentiality and privacy of personal information.

Efficiency

In an efficient system there is close compatibility and integration between the different subsystems involved. For example, the speed at which data is input should closely match the speed at which data is processed so that there is no build-up of backlogs of work on the one hand or idle processing capacity on the other. The interface with any manual procedures involved in the processing should be smooth and the system easy to use.

Effectiveness

It must never be forgotten that a computer system is not an end in itself and must be judged according to the extent to which it fulfils the needs of management. An effective system is one which helps the organisation to achieve its objectives. The more flexible the system can be in responding to changing needs, the more effective it will be.

Control

The system must provide ways for managers to exercise effective control over it. Built-in checking systems which will identify any errors at the earliest possible stage should be provided. Where it proves impossible to eliminate errors the system should have the ability to identify and correct them rapidly.

Accuracy

A computer system should be accurate, but should also be able to recognise different standards of accuracy. The accuracy of data supplied as part of a management information system will depend on the intended use of the information and the level of management to which it is supplied. At the operations level for instance, managers need detailed, high-precision information, while higher level management whose task is strategic planning and decision making, will require more generalised, summarised output.

Documentation

Every operational system must be fully documented in a consistent way, using declared standards and providing comprehensive guidance to all present and potential users.

Acceptability

To be effective a finished system must be acceptable to wide range of people whom it will affect, both inside and outside the organisation, many of whom may not be familiar with computers.

Well-fitted

The finished system must be appropriate to the working style of the organisation. This applies particularly to the design of the jobs of those who have to use the computer on a day to day basis. The system designer cannot hope to impose a high technology solution on an organisation accustomed to slow evolutionary change or on a department unable to use it.

General control principles

The information provided by a computer application can only be as good as the data that is supplied to it. If accurate information is to be provided consistently then it follows that controls will have to be applied to the raw data before it is input to make sure it is of sufficiently high quality. These controls serve four main objectives:

1   To ensure that all data is processed

2   To detect and correct errors in processing

3   To prevent and detect fraud

4   To ensure continued smooth operations even if the external environment changes

Systems designers have developed a whole battery of possible controls which can be used in different circumstances. It is probably easier to put forward some general rules which will allow the analyst to decide which control to apply, than to try to specify particular controls for particular situations.

Rules for designing controls

1.   Controls must be reliable, objective and comprehensive.

2.   Controls should be placed as early as possible in the system.

3.   The cost of the control should compare favourably with the cost of its absence, in other words, it should be cheaper than the error that it is designed to avoid.

4.   Control should be designed in the light of what would happen if the error it is meant to eliminate went undetected

5.   Place controls at the point in the system where they would be of maximum benefit.

6.   Adjust controls periodically in the light of experience.

190

7.	Fully test controls for reliability and comprehensiveness before finally incorporating them into any system.

8.	To be effective, controls must be designed to meet predefined standards.

9.	Ideally, all controls must be so simple, administratively feasible and unobtrusive, as not to interrupt the natural flow of data through the system.

10.	Controls should not only detect errors as soon as possible, but also isolate, and if possible, correct them and report on the action taken (automatic control)

11.	At every point where an error could occur there should also be a control designed to detect it.

12.	Control should, as far as possible, be automatic and part of the machine processing operation, and should not depend on human supervision and intervention.

13.	Every application must recognise that most problems arise from exceptional situations which controls must be able to recognise and deal with.

System controls

Controls are applied wherever errors might occur and so it is convenient to consider the choice and design of controls under four headings, input controls, processing controls, storage controls and output controls, which correspond with the four main stages in a system.

Input controls

The purpose of controls on input is to ensure that all authorised and only authorised data is entered and converted accurately. Typical controls used are as follows.

Prior procedures
Add lists or visual check of record
Sequence checks on serially numbered documents or transaction records
Batch control totals
Range checks - only restricted values accepted
Combination and completeness checks
Reasonableness and consistency

Verification of data conversion
Separate duties of keying and verifying
Physical control over source media
Machine locks
Screen inspection for visual verifying
On line format and key-field validation

Authorisation of input
Manual constraints, e.g. approval of purchase invoices
Machine validation, e.g. limit and reasonableness checks

Processing controls

The purpose of controls in processing is to ensure the integrity of all data throughout the internal processing stages of the DP cycle. Typical controls used are as follows.

Hardware controls
Parity checks
Updating by copying
Dumping and logging
Overflow checks
Peripheral status checks
Self diagnosis
Label checking
Write protection devices
Purge data checking

Transfer controls
Check digit verification
Range and limit tests
Presence tests
Format or picture tests
Completeness tests
Reasonableness
Consistency

Batch controls
Hash total
Trailer records
Matching checks
Consistency Checks

Program controls
File label checking
Read-after-write checks
Overflow checks
Crosscasting of column totals
Record counting and comparisons

Storage controls

The purpose of storage (file) controls is to ensure that data remains unaltered until an authorised change is made. Typical controls used are as follows.

Physical controls
Write permit devices
Limited access procedures
Librarian control

Labelling conventions

External labelling
Internal labelling
Header records
Trailer records
File control totals
Generation checking

Data security
Update by copying, e.g. grandfather, father and son technique
Periodic printouts compared with clerically held data
Control totals verified against totals accumulated on files
Periodic archiving

Output controls

The purpose of output controls is to ensure that all output is received back from the computer by the originator department, output reconciles with input, output reports of errors or omissions are acted upon, and that output destined for more than one user is correctly distributed. Typical controls used are as follows.

Logging controls

Log books of work received and delivered
Logging of distribution

Logging in of outdated hard copy for destruction

Supervisory controls

Manual verification of distribution
Amendment notices correlated with exception and error reports.
User output receipt confirmation

Exercises

Telemarketing

You've seen the advertisements on television. They sell music, hand sewing machines, books, keep fit appliances and many more. The common theme is to phone in right now and order one for yourself.

Every time you see the ad on television urging you to call 800-0800 you are being invited to join in the fastest growing segment of the shopping experience: Direct response marketing. When you call the number you are not being put through to a shop but to a room full of pleasant voiced sales people located at any one of several locations throughout the country (sometimes even in a different country). The person you speak to will simply note your order details and tell you to have a nice day. These response offices do not hold any goods and do not work for any one supplier. They simply offer a service of answering the phone and taking down your order. These are then sent on to the actual supplier who will charge your account and send you the goods in the advertised 28 days.

1. Using the output-files-input methodology design a computer based system for the direct marketing company.

2. Can you suggest any ways in which the direct marketing company could improve its present services or generate new revenue using your new system?

3. Using the headings suggested in the text, draw up a design plan for computerising a small lending library.

4. What type of output device would be the best to use for:

> A travel agent's office
> An accountant's office
> An insurance broker
> An international fashion house

5. Which of the elements of file design would you give most weight to in:

> A wages application

A holiday booking service

The credit sales ledger of a department store which is used to answer enquires and also used for producing statements each month

6. Which input method would you recommend for:

A payment of an annual insurance premium demand

Stock availability enquiries made over the telephone

A corner grocer's shop

A builders' merchant selling mostly lengths of wood?

Further Reading

Davis, G. and Olson, M. (1985) Management Information Systems, conceptual foundations, structures and development. Pub McGraw-Hill, NY.

Kendall, P. (1990) Introduction to Systems Analysis and Design: A structured approach. Pub Wm C. Brown, Dubuque IA.

Lucas, H. (1992) The analysis, design and implementation of information systems. Pub McGraw-Hill, NY.

Chapter 10 Structured systems analysis

Systems life cycle: the traditional methodology

The systems analysis methodology described so far is what has come to be called the traditional methodology. This system evolved in the early practice of systems analysis and although it can be found in daily use it is coming under increased criticism.

To understand why this should be so it is instructive to recall the origins of the systems life cycle. In the early days there were very few experienced analysts and they nearly all worked for manufacturers of computer equipment. If a company wanted a computer application the manufacturer undertook to supply the whole solution, all the hardware and any software to go with it. It was expected that the client and the manufacturer would have a long-term relationship. Hardware costs were relatively high but the manufacturer would supply any level of support needed until the application was working as specified.

A company analyst went along to the client company to assess the application and decided which of his company's range of hardware and software products would be best to use. The analyst then did a little investigating to discover what was required as output and proceeded to commission the appropriate programs. The new system was tested and altered until the client was satisfied that it was working fairly well. The analyst would remain in contact with the client for a long time after the application was first put in and would thereafter be called in if any amendments were needed.

This sort of system only worked because when computerisation was first introduced it was naturally applied to those jobs which were easy to do and which gave large and immediate savings. These were jobs such as printing electricity bills which, although handling very large numbers of records, are actually simple in concept. Basically such a bill only requires the previous meter reading to be subtracted from the present reading and multiplied by a price, and then the correct name and address to be extracted and printed out on an invoice.

Jobs like these were ideally suited to batch processing, and were mostly very successful because of their underlying simplicity and because they could do away with the need for very large numbers of clerical workers. At the time there was a great shortage of this class of worker. So the computer not only solved the staff shortage, it also avoided the need to pay large and increasing wage bills.

Given these conditions, the high cost of the computer system was largely irrelevant and any inefficiencies in the design or operation of the system could be tolerated because of the enormous savings which could be made overall.

However, these conditions do not prevail today. All the easy systems applications have already been done. Client companies have much higher expectations of what their computer should deliver. Real-time systems, where data are accepted from the user, processed and the results returned quickly enough to affect the user's activities, are now as common as batch systems, where data are collected into batches and all processed together at a specific time. Communications are a standard feature of most applications. In short the environment in which the analyst works is today much more complicated. It is argued that this calls for either a higher degree of expertise, a better methodology, or both.

Basic limitations of the traditional methodology

In today's conditions the following criticisms can be made of the traditional methodology.

Too much is expected of the analyst

A systems analyst is expected to be an expert in technical knowledge and to keep up with all the latest developments in hardware. The analyst has to be adept at handling the political difficulties associated with the introduction of Information Technology (IT) into an organisation; has to be able to overcome resistance from employees wary of job losses; and finally has to be familiar with increased communications and its problems.

Communications are poor

Once the analyst did everything. Today's complex applications make this impossible and so the analyst spends much of the time communicating ideas to users, programmers, operators, suppliers and others.

The dual aspect of the analyst's task is ignored

The job of a working analyst in fact divides into two distinct phases: logical analysis-what the system will do; and physical design-how the system will do it. Modern systems can make both roles very complex, but the traditional methodology lumps both together and assumes the analyst will be equally skilled in both, which is unlikely.

197

System complexity
It can be very difficult for a systems analyst with only limited time available to gain a rapid understanding of modern complex organisational processes and procedures. The old methodology does not provide tools for rapid in-depth investigation.

Obscure format
It is too easy for both analyst and client to be swamped with detail as the investigation proceeds. The methodology does not provide a clear way to bring out what is important while retaining sufficient detail for programming.

User inadequacy
Managers in the client company often need to be educated by the analyst before they are able to give a clear specification of what they want. The traditional methodology assumes that the problems are always clearly definable and are unambiguous.

Inadequate language
The way in which users and managers state their requirements is frequently too loose and ambiguous to be suitable for developing programming specifications.

Lack of modelling
Traditional methods produce a specification written in words , not a working model. Inexperienced managers can relate much more easily to models.

Lack of participation
The methodology assumes that the analyst is the person who will know most about the application of the proposed system and its information needs. In fact almost always the client managers know most and are experts in the application. But traditional methodology does not allow them to help design their own system.

Specification too large
For a system of any complexity the final product of analysis, the systems specification, is usually a very long written document, often running to hundreds of pages. Its sheer size means that few analysts, never mind the client's managers, would be able to give a sensible assessment of a proposal based solely on this document.

In a complex system a large specification also obscures implementation. Usually the programmer cannot work directly from the specification and has to go back to the manager for information.

198

Time-scales involved
There is an underlying assumption that the analyst has plenty of time. The whole methodology is too slow in delivering the working system.

Inadequate tools
Traditional analysis techniques are fundamentally outdated. Items such as flow charts were designed to show what in most cases are obsolete workings e.g. punched cards in batch processing. Traditional techniques make the analyst think in physical terms too soon.

Assumes always a new application
The methodology assumes that the client location does not have a computer. It is unrealistic to use a methodology which always starts from basics.

To answer these problems analysts developed many alternative methodologies. One of the first was a methodology which evolved out of a charting technique called Data Flow Diagrams.

Structured systems analysis

Structured systems analysis is a technique which divides the task of systems development in two separate stage: systems analysis and systems design, and encourages user participation throughout. It was popularised in two slightly different forms (Gane & Sarson, De Marco) and is now firmly established as a mainstream methodology.

The basic idea is that the analyst and user work together and between them design a logical data model. As the design progresses the analyst charts the movement of data using data-flow diagrams and checks its correctness repeatedly with the user until both are satisfied that it is right. Once the basic logical model of the existing system has been agreed the analyst and the manager can discuss alternatives to the present way of operating until a new and better logical design has been arrived at.

Since the logical model has been charted at every stage, the documentation is always up to date. Additionally, the analyst will use a technique called levelling. This allows important high-level views of information to be displayed together, usually on one sheet of paper, where they are not obscured by low-level detail; all the low-level detail for each process is gathered in one place where it is easily accessible to the programmer.

This means that as soon as the final design has been agreed, programming can start in a logical and co-ordinated way with no need to go back to the users for more information.

199

Some of the advantages claimed for this methodology are as follows:

- makes a clear distinction between logical analysis and physical design
- aims to involve the user at all stages to get the benefit of user experience and detailed knowledge of the application
- provides a model for the user to work with
- automatically supplies system documentation as the task progresses
- creates a bridge linking the user to the programmer, eliminating a lot of misunderstandings
- compensates for the user's lack of DP knowledge
- minimises development effort overall by not placing all the responsibility on the analyst
- speeds development time by catching most design errors very early on in the development process

The key to structured systems analysis is understanding how data flow diagrams work.

Data flow diagrams

Data flow diagrams (DFDs) are used to reduce complex data processing operations to simple diagrams. The primary objective is to first isolate and then illustrate the logical flow of information through a process, quite independent of the hardware used. System flow charts and system run charts emphasise the physical and temporal aspects of data movements by charting how and when data is physically transferred between files. Data flow diagrams show the passage of data through a process independent of the current way of organising the work and independent of the people or departments who actually carry out the procedures. The end result is a pure logical view of the process.

Data flow diagrams are very powerful. The symbols used are simple and standardised and the technique is quickly learned. They are used in the analysis and design of information processes, they get ideas across clearly to management, and are at the heart of structured systems analysis. Despite their simplicity, a correctly drawn up DFD can represent a processing system of any complexity, clearly and unambiguously.

The elements of DFDs

There are only four different symbols used (Figure 10.1)

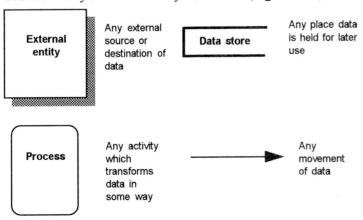

Figure 10.1 DFD symbols

External entities

These can include elements such as people, departments, companies, processes or any other thing which, although associated with the procedure under examination, is actually outside the limits of the system being examined. The objects in this classification are normally sources of data or sinks for data, and occasionally both.

A data source is anything which generates data from its own internal processes for its own purposes, and presents that data to the procedure under examination for processing. **A data sink** is anything which accepts data from the procedure and uses that data for its own purposes which are entirely outside the control of the data processing procedure being examined.

A typical source might be a company's customers who produce orders at random intervals as a product of their own internal procedures and to satisfy their own purposes and then present these to the company for processing. The company uses these external orders as data input and processes them to produce invoices and despatch notes, stock movements etc.

A typical data sink occurs when a management report produced as a by product of data processing is sent to another department who use this as raw data in their own procedures. For example, a low stocks report might be produced as part of a stock update procedure and be sent to the buying department. It thereafter ceases to be any direct concern of the stock procedure.

Processes

A process box is used to indicate any process which transforms data. Data enters a process box, is changed in some way, and leaves the process in a different state from that which it entered. The new state does not have to be dramatically different, it only has to be demonstrably different in some way. Common examples include sorting where the order of data is merely rearranged, but the output is discernibly different from the input. Similarly, adding two numbers together produces a total which is different and even inspecting an item of data input produces a piece of data output which has been inspected and is thus discernibly different from the state in which it went in.

Data stores

A data store is any place where data is held, however briefly, in any manner or in any type of device, before being made available for further processes. All computer files are data stores. A list which is referred to when checking an order is a data store, the tax rate percentage held in a program in internal memory is a data store too, as are an accountant's ledgers.

Data flow lines

The data flow arrow shows the paths along which data may flow between the other three symbols. The arrowhead must always be present and indicates the direction of flow of net data. Every data flow must be labelled with either the names of the data items it is carrying or a collective name given to the group of items as a whole when they are in that particular state.

Drawing data flow diagrams

Drawing data flow diagrams is simple. Consider the following example.

Computer Consultants Inc.

Computer Consultants Inc. organise exhibitions of the latest technology and invite existing clients by letter. A list of these clients is held in the reception area of the exhibition venue. They also advertise the exhibition in local newspapers and any local business people are welcome to attend.

When a visitor arrives in the reception hall of the exhibition, Susan Hinchley, the exhibition manager, asks for the visitor's name and checks to see if it appears on the client list. If it is there she removes the pre-printed details and asks the visitor to take them to one of the other receptionists who will use the information to issue a lapel badge showing the visitor's name and company with an indication of the nature of their firm's business. If the visitor is not an existing client then Susan gets them to complete a registration form and they then take this form to a receptionist who issues the lapel badge. Details of all visitors going in to the exhibition are retained by the receptionists and at the end of the day these are forwarded to the Marketing Manager at Head Office.

The finished data flow diagram is shown in Figure. 10.2.

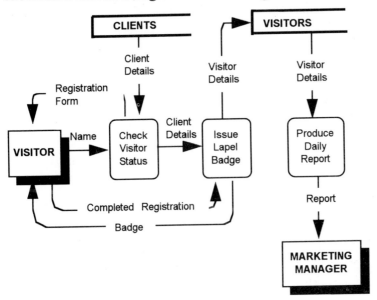

Figure 10.2 DFD for Computer Consultants Inc.

Examining CCI's data flow diagrams

The external entities and their data flows

DFDs are normally drawn so that they can be read starting from the external entity box nearest the top left hand corner. In this case this is the 'Visitor' entity.

Visitors are external entities in this DFD because the reception process has no control over who arrives or when they arrive or even if they will arrive. By similar logic the Marketing Manager is an external entity for the purposes of this DFD because although he is an employee of CCI we have no information as to what use is made of the report and the report produced plays no further part in the reception procedure.

The 'Visitor' entity is also a sink for data. When the visitor is not a client a registration form is shown going the Visitor. Although the Visitor may complete the form and present it for further processing, the way it is filled in, how long it takes and even the decision of whether to complete it or not are all matters falling outside the reception procedure. This makes it an external matter and therefore is shown as an external entity.

Processes and their associated data flows

A DFD doesn't really start anywhere or finish anywhere: it is meant to be a picture of a procedure already established and in motion. However, it is usual to draw the primary input immediately to the right of the first entity. In this case it is the data flow 'Name'. This data is shown flowing into the process 'Check-Visitor-Status'. The process is shown taking a data flow called 'Client-Details' from a data store and sending two data flows out again. One goes into another process, the other goes back to the Visitor entity.

This process box and its data flow arrows are a diagrammatic way of showing the 'logical view' of the physical actions of Susan Hinchley as she greets arriving visitors. We deal with the logical view in preference to the 'physical view' because logically speaking it doesn't matter who does the meeting, what is important is what is done as part of the procedure.

Similarly, it is immaterial in what manner the visitor is greeted, or whether they have an invitation letter or not, or whether Susan recognises them or whatever. The important thing is that a name is obtained. The process cannot operate without that; it requires no other piece of data to operate effectively so the name is the only data item shown on the data flow. Everything else is irrelevant and is therefore ignored in the logical view.

Data at rest: data stores

The process next compares the name obtained with the list of clients who have been asked to attend. This is shown by an arrow from the 'Clients' file going into the process. (Consider the terms data store and file to be interchangeable for now.) The data store symbol is used because although the names are in the form of a list, the physical form that the storage takes is unimportant at this stage. The name list could be on index cards, on a floppy disk or just held in Susan Hinchley's head - every kind of storage uses the same symbol since the logical effect is the same, i.e. data is held in a way that allows it to be retrieved when wanted.

The arrow is shown coming from the data store because client details are being extracted from it, but in order to find out whether a name is present or not at some point the visitor's name must have been presented to the store for comparison purposes. In programming terms this is called the search key.

This suggests that perhaps there should be an arrow showing the name going to the file as well.

However, DFDs only show the net effects when accessing a data store. The logical effect of consulting the store is to produce the client data if it is there. The 'how' of it is a physical consideration and is omitted.

Data in motion: data flows

Data flow lines show the minimum amount of data. This is to make the diagram as readable as possible by avoiding clutter. For example the data flow line coming from the 'Clients' data store is labelled 'Client Details'. The client details will actually consist of at least two pieces of information, Client_Name and Industry_Type, Since there are only two data items these could be added to the diagram and still leave it reasonably clear. However the 'Completed Registration' data flow will hold many data items and listing all those on the data flow line would certainly obscure the logic. So wherever necessary data flows are given a collective name. The details of what is actually being transferred under that collective name are stored separately in the data dictionary.

This simple example also shows another feature of data flow diagrams. They can be adapted to show the movement of physical items. The flow labelled 'Badge' refers to a physical object, not a   logical data flow. This use is acceptable on high level diagrams where the overall operation is being examined, should be avoided in all other cases.

The principles underlying DFDs

Avoid excessive detail
The primary purpose of a DFD is to lay clear the logic of an existing system so that it can be critically examined with a view to designing a better system to replace it. The enemy of clarity is excessive detail. There is no need to spell out exactly how something is done if the main purpose of the examination is to determine whether to continue doing it or not.

Leave out the error conditions
The data flow diagram is a communication tool, designed to illustrate ideas clearly and economically. Putting too much information on it is a mistake. In the CCI example there are no routines to handle the case where someone turns up and claims to have already completed a registration form but is not listed in the client file. These situations of course have to be handled, but they are

205

not shown on the main DFD. Error conditions are normally dealt with on a lower level DFD to keep the main process logic free from clutter.

File handling

It is unnecessary to show the process which created a file in the first place and it is unnecessary to show the routine maintenance needed to keep it up to date. All files have to be created and maintained so including these does not help an understanding of the process being studied.

Think logical not physical

A case in point is the arrow which takes 'Client-Details' from the process 'Check-Visitor-Status' to 'Issue-Lapel-Badge'. The description merely says 'she removes the pre-printed details', with no indication of what form these details take. The visitor then takes them to one on the other receptionists. How many are there? And how does he choose one and not another? Once again the answers to these questions are of no importance. The important point is the logical step of providing prepared client data to the Issue-Lapel-Badge process, not the physical act of walking to a person and handing it over - the logical result would be the same even if the information was telephoned to the person issuing the badge.

The perpetual motion machine

The process called 'Check-Visitor-Status' is obviously nudged into action by the arrival of a visitor who provides a name for input into the process. The 'Issue-Lapel-Badge' process is triggered by the presentation of Client-Details as its primary input. Have a look at the DFD and see if you can find what sets the 'Produce-Daily-Report' process into action.

There is no primary input to this process since by implication it is a batch process which is turned on by some agent outside the process at a predetermined time. In a DFD you do not show this 'time actioned' agent since the assumption that the process is running all the time takes care of the problem.

(This consideration also nicely points up the underlying similarity between real time and batch processing from the logical point of view. If we assume that the report is to be updated and presented on line every time a new visitor is issued a badge then the problem disappears. From a logical point of view there is no essential difference between batch and real-time.)

Show the essential logic only

The procedures involved in issuing a lapel badge are carried out by any one of a number of receptionists, yet the DFD shows only one process. Each of these receptionists individually gathers visitor data and accumulates it until the end of the day and yet the DFD shows only one file.

The reason for this is that despite the fact that many different people are working in different areas for different visitors, logically speaking there is only one task being done, issuing badges. We pay no attention at all to the way the job is physically organised and only show the logical processing.

At the end of the day somebody goes round collecting all the different piles of visitor details and then processes the data to produce the report. However, the fact that the data is in different piles is only a consequence of a particular physical way of organising the job. Logically all that data constitutes one file because it is identical in format and produced from logically identical processes. So for the purposes of the DFD there is only one process and only one file although there are physically many processes and many files.

A worked example The Aintree Hotel - enquiries

By now you should have a good idea of how to read a Data Flow Diagram and be ready to tackle simple examples. Consider the case of The Aintree Hotel. Here is a description of the Enquiry process as given by the general manager, Leslie Almeida.

'Usually the first thing we get is an enquiry from a prospective customer asking us if we have a room and how much it will cost. We look in our vacancy register to see if there is a room free on the dates required and if there is the clerk looks up the price for that room in that month. We send a letter back to the customer with this information. We also put the enquirers letter into a pile and go through these in about three weeks time and if we have not heard from the customer by then we send a reminder. The procedure for telephone enquiries is much the same.

Drawing the DFD
Every DFD consists of processes, data flows, data stores and the external entities the process is meant to serve. Start trying to identify the various elements.

As a first step go through the process description and try to identify the external entities. Typically there are only one or two of those.

In this case it should be apparent that there is only one external entity, the Customer. Draw a circle round the first occurrence of the word 'customer' to make it stand out clearly.

Next look for data stores. The actions 'look into', 'look up' and 'put into' all indicate the existence of stored information so go through the narrative and underline the 'file names' of 'Vacancy-Register', 'Price' and 'pile'. There may be others, but this will allow a start to be made on drawing the DFD.

Draw an entity box on the left hand side of the paper and write in the word 'customer'. Draw a process box to the right of that, join the two with a data flow arrow and label the arrow with the name of the main or 'primary' data flow coming from the entity.

From the procedure description find out what happens to the primary data flow and think up a process-name which summarises the processes. The process-name normally consists of a strong active verb followed by an object, ideally made up only of an adjective and noun. In this first process we want to find out if there is a vacant room on the date requested so the verb can be 'Check' or 'Find' or 'Establish' or some other direct command word. This verb will be applied to an object phrase such as 'Room Availability' or 'Bed night Vacancy' or 'Room Status'.

The exact choice of words is largely a matter of personal preference, always provided that the name is a clear unambiguous description of the process being carried out. Unacceptable process-names would include 'Process Enquiries' (too vague), 'Handle customer letters', (does not describe the purpose of the process), and 'See if any room free' (too long). You may have to have several tries before settling on a process name that is just right. The draft DFD is shown as Figure 10.3.

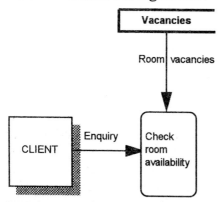

Figure 10.3 Draft DFD

The next step is to establish the data flows into and out of the process we are dealing with (the 'primary' process). Most processes either put data into files or verify data from files and identifying the file(s) involved is the easiest way to start the next stage.

The process Check-Room-Vacancies takes data from a file named 'Vacancies' so this data store can be drawn anywhere convenient to the process box and the data flow labelled. Naturally, the process has to do something with the incoming data and has to produce at least one output.

The primary output of Check-Room-Vacancies is data about rooms free on the date requested and this data forms the primary input for the next process Find-Room-Prices. Therefore draw a process box for Find-Room-Prices and a data flow linking the two.

Before going on check that nothing has been omitted. In the process description it states that 'if a room is free' certain things follow. What happens if there is no room free? In that case there is no point in finding a room price and no point in any further processing. The process description does not say what actually happens, but presumably a letter is sent back to the enquirer regretting that there are no vacancies, so the DFD should appear as in Figure 10.4.

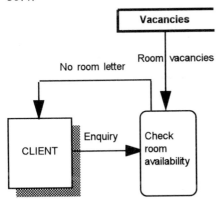

Figure 10.4 DFD for room vacancies enquiry

If there is a vacancy of the right type of room on the date wanted then the room must be priced. This procedure takes the enquiry as its input and consults the room tariff to get the appropriate figure. This is shown in Figure 10.5. Note that only one flow line is shown. There must be some searching mechanism used to find the appropriate record. The process will have to pass the values of date and room size to the search mechanism but this flow is incidental to the logic. We are only interested in the net data flow. The important thing is the price coming out of the tariff file, so that is the only data flow that is shown. Since the offer can not be confirmed immediately the

209

incoming letter must be put on hold somewhere so there logically must be a data store. This is shown as 'Offers Made'.

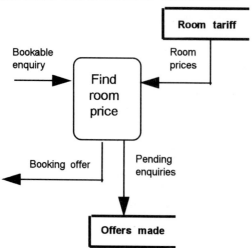

Figure 10.5 DFD for room tariff

The stored letters remain in the file for three weeks when a reminder letter is issued (Figure 10.6). Logically there must be a another process for books which are accepted by the customer within three weeks. The analyst would note this omission and bring it up for discussion with the problem owner. The DFD for this part of the procedure does not make any reference to the three weeks waiting period as this does not affect the logic of the procedure. There is no difference between issuing a reminder immediately or issuing it in three weeks.

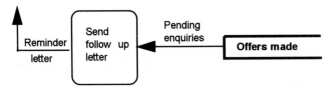

Figure 10.6 DFD for reminder letters

The finished DFD might look something like Figure 10.7.

Rules for drawing data flow diagrams

Read the whole process through a few times and try to get a clear picture in your mind of the activities that are being described. (If you know how to draw a Rich Picture that helps. Instructions are given in the Checkland methodology in chapter 10.)

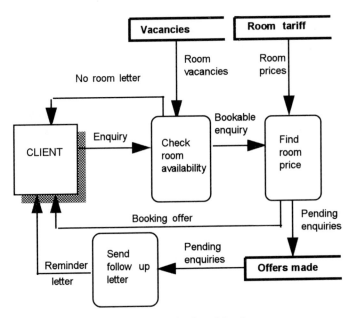

Figure 10.7 Completed DFD for hotel booking

Identify the sources and sinks. There are normally very few of these. Draw a circle round the one 'key word' for each of them.

Provisionally identify any data stores and underline them. They may be mentioned directly or may only be implied by the use of 'storage' verbs such as 'read' 'look up', 'put into', 'check', etc.

Start by drawing an entity box towards the top left hand corner. Write in the name of the external actor who seems to start the whole thing off.

To the right of that draw in the first process box and link the two symbols with a data flow arrow

From the description find what appears to be the primary data flow coming in from the source and label the data flow.

Try to find a phrase which describes what happens to the primary data flow and provisionally name the process.

Most primary data flows are either put into data stores or are checked against data stores. Identify that store and link it up to the process with data flow in the appropriate direction.

If the data flow is coming in from a data store then there must be a data flow out and that will identify the next process. Draw that in any convenient

211

position, find a phrase that describes what happens to the data flow, label the data flow, name the process and carry on from there.

Make sure that when the initial process involves an IF... THEN you deal with both outputs.

If the initial data flow is into a data store then you must look to the procedure description to establish what comes next and draw a data flow either from the store to the next process or from the first process to another process.

Carry on from there treating every new process as if it were the primary process until this first draft of the diagram is complete.

Finally read the description again and check that you haven't left out any flows to or from the sources and sinks.

Now check your draft against the following principles:

- Every data flow line is labelled

- You cannot have data going from a store to a store. There must be a process in between.

- Every output from a data store is to a process.

- Entities only ever connect with processes.

- No decision conditions are ever shown.

- No duplicated files

- No crossed lines

These last two rules are sometimes broken. In general however, flow line crossing can be avoided by redrawing the DFD and repositioning the processes relative to each other. Moving a data store to the centre of the DFD often eliminates the need for duplicate occurrences. If there is still a tangle of lines it probably means that there are two separate processes going on.

DFD independence
- Each process must be regarded as entirely independent of any other process

- Must be capable of accepting its inputs from any source

- Must be capable of sending its outputs to any other process irrespective of how that particular process is organised.

- The data flows going into a process should be the minimum needed by that process to produce its outputs.

212

- The data flows coming out of a process must be only those capable of being formed from the data flows going into the process. Time, date and sequential numbers are assumed to be available to all processes.

- A process is always running, it never starts or stops as far as the DFD is concerned. No indication of time or trigger events is shown on the DFD.

Ordering and persistence

- The first item into a data flow is always the first item out of the data flow. Other wise the order must have been changed and that must have involved a process.

- Using a data item from a data store does not erase it.

- Using an item from a data flow does erase it.

Data dictionary

The DFD succeeds as a tool of analysis largely because it is deliberately kept clear of detail. However, that detail is needed, and must be recorded somewhere. The data dictionary is the place where the detail is kept.

A data flow diagram must always be accompanied by a data dictionary. Data dictionaries can be compiled manually by the person drawing the DFD or they can be a component of a sophisticated CASE tool used to produce the DFDs. No matter how it is done the principle is the same. To keep things simple we will assume a manual data dictionary is being maintained by the DFDs designer. The normal way of doing this is on file cards. There is one card for each DFD object and the cards are classified according to the object type and then sorted alphabetically.

The data dictionary has entries for each of the four elements of the data flow diagram. There are separate entries for flows, processes, entities and stores. Using the data dictionary enforces consistency in the DFD. It prevents duplicate procedure names and ensures that there is sufficient information about each data element found in the DFD.

Flow entries

The most obvious use for a data dictionary is for removing excess detail from the flow lines. This is done by assigning collective names to the various elements making up a flow. For example in the CCI DFD (Figure 10.2) there is a flow from the Check_Visitor_Status process to the Issue_Lapel_Badge process. The data label on this flow is 'Client Details'.

The term 'Client Details' is correct and needs no further expansion to understand the logic of the process. However, if this procedure is to be converted to a computerised solution then 'client details' is too vague. A programmer needs to know exactly what makes up client details, what data elements must be present, which are optional and might be there and what the individual data types are. This information is recorded in a data dictionary data flow entry. A typical card is illustrated in Figure 10.8. The 'client details' name is underlined to show that it is a compound item made up from other data elements.

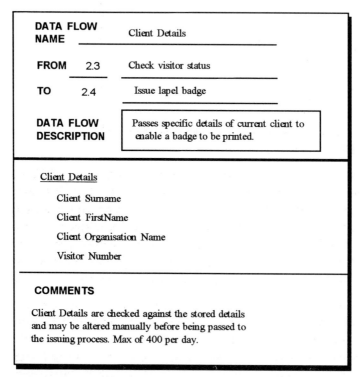

Figure 10.8 Data flow entry card

A **data element** is defined as a data item which cannot be usefully decomposed into to further, simpler elements. The data element 'Client Surname' cannot be broken down any further, it is at the lowest level of the data dictionary. Each data element will have its own entry in the data dictionary. An example is shown in Figure 10.9. The data element entry holds all the details a programmer would need to handle the data element in a

214

programming language. There may be one or more aliases for a given data element.

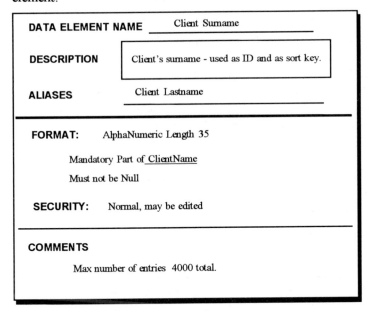

Figure 10.9 Data element entry card

Organisations often call data items by different names in different departments. Each alias would have its own entry in the data dictionary pointing the user to the correct entry to use. It also needs to be recognised that the definition of an item of information as a final level data element is often subjective. A date can be regarded as either an irreducible data element or can be broken down further into day, month and year. A telephone number may used as is or could be broken down into area code and line number.

Data elements are often grouped into **data structures**. These are data elements associated with some particular entity or relationship. Data structures may or may not be made of the same elements as are found in the data stores. It is useful when analysing an application to construct data structures even if it is known in advance that they will be physically implemented in a different way. A typical data structure would be all those data elements associated with a client. This would include name of the client, name of company, one or more addresses for correspondence and deliveries, perhaps some historical data about purchases or preferences and many other items.

There are many typographical conventions in use to show which parts of the data structure are mandatory (must be present) and which parts are optional. For example the entry for the data flow 'Name' might look like Figure 10.10.

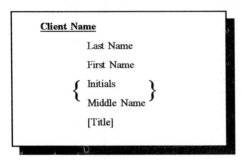

Figure 10.10 Data structure entry

The 'Client Name' entry is underlined to emphasise that it is a composite. The 'Last Name' and 'First Name' entries are mandatory. The 'Initials' and 'Middle Name' entries are in curly brackets to indicate that one of them must be present but not both. The 'Title' entry is in square brackets to show that it is optional: the data group 'Client Name' is valid even if there is no value present for 'Title'.

In some data elements there may be repeated values. These are commonly shown by placing an asterisk beside the element and a number representing the range of repetitions. For example an order may have many order lines.

Order
        Order date
        Customer Name
        Order Line *(1 - 15)

In this example an Order must have at least one order line and may have up to fifteen order lines. Details of what constitutes a valid order line would be found under the appropriate entry.

Process entries

Every process must be documented to show its inputs and outputs, and to express the logic of its internal operations (Figure 10.11).

The process logic can be described by a Decision Table, by a flow chart or most commonly, in Structured English.

The procedure logic's Structured English will be expressed to a degree suitable to the target audience. Some process logic will be indistinguishable

216

from programming instructions, some will be at a much higher level and merely restate the procedure's steps in a condensed version.

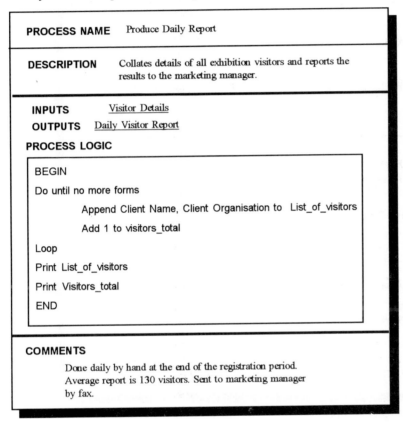

PROCESS NAME   Produce Daily Report

DESCRIPTION   Collates details of all exhibition visitors and reports the results to the marketing manager.

INPUTS   Visitor Details
OUTPUTS   Daily Visitor Report
PROCESS LOGIC

BEGIN
Do until no more forms
      Append Client Name, Client Organisation to List_of_visitors
      Add 1 to visitors_total
Loop
Print List_of_visitors
Print Visitors_total
END

COMMENTS
Done daily by hand at the end of the registration period.
Average report is 130 visitors. Sent to marketing manager
by fax.

Figure 10.11 Process entry

Data store entries

This is primarily a list of the data elements held in the store (Figure 10.12). Data elements coming out of a store must of course be in the store and data elements coming in from a flow must be held there. There may also be some system variables needed such as the date and time, or there may derived data such as record IDs to be stored. So the data store can be derived by adding all the incoming data elements and then checking the results by examining all the outgoing elements.

The data store is a listing of all the elements logically required. It is unlikely that the final physical organisation will be identical to the logical requirements. The degree to which the physical organisation is shown will depend on the existing form of the file.

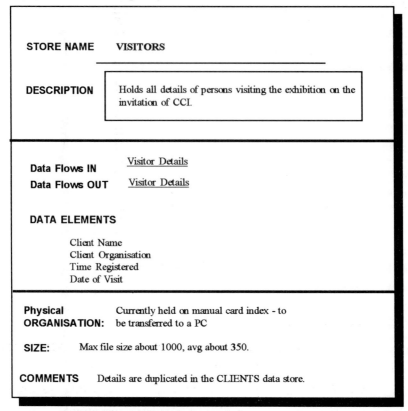

STORE NAME   VISITORS

DESCRIPTION   Holds all details of persons visiting the exhibition on the invitation of CCI.

Data Flows IN   Visitor Details
Data Flows OUT   Visitor Details

DATA ELEMENTS

Client Name
Client Organisation
Time Registered
Date of Visit

Physical ORGANISATION: Currently held on manual card index - to be transferred to a PC

SIZE: Max file size about 1000, avg about 350.

COMMENTS   Details are duplicated in the CLIENTS data store.

Figure 10.12 Data store entry

External entity

The external entity is by definition of no importance to the logical operation of the process being analysed. However, it should be included for completeness and because it is essential where the DFDs are being drawn using a CASE tool.

Many CASE tools have logic checking features which ensure that flows are connected to a defined object. If the defined object is not a process or a store then it has to be an entity and the entity must have an entry in the data dictionary.

The entity entry simply names the entity and lists the flows originating or terminating there (Figure 10.13).

218

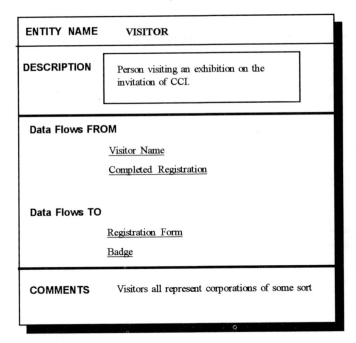

ENTITY NAME	VISITOR
DESCRIPTION	Person visiting an exhibition on the invitation of CCI.

Data Flows FROM

        Visitor Name

        Completed Registration

Data Flows TO

        Registration Form

        Badge

COMMENTS	Visitors all represent corporations of some sort

Figure 10 13 Entity entry

Levelling and balancing

Levelling and balancing are ways of ensuring that DFDs retain their simplicity. Consider the following example (see Figure 10.14):

> Richmond Rockhounds is in the business of supplying geological specimens to colleges around the country. Orders are received daily by post or telephone. Each order is checked to see whether the items requested are available by inspecting the catalogue. Then the customer credit worthiness is verified. An orders pending list is updated to hold all the valid orders. The company holds very little inventory preferring to contact a world wide network of wholesalers when a sample is needed. So in order to fill the orders a request is sent to one of the collectors whose details are kept in the suppliers list.

> Geological specimens come in irregularly and have to be allocated to the right college. As the specimens arrive each customer's order is assembled. Incoming samples are first verified with the purchase requests and if correct are assigned to the pending customer orders. When the order is complete the customer details are extracted from the accounts records to provide the name and address of the college and a

despatch note is raised which is sent out along with the collection of specimens.

Inspecting the DFD for Richmond Rockhounds in Figure 10.14 reveals that there are conflicting levels of detail present.

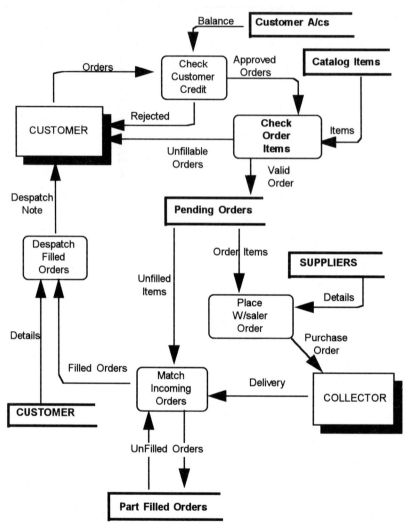

Figure 10.14 DFD for Richmond Rockhounds

Some procedures such as 'Check Customer Credit' are simple and more or less complete as given. Other procedures are more complex. The 'Match Incoming Orders' procedure must contain more detailed procedures. What is to be done about partially filled orders, or those which cannot be supplied within a given time? How are payments to and from the company handled? If all these factors were to be added to the DFD it would be overwhelmed with detail. And lose its principal advantage: simplicity.

In order to get round this problem DFDs are levelled, that is they are drawn from the top down in ever increasing detail. Look again at the Rockhound DFD. There are actually several separate sub systems within that DFD. Subsystems can often be found just by inspection. The existence of a subsystem is revealed where a there is a 'clump' of processes and stores with many interactions but only two or three flows in or out.

Look at the DFD and image a line drawn across it just above 'Pending Orders'. It should be evident that there are two major subsystems here. The upper subsystem has an input of Customer Orders and an output of orders classed as valid or invalid. Similarly another subsystem can be defined by drawing a boundary round the 'Despatch Filled Orders' and 'Match Incoming Orders' and their stores. This gives a subsystem with two inputs and one output. Examining the inputs and outputs will reveal the nature of the transformation going on inside the boundary. This subsystem could be renamed 'Order despatch' or similar. This leaves only one process which really constitutes a 'Procurement' subsystem.

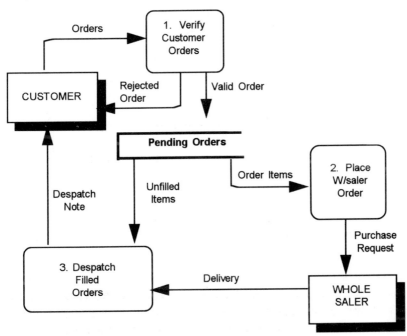

Figure 10.15 Consolidated DFD

221

The original DFD can now be redrawn to show only three procedures linking the same entities and all three linked through the central data store.

The result of combining the processes into higher level subsystems is shown in the Consolidated DFD (Figure 10.15). This DFD still shows the same logic. But it brings out more clearly the relationship between the customer and the wholesaler and emphasises the importance of the pending orders file. Try locating the Pending Orders file in any of the processes and it becomes impossible to retain the clarity of the logic. Notice also that no data has been lost. All the flow lines are in place exactly as they were in the original DFD. The exception is the rejected orders flow line, which has combined two flow lines into one. The reason for the rejection is not important at this level of abstraction. What is important is that the process is seen to able to distinguish between valid and invalid orders however they might be defined.

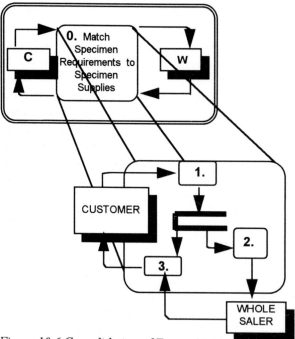

Figure 10.6 Consolidation of Figure 10.15

This process of consolidation can be taken one stage further. The three procedures can be combined again into an ever higher level DFD. Figure 10.16 shows the process used to produce the **context diagram** shown in Figure 10.17. If it is correctly derived it shows what the organisation is about, its fundamental nature. This organisation is basically about matching the needs of colleges to the supplies available. How it goes about doing this is purely a matter of detail. Once again there is an exact match between the data flow lines on this diagram and those on the previous level DFD. This process of combining or expanding DFDs is known as levelling. The discipline of maintaining the data flow lines at each level is known as balancing the DFD.

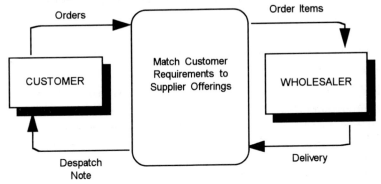

Figure 10. 17 Context diagram

We now have three levels of data flow diagram in increasing level of detail. The context diagram can be expanded into three major processes. Each of these can expanded into lower level processes. To keep track of the various processes they are numbered to show their level and their sequence within that level. The context diagram is always level zero. In this example the second level processes could be numbered 1, 2. and 3. Let us assume the Verify Customer Orders procedure is labelled as procedure 1. Then when it is decomposed it will expand into two separate procedures: the 'Check Customer Credit' procedure will be labelled as 1.1 and the Check Order Items procedure will be labelled 1.2. If the Check Order Item was itself decomposed into three more procedures these would be labelled 1.2.1, 1.2.2 and 1.2.3. In this way it is easy to keep track of the level for any given procedure.

The process of decomposition can be carried to any degree of refinement required. However, at some point, just as there must be a top level, there must be a bottom level, some level below which the processes cannot be decomposed any further. The lowest possible level of procedure logic is known as the **functional primitive.** It is the logic of this functional primitive which is displayed in the data dictionary.

CASE tools and software engineering

Data flow diagrams are an excellent communications and analysis tool. They are also easy to draw and read. They do however have one serious drawback. As soon as the analyst sketches out the logic and shows it to a manager, the manager wants it changed. Changing DFDs can be tedious because changing one element often means rearranging other parts of the chart. It also means changing the data dictionary entries and ensuring the consistency of the data.

The difficulty of maintaining DFDs led many analysts to stop using them as a way of analysing and documenting systems. (Sumner and Sitek, 1986). Fortunately there is now a way of overcoming this problem. The easiest and best way to produce data flow diagrams is with a CASE tool. CASE stands for Computer Aided Software Engineering.

CASE products cover a wide spectrum of systems design tasks. At one end are simple diagramming tools which are drawing packages adapted for easy production of structured systems charts. At the other end are sophisticated comprehensive packages which derive designs from a statement of the organisation's objectives. These help the designer to define the business concept, specify file contents, trace the procedure logic and simplify the design of interactive screens and forms. Most maintain the data dictionary as a by product of the charting process. Some go a step further and actually produce code from the procedure logic which can be compiled and run with the minimum of programmer input.

CASE tools are particularly good at drawing DFDs. There are only four symbols used so these fit in well with a graphical interface and 'drag and drop' methods. Many packages allow the user to select an object with a mouse and move it to a new location while still keeping its flow lines attached. Some products will automatically rearrange the existing objects on a DFD to make room for a new object.

A good CASE tool makes exploding and condensing processes simple. Usually all that is needed is to click on a process and this will open up a window to reveal the subcomponents of that process. Alternatively clicking on the boundary collapses the processes into a higher level process box. Processes are linked to each other and numbered automatically. The best products offer extensive consistency checking. Everything added to the DFD is automatically checked against the data dictionary. It is impossible to give the same name to two different processes. Data flows are automatically tied to the same dictionary entry so identical flow names are forced to have identical data elements. Clicking on the flow line will open up the dictionary entry for inspection or editing. Processes are checked to ensure that there is a least one input and output.

Some CASE tools incorporate elements of artificial intelligence so any attempt to draw a flow line between two entities will be rejected. Flows line entries are checked to ensure that all data elements flowing into or out of data stores are in fact part of the data store's data structure. Once the processes have been mapped and linked with flow lines the CASE tool accepts process description in Structured English and stores these in the data dictionary. The Structured English modules often check the logic structures for syntax errors and will report a missing ENDIF or a FOR without NEXT, for example.

The availability of CASE tools led to the introduction of Joint Applications Design (JAD). The best tools are fast enough to allow the analyst to build the data models interactively while the manager is describing the process. This allows both to check the model on the spot and clear up any inconsistencies right at the beginning.

CASE components

Many CASE products incorporate tools which are indistinguishable from the fourth generation language tools associated with database languages.

Screen generators
These are modules which take a file definition and extract the data field information from it. The module then derives a default screen design displaying the fields neatly arranged on the screen. Each field is labelled with the field name and is of the correct length and data type. The screen is ready immediately to accept entries to display existing records for editing.

Report generators
These perform the same function for printed reports. The user simply has to specify which file or files holds the data wanted and then enters any conditions which apply such as department number or a range of dates the report is to cover. There is virtually no programming required so in many cases the end users can specify the output themselves.

Application generators
Much of the work done on computer systems is predictable. Every file needs some way to display its contents, every file needs a program which will allow access to its fields for updating. Applications generators automatically create programs which will do this sort of routine work. Even quite complex procedures can be set up using default values. For example sending out statements to customers are standard in most companies. An application generator can produce the skeleton of a working program which can be modified to suit the particular needs of the organisation. All the designer has to do is change some of the parameters and tell the application which files hold the necessary transaction and master file data. The resulting programs

225

are not elegant or very efficient but they do perform the function required with the minimum of programming.

Software engineering

This is a concept which specifies procedures and standards for program production which if used consistently will produce robust and error free software much as an engineering workshop produces physical goods on time and on budget. The basic idea is to get away from the notion of software production as an art and to build programs according to a predefined schedule, making use of standardised subroutines and eliminating the possibility of errors by rigorous design checking.

Not everyone is a believer in software engineering. Fertuck comments 'Some people see Software Engineering as an oxymoron, like military intelligence or telephone service'.

Exercises

a) Draw a computer run chart of the following cases.

b) Draw a data flow diagram of the procedures.

c) Express the logic in structured English.

1. The Aintree Hotel - Bookings Procedures

When a guest sends us a booking, with deposit, we change the vacancy list to show one less and enter the customer details into the reservation file. The cash from the deposit is sent to the accounts department. A letter of confirmation is sent to the customer confirming the details and we also open a guest account in our ledger.

This guest account holds all the details of meals which a guest has signed for in the restaurant and drinks which have been charged in the bar. The vouchers from the bar and restaurant are applied to the guest account daily in batches. Every Saturday a statement is produced for each guest and a copy of this goes to the accounts section for inclusion in their weekly figures.

When the guest checks out we copy all the details from the guest account onto a statement and give this statement to the customer for payment. The customer actually pays the cashier in the accounts department.

2. Cashing a cheque

Before a customer can draw out cash from a current account they have to get their cheque approved at the ledgers counter. The customer gives over the cheque to the ledger clerk who goes to the card cabinets and verifies the signature, we're a very big branch here and can't know everybody. If the signature is different to the one on the card then the clerks will discretely call security. Usually of course there is no problem and so then the clerk validates the cheque itself. This involves making sure that the words and figures agree and the date is OK. If there is a mistake on the cheque then the clerk will ask the customer to amend it.

If the cheque is valid then the clerk will look up the customer's balance. If there is sufficient in the account then the check is stamped and initialed and the customer can proceed to the cash desks. If the customer is already overdrawn then they are asked to take the cheque to the manager's office. She will grant an overdraft or not according to her rules - the ledger clerks are not allowed to take any part in this. The only other case arises where the customer is asking for more than the account holds. In that case the customer just changes the amount.

3. Willis Wholesale Pharmacy

On our toiletries we do heavy sale or return marketing exercises backed up with special offer packs and so on, and so we get a lot of returns in the normal course of events. All returns are first handled by the warehouse staff. Their job is to ensure that the returned goods were actually sold by us and the quantities found in the cartons are the same as those quoted on the documentation. When they have established this Mr Rutherford, the warehouse supervisor, writes out one of our return debit notes and attaches this to the original documentation. He also keeps one of the carbons for his own records and sends a copy back to the customer by way of a confirmation of receipt. He has to decide himself what to do in cases where there are there are large discrepancies between the numbers claimed to be returned and the actual quantity received by us. Sometimes he sends the whole lot back, sometimes he accepts them.

When we are updating our customer records in the office we use a terminal to enter the product details from the returns debit notes. All debit notes are collected into batches of 20 to 30 and Jane totals up each batch using an adding machine. Then we run the debit note entry program, (providing there are at least two batches ready) which checks the entered values against the batch totals and stores the valid batches ready for the next stage. When all the batches have been run through or returned for resubmission we then run the data validation program which checks the validity of all the product fields in the transaction records. If they are all OK then they are sorted into ascending order by the sort utility and finally the update program runs the validated records against the customer master file. At each stage of the procedure error listings and proof sheets are produced as appropriate and then the whole cycle starts again with fresh goods returned notes coming in.

4. Blenheim Development Bank

In the Blenheim Development Bank the loan application system works like this. The bank's customers send in letters on all sorts of subjects, so first we go through them all and take out all the loan applications. The other correspondence is just passed on to the general office. Once the loan applications have been extracted, we have to make up a loan application folder. This consists of the loan application letter, plus the customer's statements for the previous three months from the transactions file, and any previous correspondence with the bank. The loan folder is passed to the under-manager who makes a first assessment of the application. Usually he can approve or reject straight away. If the loan is rejected he writes a letter to the customer. Sometimes he cannot approve the loan because he needs more information and so he will write to the customer requesting further details. In both these cases the loan folders are filed back where they came from. If the loan is approved the loan application is passed to the funds manageress who decides what interest rate to apply. She examines the application to determine the amount of the loan needed. She compares this with the amount of funds available and deducts the amount of the loan commitment from the funds available figure. She sends a letter of approval to the customer and a copy of this goes the general manager. The loan application papers are then filed away.

Further Reading

Fertuck, L. (1992) Systems analysis and design with case tools. (Pub Wm C. Brown, Dubuque, IA)

Page-Jones, M. (1988) Practical guide to structured systems design. Prentice-Hall, NJ.

Peters, L. (1988) Advanced Structured Analysis and Design. Prentice Hall, Englewood Cliffs, NJ.

Powers, M., Cheney P. and Crow, G. (1990) Structured systems development. Pub Boyd and Fraser, Boston, MA.

Chapter 11 User centred design

The systems life cycle and structured systems analysis are both methodologies of the 'hard systems' type. That is to say they both look at the requirements of the processing and try to determine the best mix of hardware and software for solving that particular problem. In other words they present 'hard', technology based solutions to problems.

Not all methodologies are hard, however. Other methodologies including 'soft' methodologies take account of the human factors that affect organisational systems.

The difference between the hard systems methodologies and other design techniques is similar to the difference between programming and systems design.

Programming is a fairly straightforward process. You can normally tell whether the result is right or wrong and when it is finished. In contrast, systems design revolves around personal contacts and very often involves conflict and compromise. It is often difficult to know when the process is completed.

Methodologies which are suitable to a data-centred procedure such as programming may well not be as successful when applied to other areas. In particular hard methodologies allow for very little feedback from people who will be using the system or participation in its development. Users tend to feel that the solution is being imposed on them rather than belonging to them. To overcome these problems a number of alternative methodologies have been developed.

Prototyping

If you were asked to design the ideal car you probably would not know where to start. But if you looked over a range of cars you could easily pick out the features you liked. So if you teamed up with an automobile engineer you could probably work out a specification for your ideal car in a relatively short period of time. This is essentially the way in which prototyping builds computer systems.

Prototyping is a method of design where the analyst and the user interact in rapid development cycles, producing a series of increasingly better solutions until the manager's information needs are satisfied.

Problems with the life cycle model

Prototyping is a response to the problems of the life cycle model. The life cycle model probably causes as many problems as it solves. It is really a rule of thumb method which grew out of experience with early computer systems. It works reasonably well where applications are routine and predictable with fixed output requirements. But with real time applications and extensive user interaction the method often fails. The basic problem is that delivered systems do not match user requirements. Sometimes this is because the analyst has not fully grasped the nature of the problem, in other cases the time to delivery is the problem.

One solution is to stay with the life cycle model and to study the procedures in greater depth in order to understand user needs better, but this brings its own problems. Investigating a complex modern system takes time, lots of it. And for most of that time the analyst isn't actually doing any useful work, but simply learning the procedures , duplicating knowledge already held by users, and producing no real output.

The alternative is prototyping. There is in fact nothing new about prototyping. To an extent every system is prototyped, and originally all systems were built on a trial and error basis. However prototyping starts from a different base position. Prototyping:

- Accepts that today's applications will be inherently complex and require user interaction - the simple record handling systems have all been done.

- Uses the accumulated experience of managers and operators, rather than expecting the analyst to know everything

- Does not assume we start from a 'green field' site. Most organisations already have some computer power installed. Most people have a broad idea of what to expect from computers.

- Uses the microcomputer as its starting point, not a mainframe.

The basic prototyping cycle

Most computer applications consist of fairly simple requests for data in the form of reports to management summarising data held in files. If these files already exist for some other purpose then the analyst can use a high level programming language to produce reports quickly with the minimum of investigation.

One of the problems of designing management information systems is that, in general, managers can't state their requirements clearly enough to allow an accurate program to be written first time. However, if managers are shown one or more possible solutions they can almost always distinguish the features they find useful, and identify features which are missing.

Modern high level languages, often called fourth generation languages, are easier to use and more powerful than older languages such as COBOL or BASIC. In the right circumstances these allow a programmer to write applications very quickly especially when the data files already exist. This means that an analyst can sit down with a manager and get a rough idea of the requirements. Once these are known, a rapid search of the system will reveal which existing files hold the relevant data. The analyst can write a 'first cut' attempt at meeting the manager's stated requirements, and then present this for the manager's evaluation, usually by the next day.

Obviously it is unlikely to be exactly what the manager had in mind, but the manager should be able to look it over, decide what parts are wrong or irrelevant and which are useful. The analyst will note the manager's references and go off to write a second attempt, returning with the revised solution within a very short period. Since the second attempt will incorporate the feedback from the manager it should be much closer to what the manager actually needs. This process continues with the analyst and manager refining the application until the manager has what is wanted.

The cycle of problem description, initial solution attempt, discussion and revision should normally take no more than 48 hours at the early stages. This keeps the problem fresh in the end user's mind and maintains interest and commitment. If the prototyping iterations are spread over weeks or months then much of the advantage is lost. Many database languages can produce a fully validated data entry and query screen in seconds so the prototype is often built on the spot and refined interactively, and then left with the manager :for testing and evaluation.

The prototyping philosophy

Some people use the word prototype when they mean model. In fact, the essence of a prototype is that it is a working system. A model is simply a description of a system. The prototype may be crude and incomplete, but it *does* something. Prototyping means more than just showing users mock-ups of the program screens and asking for comments.

Prototypes in practice

Prototyping is a powerful, flexible design methodology, aimed at developing a simple system which is refined and refined until the user is satisfied.

Thereafter at some point the system is either abandoned, partly integrated, or becomes the production system. The approach depends on he nature of the system being prototyped.

Ill defined problems

Prototyping can be reserved for use only where the users themselves are unable to state their requirements. or used where the design team is undecided as to the best way to build a system. Another approach is to prototype within the standard method and use it to explore untested complex features involving user interaction, and develop the rest normally.

Partial systems

There is no obligation to use prototyping in isolation. A prototyped module can fit within a larger system, or several parts can be developed simultaneously. Alternatively the programming team can switch to standard methods once a 'core' has been prototyped.

Deriving a specification

Analysts are often asked to deal with poorly described problem situations. Prototyping can be used to demonstrate to the user some of the capabilities of computing and use the user's improved perceptions to get a specification started.

Experimentation

Prototyping is an ideal way to try things out. It allows immediate testing of alternatives and new ideas. It is often quicker to build a prototype application than it is to write out the specification for it.

Specify output

One form of prototyping aims to allow the users to help design the output. The idea is that the output is what systems design is all about. The user and analyst develop a design which will deliver the needed output. Once it is clear what they want the programming team can then go back to using a formal method to produce the output specification.

Total methodology

Prototyping has the potential to evolve a complete operational system, with full user :input all the way to the final system.

Advantages of prototyping

The process reduces application development time.

Microcomputers can be used as development platforms for target mainframes.

232

It is possible to test ideas without incurring large costs.

The manager very quickly becomes educated in what is possible and what is not.

It allows users to try out a number of alternatives: that is it allows them to program and present alternatives.

It gives users direct knowledge of systems performance and capability.

It makes acceptance of the finished system more likely.

It increases analyst productivity and utilises the user's skills and knowledge..

Since there is a close interaction between analyst and manager the problem of remoteness is removed.

The manager is encouraged to think of ways of solving day to day problems instead of leaving responsibility for this to the DP department.

The user always has a working system.

Disadvantages of prototyping

It is easy for a prototyping project to go out of control.

It is difficult to manage; how much time and resources to allocate to functions?

It depends too much on the personal skills of the individual analyst. It assumes there is one analyst and one user and also assumes there is time for one-to-one interaction.

Users cannot easily specify or check complicated logic.

It is difficult to predict how long a system will take to deliver and difficult to tell when a system is finished.

Different end users may demand incompatible features.

No account is taken of downstream effects. Users may not be aware of how their chosen design will impact other peoples jobs.

It is not suitable for very big projects.

The process is addictive: the urge to continue to improve and refine can lead inefficient use of time.

Prototyping also requires a particular environment.

There needs to be suitable hardware to run it on.

Problems with prototyping

In practice prototyping is not always the preferred methodology. Many experienced practitioners prefer more formal methods. This is because there are many problems with prototyping that must be addressed:

Inefficient
Many analysts start with the intention of discarding the prototype once the lessons have been learned from it. By their very nature prototypes are often pulled together from existing code libraries and end up inefficient, poorly designed and badly documented.

Poor fit
There is also the danger that a prototyped solution will not integrate into other operational systems or will incorporate techniques which are impractical and will not scale up directly.

Speed
The prototype may take longer than normal methods if the 'quick and dirty' version has to be rewritten.

Resistance
The reworking can lead to user dissatisfaction because the experience of rapid delivery in the early stages leads to unrealistic expectations. Users may be unwilling to give their time to designing an application with a high probability of being discarded. Interruptions to work are a problem since prototyping is very heavy on user time.

Testing
Where the analyst chooses to prototype the entire system, it often means a greatly extended evaluation time. The 'live' data may be very different from the test data used to show users the proposed systems

Poor design
Many analysts also argue that prototyping reduces the quality of systems analysis overall since prototyping implies continuous piecemeal development. The process may simply automate bad practice. A total bottom up redesign might be more effective in the long run. Many question the assumption that precise requirements are not always definable.

Silver linings
But some of the problems with prototyping have positive as well as negative aspects:

- Users can see the output of the final system. But is this the right criteria to judge by?

- Rapid feedback leads to user satisfaction. But does user satisfaction equate with good design?

- Users do not know what they want and prototyping lets them choose between alternatives. But how many alternatives, and which alternatives are excluded in advance and never get offered?

- Provides a learning vehicle and participative approach. But to what extent is this real participation? Do users have the right to say no? To insist on one particular alternative?

Prototyping has many advocates but it must be stressed that prototyping is no substitute for good analysis.

Information centres

What is an information centre?

The introduction of microcomputers led to the phenomenon of end user computing (Davis and Olson, 1984). Microcomputers made it possible for non computer people to design and operate their own programs. In many cases the application of user driven computing led to increases in efficiency; in other cases the results were just the opposite.

IT managers recognised the potential benefits of having end users build and maintain personal information systems but also saw that there was scope for the provision of professional services. Many companies have set up information centres to help end users. The basic justification is that providing computing power will pay off by helping people get more from their job. It is one way of overcoming the scarcity of skilled staff by freeing DP staff from dealing with minor queries. Information centres are usually offered as a service to users, who are not obliged to consult the centre if they choose not to.

Organisations have set up information centres in many different forms. They all have the basic aim of enabling people who need some computing knowledge to do their jobs but who are not computing professionals.

In some organisations the information centre is set up as an internal 'shop' which takes orders and sells selected hardware and software to its client departments. This allows the organisation to negotiate bulk discounts, arrange site licences, enforce a standardised range of equipment, and keep a record of the IT in use. The idea is to offer computer users a single place where they can get information and help whenever they want it. Many are set up as 'walk in' consultancies.

An information centre typically offers advice on purchase, on hardware compatibility, will help users who are unable to get their application working, and will arrange for the transfer of data from one format to another or between the corporate mainframe and the user's machine. More sophisticated information centres may offer a complete programming service, writing programs for users or advising on how to go about designing their program.

In many cases all the user wants to do is use packaged software: they may need some help in getting it set up, especially if files are held centrally. The information centre staff may be able to set up menu systems or automatic log-ins to the corporate database.

It is usual for the centre to give beginners introductory training on the use of computers. They generally support all the major packages for word processing, spreadsheets, presentation graphics and databases (Senn, 1990). Some have formal training schedules which new staff are required to attend. Training may be classroom based, designed and delivered by information centre personnel. Or it can designed and organised by them but delivered by external consultants. The information centre should also be able to offer guidance on the courses offered by third party training organisations and may also co-ordinate product presentations by vendor companies.

As well as being a centre of expertise, the information centre can hold copies of training manuals, computer based training programs, videos and other self learning materials.

The information centre should keep users informed of developments such as new releases of software, hardware upgrades and utilities which might be of interest to users of particular packages. The information centre staff may also be made responsible for wider issues of training and familiarity Many information centres issue newsletters to keep users in the picture. They may issue periodic reminders to users of the importance of making backups and maintaining system security.

Futher Reading

Avison, D. E. (1985) Information Systems Development: A database approach. Blackwell, Oxford

Panko, R. (1988) End user computing: Management, applications and technology. John Wiley, NY.

Wood-Harper, A.T., Antill, L. and Avison, D. (1985) Information systems Definition: The multiview approach. Blackwell Scientific, Oxford.

Chapter 12 Soft methodologies

Checkland methodology

The progression along the axis from data-oriented systems design to people-centred systems design is continued in other soft methodologies. One of the best known and most used soft methodology is the methodology developed by Peter Checkland which bears his name.

The Checkland methodology is not a methodology which will directly derive a computer system design, but that is not its intention. It is methodology designed to provide understanding of, and suggest viable solutions to, 'fuzzy' and ill defined problems.

On the one hand, some problems are capable of being defined exactly and relatively easily. A computerised application only needs to conform to its internal rules and work reliably. Examples of such applications are accounting packages and programs to produce invoices and statements. On the other hand, many computer systems fail because the original problem was misunderstood or the solution that the analysts came up with only answered part of the question.

The Checkland methodology is strongly participative, like prototyping and Ethics, with all the benefits that participative methodologies bring. However, the methodology concentrates on defining and analysing the problem from the perspective of the various stakeholders in the system. The people involved in any system that is under investigation are not just the analyst and the end users.

There are many other stakeholders. There will be different classes of end users. There will be a management structure. The system may directly impact on customers or suppliers. And its success may depend on effective interaction with related departments and their own information systems. Each stakeholder will have a different perception of the system and different needs. The perception and needs of each stakeholder needs to be taken into account in arriving at any solution.

Although the interest here is in how it can help in the definition and design of information systems, the methodology is aimed at more general problem solving and can be applied to any type of problem. Some of likely candidates would be:

- How should we decide what products to concentrate research on?

- Staff turnover is high. What should we do?

- Some of our operators want to work from home. It is feasible?

- Should we move towards outsourcing our computing services?

The common feature of these kinds of problem is that there is no simple immediate answer. Many people are involved in any possible solution and success will probably depend on getting their commitment to change.

The strength of the Checkland methodology is that it considers the problem definition itself to be a problem and insists on recording the views of all the stakeholders. It challenges the assumption that the problem is as defined by management. It recognises from the start that there will be competing views. For example a company might be plagued by low productivity. The management view might be that workers are lazy and the solution is an improved monitoring system to keep them at their machines. The employees view of the same problem might be that it is lack of past investment that is holding down productivity and the workers are in fact doing a heroic job in producing what they do with the tools they have.

The starting point

The starting point of the methodology is to try to build a systems view of the organisation or the subsystem of interest. The analyst tries to determine what the system is about, what it is trying to achieve, what purpose the particular subsystem serves. This is not as straight forward as it seems. Consider the purpose of a police force? Is it to detect crime or prevent crime. Both are relevant but require different systems.

Rich pictures: identifying relevant systems

So the first task is to identify relevant systems. Relevant systems arise out of an analysis of a rich picture. Figure 12.1 shows a rich picture drawn for the Fashion Footwear example used to illustrate fact finding methods earlier.

Rich picture for the Fashion Footwear situation

A rich picture is a pictorial representation of what the organisation is supposed to be doing, what the current situation appears to be, how the actors see things. The Figure shows a rich picture for Fashion Footwear.

The objective of using a rich picture is to suggest some potentially fruitful ways of viewing the situation. By identifying the issues the rich picture helps problem solvers come up with conceptual views of the problem, which may give an insight to possible solutions.

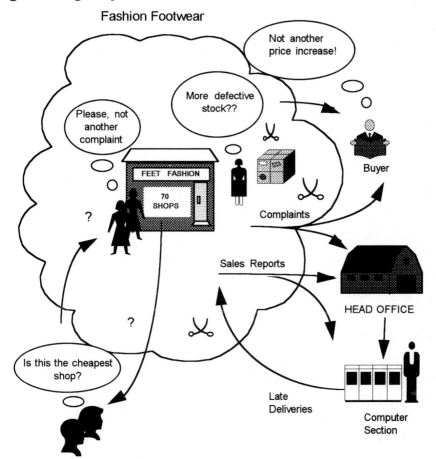

Figure 12.1 Rich picture

Drawing rich pictures

There are no right or wrong ways to draw rich pictures, only ways which are more or less clear. The whole point is clarity of communication. It should be self explanatory and easy to understand

1. Draw a large cloud representing the boundary of the system.

2. Add in the people who are of concern within the system

3. Add in the people who operate or control the system.

4. Add the people and things which affect the system from outside.

5.   Show relationships by arrows. Label the arrows if it helps.

6.   Identify actual or potential conflict

7.   Put in 'think' bubbles of the main people's worries, concerns, issues.

8.   If necessary expand parts on to separate sheets.

9.   Make important things big.

10.   Use any symbols you like as long as they are clear and vivid. (use eyes, ears., reports, lorries, crossed swords, houses etc.)

11.   Show hard and soft facts.

Rich pictures are drawn up in order to bring out hidden assumptions, conflicts, worries and other 'soft' information. The analyst will sit down with one of the actors and will sketch out the rich picture as the person describes the problem situation. They will then together revise and refine the rich picture until the actor is happy that it represents their particular view of the process and its problems. The analyst can then repeat the process with another person, either drawing a fresh rich picture and comparing the two afterwards or can show the first rich picture and ask for comments. Either way the analyst and the participants should get a much deeper appreciation of what is going wrong and how different people see things. Where things begin to look overcomplicated and take up room on the page the analyst can divide the problem into subsystems and treat each as a separate situation.

Rich pictures on their own are a powerful tool for capturing and assessing soft issues. The Multiview methodology (Wood-Harper et al., 1985) takes advantage of this and uses rich pictures as a main component of the analysis along with many of the concepts of socio-technical systems design. They suggest the following rules for analysing rich pictures and have codified the benefits of their use.

Analysing rich pictures

Things to look for include

• Primary Tasks- does the picture show the main tasks being done?

• Structure - are all relevant organisational structures shown?

• Process - does the picture show all the processes involved in the problem?

• Climate - Is there a good fit between the task and structures meant to control the performance of the task?

- Issues - have the issues, worries, complaints been noted?

Wood-Harper points out that the issues can be more important the tasks and if left unheeded can wreck the implementation altogether.

Benefits of rich pictures

There are many benefits of rich pictures including:

- Restricted space forces decisions on what is really important
- Allows people to visualise and discuss their role.
- A basis for partitioning sub systems
- Allows expression of worries and highlights areas of conflict
- Can help clarify the owners of problems
- Establishes problem boundaries.

Even if the use of rich pictures went no further than this, they would be a valuable tool. Checkland, however, has provided a more structured approach to the use of rich pictures. In the full methodology, deriving the rich picture is only one step an iterative process. The Checkland methodology consists of several stages (Checkland and Scholes, 1991):

1. Identify the problem
2. Create a rich picture
3. Identify the tasks and issues
4. Create a logical model
5. Compare model and reality
6. Consider the options
7. Act to improve the situation

The Checkland methodology's seven stages

The first stage is where the problem situation is partially defined awaiting analysis.

The next stage is the creation of a rich picture and the isolation of the primary tasks and issues, as has been discussed.

In the third stage each task and its issues are identified and named as a relevant system.

The third stage: identify relevant systems

A relevant system is one which helps the analyst and users think about the issues in the problem situation. It is one which either performs one of the tasks identified or would prevent the issues arising. The relevant system may or may not be a formal part of the overall system. Some of the actors may not recognise or accept what are clearly relevant systems to other actors.

Construct a root definition

For each relevant system a root definition is constructed. The root definition is a rigorous description of what the system has to do, who is going to do it, and who is responsible for its being done. It also defines who it is being done for, what rules the system operates under and the wider environment under which all this is happening.

For example consider the Fashion Footwear situation. Analysing the rich picture (Figure 12.1) suggests possible relevant systems based on the issues identified. The issues appear to be 'problems with defective goods', 'late deliveries of best selling lines', 'slow replies to complaints', and 'no responses to defective footwear notices'. The primary tasks appear to be selling shoes, reordering shoes, reporting sales and returning defective shoes. Many of these appear to be connected and suggest systems which are producing unacceptable variances. Suppose we decide that one task is the reordering of shoes. An idealised shoe ordering process might be defined as follows:

> A shop manager owned system, operated by the shop staff, designed to replace shoes sold with similar shoes, in good time and with the minimum of administration, under the assumptions that what sold before will sell again.

The root definition is a matter of trial and error but can be checked against the questions of who, why, for whom, etc. asked above. A more formal checking process is summed up in the word CATWOE. This acronym stands for

- Customer - who is the system operating for? In the case of the shop it is presumably for the shareholders. In the case of the re-ordering system it is assumed to be for the benefit of the manager or the shop staff.

- Actors - who is involved in carrying out this process? In this case it is the shop staff.

- **T**ransformation - What is the process supposed to do? What are its inputs and outputs?

- **W**eltanshauung - This word roughly translates to 'world view' or all the things we take for granted (Wood-Harper, 1985). It is the set of assumptions or attitudes which the process is operating under. One part of the weltanshauung of a shop would be that is profit driven and must comply with local laws and regulations.

- **O**wners - who is the problem owner? Who is responsible if system doesn't function properly?

- **E**nvironment - what conditions is the system experiencing which may have a bearing on its viability?

The advantage of the CATWOE check is that it enables the root definition to be interrogated and very often suggest missing or incomplete relevant systems. For example the root definition for the reordering process suggests that part of the weltanshauung is that what sold before will sell again. This is not necessarily true. Fur boots may sell steadily all winter but will not necessarily keep selling through the summer. So this suggests that either the relevant systems, the reordering procedure, is incomplete, or there is a sales forecasting system missing. If the sales forecasting system is accepted as a relevant system then applying CATWOE will force a consideration of who owns the system. Is sales prediction the responsibility of the shop manager or the buyer or somebody else in Head Office?

The root definition is finished off by testing to see if the definition is internally consistent, is clear and unambiguous and if it is understood and accepted by others.

The fourth stage: build a conceptual model
Completion of the root definitions leads to the next stage, the creation of logical models for each relevant system. The conceptual model specifies all the steps and activities needed to carry out the task specified in the root definition. The root definition is deliberately kept at a general level so the conceptual model can be an 'idealised' solution, a logical view of the processing required to carry out the system. The process of designing the logical model will bring out weaknesses and omissions in the root definition and leads to a circular process until the root definition and the idealised operationalisation of that definition are defined.

The utility of the conceptual model itself can be checked out by applying what Checkland and Scholes call the three 'E's

243

- Efficacy - does the means chosen actually work in producing the output?

- Efficiency - Is the transformation being carried out with the minimum of resources?

- Effectiveness - Is the transformation actually achieving the longer term aim?

The fifth stage: comparison with actuality
The next stage compares the ideal solution with what is actually in place. The actual systems may be very close to the ideal systems or they may be totally missing. The comparison is always instruction and often reveals real world constraints which were not allowed for in the conceptual models and which necessitate a return to the previous stage.

The sixth stage: debate the options
The outcome of the comparison will generate the next stage. Any variance between what exists and what is needed will throw up opportunities for action. There will normally be many possible actions and many possible ways of doing those actions. This process should generate a debate among the actors until agreement is reached on how best to proceed with change.

The seventh stage: take action.
The final stage implements the action and after a period observes the effect on the problem situation.

The description given here might suggest a rather longwinded process but in practice the drawing of rich pictures and the creation of relevant systems can be done quite quickly. Certainly there are few better ways of getting right to the heart of the matter and ensuring that you are tackling the right problem. And choosing the right problem is at least half way to getting the right solution.

Ethics

The participative approach used in prototyping has been made the central theme of some design methodologies. One of the most influential is the Ethics methodology. (Mumford, 1985)

Ethics stands for: **E**ffective **T**echnical and **H**uman **I**mplementation of **C**omputer based work **S**ystems. The methodology has three objectives:

- Enable users to design the systems which affect them.

- Let design groups set specific job satisfaction objectives.

- Surround any new technical system with a compatible, well functioning organisational environment.

Ethics starts with the concept that a successful system will only arise where the social and organisational needs of the work group are given equal weight with the technical aspects. This concern for balance is known as the socio-technical approach.

'A socio-technical approach is one which recognises the interaction of technology and people and produces work systems which are both technically efficient and have social characteristics which lead to high job satisfaction.' Enid Mumford.

Mumford list the following as commonly accepted socio-technical principles

- The work system is the basic unit, not the operations making it up.

- The work group is the primary social unit, not the individual job holder.

- Internal regulation is by the work group itself.

- Because the basic unit is the work group individual jobs can be multi-skilled.

- Emphasis is placed on the discretionary elements of jobs, not the prescribed part.

- Work organisation aims to increase variety of work, not decrease it.

- People are complimentary to machines, not subservient to them.

These principles are at odds with what is observed in most hard systems designs. The socio-technical approach means accepting a radically different approach to the design of information systems. It must be recognised that individuals and groups have their own needs and agendas and these must be taken into account if employees are to accept change enthusiastically. Imposed change will cause resistance and will work against the successful implementation of the design.

Mumford sees the process of design as a four step process:

First, *objectives* for the system are set by the people most affected by the new system.

Then a process of *adaptation* must be fostered. Change involves people and requires a degree of negotiation. The outcome will typically be a compromise with everyone can live with, rather than a purely rational technical 'best' solution.

245

The third stage is *integration*. This is action taken during design and implementation to ensure the new situation reaches equilibrium.

The final stage is *stabilisation*. This requires processes for socialising and educating new group members, methods for controlling tensions when the fit between variables slips and a mechanism for resolving conflict over divergence.

Integration

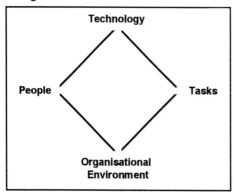

Figure 12.2 The constituents of the Ethics methodology

Leavitt's (1965) diamond model (Figure 12.2) can be used to illustrate the basis of the Ethics methodology. Leavitt asserts that all organisations have to achieve a balance between four elements. These are:

> the actors
> the tasks
> the technology
> the structure

If any one of these elements is disturbed, the others must be adjusted to compensate until the whole system is back in equilibrium.

The traditional way of designing information systems concentrates primarily on the task and technology elements of the situation. In large measure the people side is ignored and the issues of supervision, control and ownership are left for the people involved to work out after implementation. The socio-technical approach give full weight to the needs and perceptions of individuals and uses this to influence the design of the task using existing or proposed technology but in its traditional form does not encourage alternative choices of technology directly.

The Ethics methodology is designed to encompass all four elements (actors, tasks, technology, structure) at once. This should produce a balanced design which delivers the best technical configuration possible in the circumstances. At the same time it will ensure the best social and organisational structure compatible with the task requirements and put into place mechanisms which will maintain equilibrium.

The steps of Ethics

1. Diagnose business and social needs and problems.

2. Set efficiency and social objectives

3. Develop a number of design strategies

4. Choose the strategy which *best* fits both sets of objectives

5. Design this in detail

6. Implement the new system

7. Evaluate it once it is operational.

Diagnose business and social needs and problems

One of the key elements of the hard systems approach is that it takes the problem as granted. It is whatever the problem owner says it is. The 'softer' approaches start from the premise that problems have to be defined and are subject to different perceptions. You cannot produce an effective design unless you are tackling the right problem.

Set business efficiency objective

One of the key elements of the hard systems approach is that it takes the problem as granted. It is whatever the problem owner says it is. The 'softer' approaches start from the premise that problems have to be defined and are subject to different perceptions. You cannot produce an effective design unless you are tackling the right problem.

Ethics uses the concepts of variances to investigate the business problem. A system is set up to perform some task to a predetermined level. Any deviance from that pre-established level of performance is called a variance. When a system's variances deviate too far from the norms you have a problem situation. Variances are of two types.

Key variances are systemic: they occur as a direct consequence of the goals and functions of the system. They are part of the nature of the system, inevitable. A systemic variance might arise where sales are made on credit.

247

By the very nature of the selling process there will be some bad debts. These are a problem, but a problem which can only be eliminated entirely by changing the process to one where no credit is offered.

Operational variances stem from organisational inadequacies, and the poor procedures which have been installed. These are always avoidable. Operational variances occur where an employee takes a wrong action because of misunderstanding the system or where one person is overwhelmed with work and the backlogs affect many others.

Business efficiency objectives are therefore aimed at designing out key variances and preventing the occurrence of operational variances.

Set social efficiency objectives
At the same time that the business task efficiency is being defined, the methodology attempts to establish a standard for the job satisfaction level of the people involved. Job satisfaction is derived from a number of different factors. By deliberately building in these factors jobs, can be designed to integrate into the business efficiency needs.

Workers need their own personal skills and knowledge to be used and to feel they are being developed. They want to get a sense of achievement from their work. They need to feel that they are being rewarded fairly and that they are properly supervised. The job itself needs to be varied and interesting and the task has to be one which fits with the workers' personal values and beliefs. Some of these objectives are the opposite of simple technical efficiency objectives. A possible design might call for a operator to learn a simple repetitive task such as typing in data read from a customer order. But if that is all the operator does all day boredom or resentment will soon set in and the operator is likely to work at less than optimum efficiency. By considering job satisfaction needs at the outset this type of problem can be entirely eliminated.

Develop a number of design strategies
Once the social and business objectives have been determined, a number of alternative implementations are developed. There will be many ways of achieving the business efficiency requirements of the system.

There will be many possible ways of organising the flow of work and many different ways of structuring the supervision and control of the work group. For example the computer system could be a centralised mainframe with a single database accessed remotely through terminals, or a distributed database could be physically held in divisional offices or the work could be devolved down to individual PCs holding self contained data or any combination of these.

248

There will also be various degrees of automation possible and trade-offs between doing things manually and fully computerising them. Similarly information could be accessed by regular reports or through limited menu choices or by users constructing their own queries.

The social and job organisation has many alternative formulations too. There could be a centrally controlled administration which monitors how and when individual tasks are performed. Alternatively, responsibility can be devolved to local level where work groups decide for themselves how best to organise the work and where different groups might organisation themselves in if totally different structures. Some organisations are more comfortable with control from Head Office, others prefer a more independent way of operating.

These design strategies are typically devised by the work groups themselves, aided by an analyst trained as a facilitator. The work group supplies the detailed knowledge of the operation and the analyst supplies technical knowledge and puts forward possible configurations for the groups to consider. The strength of the process is the high degree of participation and the sense of ownership of the new system.

Choose the strategy which best fits both sets of objectives
The outcome of the discussions is a list of practical alternatives for organising the task and a list of acceptable ways of organising the work group. The next step is to match all the possible technical alternatives with all the organisational alternatives. Some combinations will be impractical, some will be attractive. The alternative combinations are discussed and the best combination is chosen to be implemented.

Design the new system in detail
Once the outline of the design has been agreed the normal process of systems analysis and design continues except that at every point the work group is consulted and participates in the development process.

Further Reading

Checkland, P. (1981) Systems Thinking, Systems Practice. Wiley, New York.

Checkland, P. and Scholes, J. (1990) Soft systems methodology in action. Wiley, New York.

Mumford, E. (1983) Designing Human Systems. Pub Manchester Business School.

Patching, D. (1990) Practical Soft Systems Analysis Pub Pitman, London.

Wood-Harper, A.T., Antill, L. and Avison, D. (1985) Information systems Definition: The multiview approach. Blackwell Scientific, Oxford.

Chapter 13 Data centred design

One way of designing information systems is to chart the movement of data as it travels from process to process and to produce a program specification for each process. An alternative way is to think of the organisation as consisting of a collection of data stores. In this view all processing is regarded as a series of events which change the contents of the data stores. By defining the data stores correctly, any possible event can be handled. Instead of asking 'what programs are in use now?' and setting up the files to support them, the analyst designs a database of files capable of supporting every possible program. There are two basic approaches to defining the data stores. One method is called data analysis, the other is normalisation. Each approach delivers essentially the same result.

Normalisation

The objective of normalisation is to produce database files of the simplest structure. When designing a database there are many possible ways of organising the data elements into files. Some of these are more efficient than others. Ensuring an optimum design needs an objective test of the way the data is organised. Applying the techniques of normalisation provides this test. It ensures that data storage is efficient and helps eliminate potential problems.

Table 13.1

Emp. no.	Name	Pay rate	Dept	Dept name	Location	Sales
E2	Smith	23 000	12	Repairs	City	30.6
E3	Chung	22 000	25	sales	Belair	8.0
E4	Jones	23 000	12	Repairs	City	17.9
E6	Green	28 000	25	Sales	Belair	2.3
E8	Mason	60 000	30	Spares	Levin	67.8
E5	Patel	29 000	25	Sales	Belair	30.2
E9	Varna	30 000	12	Repairs	City	14.8
E10	Klein	16 000	12	Repairs	City	25.6

Simply listing all the data elements used in a process will not necessarily give a suitable file layout. Let us suppose that a file was set up to hold employee details and their departments (Table 13.1). Although this structure holds all the data needed there are a number of problems due to its internal organisation.

Data redundancy
A lot of data is unnecessarily duplicated. For example, in Table 13.1 the values 'Repairs' and 'City' repeat every time a '12' appears in the department field.

Inconsistency
Due to data duplication there is nothing to prevent one record showing department 12 as 'Repairs' while another shows it as 'Sales'.

Integrity
If employee E8 leaves and that record is deleted during normal file updating then all trace of the Spares department disappears.

Poor structure
Suppose the company decides to open another sales office in Greenvale. Entering the new department would mean that you would have to create a 'dummy' employee first.

Examining this table reveals that it is not just a simple collection of data elements: it in fact contains several hidden dependencies. There appear to be two separate logical data sets, one set associated with the Employee field, the other centred round the Dept No field. These data sets are mapped out in Figure 13.1.

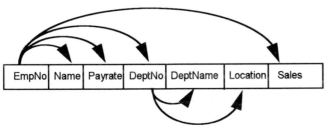

Figure 13.1

All these update, insertion and deletion difficulties can be eliminated. Normalisation separates out the dependencies and reduces the data set to simpler tables.

For example normalising the Employee file produces two smaller tables (Tables 13.2 and 13.3) representing the logical groupings 'Employees' and 'Departments'.

Table 13.2 Employees

Emp. no.	Name	Pay rate	Dept	Sales
E2	Smith	23 000	12	30.6
E3	Chung	22 000	25	8.0
E4	Jones	23 000	12	17.9
E6	Green	28 000	25	2.3
E8	Mason	60 000	30	67.8
E5	Patel	29 000	25	30.2
E9	Varna	30 000	12	14.8
E10	Klein	16 000	12	25.6

Table 11.3 Departments

Dept	Dept name	Location
12	Repairs	City
25	Sales	Belair
30	Spares	Levin

Even in this small file, normalisation saves storage space and eliminates the previous problems; yet none of the data has been lost. It is still possible to tell the department name and location of every employee. Or, given a department, identify all employees. However, it does need additional processing to provide the answers. There is always a trade off between storage efficiency and processing overhead.

Normalisation is done in steps. The first step is to examine the proposed data structure and remove any repeating groups. A repeating group occurs where a data structure can contain one or more instances of a different, related data structure. A structure with no repeating groups is said to be in first normal form.

The next step starts with a structure in first normal form and inspects it to see if there are any partial dependencies present. A partial dependency occurs where a data element is associated with part of a record's key, but not with the whole of the key.

The third step starts with a structure in second normal form and tests for transitive dependencies. A transitive dependency occurs where a data element is associated with some other data element which is not part of the record's key.

At every step the process can be reversed and the original data structure can be recreated from any of the normal forms. The process never creates or destroys any data. The end product is a logical representation of the original data structure which can be used as a file definition and which will efficient and free from insert, update, and delete problems.

The normalisation process is based on the concept of functional dependency. **Functional dependency** means that the value of one data element determines the value of some other data element. For example each employee in the file has one employee number and one last name and one pay rate at any particular time. Given that the key field, the employee number data element, is always associated with just one employee, if I know the employee number then I know the last name with certainty. I also know the pay rate. Last name and pay rate are said to be functionally dependent on the employee number.

On the other hand, if I am given a figure which represents some employee's pay rate, I cannot with certainty identify one and only one employee. There may be several employees with the same pay rate. The pay rate does not functionally determine the employee number or last name. Even if by chance all the pay rates were unique this still does not imply a functional dependency because the relationship is one way only. The employee number does identify a given pay rate, by design. The pay rate is not designed to identify a particular employee even if in some circumstances it may do so. There is always the possibility that there will be duplicate pay rate values in the future.

A **data structure** is the name given to any logical set of related fields. Your name and address is a data structure consisting of First Name, Last Name, Street Name, House Number and so on. To demonstrate how normalisation works we will extract a data structure from a typical business form.

Figure 13.2 shows a job card from a garage used to record details of service jobs on cars. As a job progresses the mechanic fills out the card with the materials used. The first thing to do is to extract all the relevant data elements from the card. The first thing to look for is an identifier, something which identifies this job from every other similar job. In this case the obvious candidate is the job number. It is assumed to be unique for each job. This will be used as the key. The other data elements are then copied down in order. A listing of the data elements is shown at the foot of the figure.

Some of the entries can be collectively grouped as 'header' data. These entries relate directly to job number and can only ever take one value. The operator name, job description, make of vehicle and insurance value are of this type. Other entries can repeat many times.

There are four lines shown for materials used on this particular job. Each materials line consists of a part number, a description and a quantity used. These are examples of repeating groups.

The job card type of data structure consisting of header data and repeating groups is very common in business application. Purchase orders for example, have header information and then a variable number of lines showing details of the products ordered.

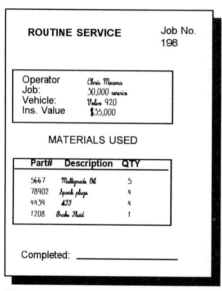

Figure 13.2

Data structures containing repeating groups are often referred to as 'non-flat files' Conversely a data structure without repeating groups is called a 'flat file'.

Non flat files are difficult to work with because of the unknown number of repeating groups they may contain. The first task in normalisation to reduce all data structures to flat files. An example of the job card represented as a flat file is shown in Table 13.3:

Table 13.3

Job no.	Operator	Job	Vehicle	Value	Part no.	Descr.	Qty
98	Moana	serv	Volvo	35 000	5667	Multigrade oil	5
98	Moana	serv	Volvo	35 000	78902	Spark plugs	4
98	Moana	serv	Volvo	35 000	4439	ATF	4
98	Moana	serv	Volvo	35 000	1208	Brake fluid	1

The flat file is obviously very wasteful of space since it has to hold the header information once for each instance of the repeating group. It is also likely to be subject to all or some of the problems found in the Employee file example. The process of normalisation avoids these difficulties.

Normalisation in action

Identifying the dependencies.

Normalisation starts by identifying the dependencies in the original data structure. There are two separate but linked data structures on the job card shown in Figure 13.3. One is keyed on the Job No. and the other has the Part Number as key. There is also a relationship between the insurance value and the vehicle type.

JOB CARD

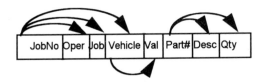

Figure 13.3

Once the dependencies have been identified the first step in the process is to 'break off' the repeating groups and put them into their own data structure. The result is two separate structures.

The key field of the job card is still the job number. The new key of the repeating group is a combination of the job number and the part number. The use of two data elements (or fields) to uniquely identify an item is known as **concatenation** and the combined key is called a concatenated key. Once the repeating groups have been separated out each of the resulting tables is in first normal form, by definition (Figure 13.4).

The second step involves identifying and removing any partial dependencies. There is a partial dependency in the Parts Used structure in Figure 13.5.

255

JOB CARD

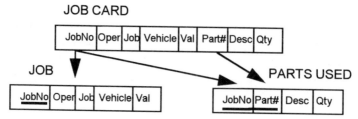

JOB   PARTS USED

Figure 13.4

There is always the possibility of a partial dependency when a concatenated key is present. In the Parts Used structure the quantity used is determined completely by the job number and the part number together. Knowing only the job number is not enough to determine the quantity. Knowing the part number on its own is also not enough to know how much was used - parts are used in different quantities on many different jobs. But the combination does uniquely identify a particular quantity of a particular part on a given job.

PARTS USED

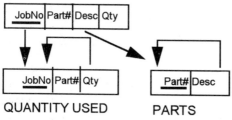

QUANTITY USED   PARTS

Figure 13.5

The same is not true of the description in the Parts Used structure. Each part has a description. The description is independent of the job number. If I know the part number, I can determine the description. The job number is irrelevant, the part's description does not change according to what job it is used on. In normalisation terms we say the quantity is *fully dependent* on the key, the description is only *partially dependent*. Notice that a partial dependency is only possible when a concatenated key is present. The job structure has only a single valued key and so cannot have partial dependencies.

Removing the partial dependency is simple. Remove the partially dependent data element from the structure and create a new structure containing the data element itself and the part of the concatenated key which controls the dependency. So Parts Used is split into two smaller structures called Quantity Used and Part.

We have now created three data structures from the original: Job, Part and Quantity used. The third step in normalisation involves inspecting all the sub structures for transitive dependencies. A transitive dependency arises where a data element is dependent on some other data element which is not itself part of the key. This situation is found in the Job data structure. The value of the vehicle for insurance purposes is dependent on the make and model of the vehicle and has nothing to do with the job number (Figure 13.6).

JOB

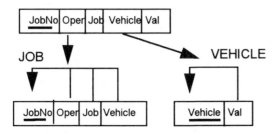

Figure 13.6

The Job structure is in first normal form (1NF) because it has no repeating groups in it. It is also in second normal form (2NF) because it contains no partial dependencies. It is not in third normal form (3NF) since it does in fact contain a transitive dependency.

The final step of normalisation, then, is to remove any transitive dependencies. This is done by breaking out the data element and the value which determines it from the 2NF structure and using these to create another data structure.

The end result of the three steps of normalisation has been the creation of four smaller and simpler data structures: Job, Vehicle, Quantity used and Part. A final inspection will reveal that every subsidiary structure is now in third normal form. That is to say there are no repeating groups, no partial dependencies and no transitive dependencies.

The process of normalisation results in data structures which can be used to determine the optimum layout of data files, either for single programs or as the foundation for a database (Codd, 1970). The normalised files derived by the three step process will normally be sufficient for the purposes of analysis. In rare circumstances the analyst may have to apply additional tests to reduce the dependencies further into fourth normal form, and there exists a fifth normal form but this is largely of theoretical interest.

The normalised data structure contain all the data elements found in the original and the original could be reconstructed from the 3NF forms. The advantages of reducing structures to 3NF is that it is a guarantee that the data storage requirements are the minimum needed. In the original the insurance value was stored on every card. In the normalised files the value is stored only once in the Vehicle file and any changes in value require only a single update.

There is also a guarantee that any question which is possible to ask of the original data can be answered from the normalised structures. For example to find out the value of all vehicles worked on by a particular mechanic simply scan the Job file to find the records for that mechanic. Note the types of vehicles and the number serviced and use the information in the Vehicle file to supply the values for calculation. At the same time there is also a processing overhead to fetch the data and combine it from different files, but in most instances this trade off is worthwhile.

Data modelling

The outcome of normalising this simple record structure is a data model. A data model is a logical view of the organisation and the objects of interest to the organisation. Normalisation derives the objects directly. The four objects produced by the normalisation can be translated directly into a conventional data model (Figure 13.7).

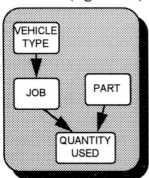

Figure 13.7 Conventional data model

Data models consist of **entities** and **relationships**. An entity can be thought of as something which exists independently and has a number of features, called attributes, which can singly or in combination uniquely identify one particular instance of that entity. An employee could be an entity, for example. An employee has a name, or an employee number to tell one employee from another. An employee can exist independently of jobs or departments even though they may associated with them. Similarly a Part is an entity, something which exists independently of any processes it might be involved in.

In the view of the data shown in Figure 13.7 there are three entities, things of interest, and two relationships, a link between two or more of the entities. There is a job entity, a parts entity and a vehicle entity. Quantity used is not an entity as it cannot exist independently of Part or Job.

Entities interact through relationships. There are two relationships implied in the Job card example. One is the link between parts and the job number those parts were used on. The other is the relationship between job and vehicle type. In the figure these relationships are shown by arrows. The direction of the arrow head is significant. When an arrow head is shown going into a relationship it means the key field of the entity will be stored in the relationship. The Quantity Used file is actually a relationship between the entities Job and Part and therefore has the key fields of Job and Part stored within it. The relationship between Job and Parts is shown as a separate object because of the nature of the relationship. A part can be used on any number of jobs and a job can use any number of parts. It is this many to many relationship which is being captured in the Quantity Used data structure shown in Table 13.4. This gives a two way link so that you can tell which parts were used on a particular job and also which jobs any particular parts were used on.

Table 13.4

Job no	Part no	Qty
198	5667	5
198	78902	4
198	4439	4
198	1208	1
199	5667	3
199	78902	4
200	5667	5
200	3398	3

The Job to Vehicle Type relationship does not have a separate table because it is a one to many relationship. There are many different vehicle types but only one vehicle type can ever appear on a given job card. Under those circumstances there is no need for a separate relationship table. If the key field of the Vehicle Type file is stored in the Job file then any details of that vehicle type can be found by reading the appropriate record in the Vehicle Type file.

Data modelling consists of defining entities and examining the relationships between them. Normalisation gives the entities and relationships directly but will only show those entities and relationships for which the organisation already has data structures. Data modelling starts with the entities and determines which relationships need to exist.

For example it is obvious that a mechanic carries out the servicing of particular cars. There should be an employee entity to hold all the details of the employees. If this were added to the model there will be a link between the employee entity and the job entity. For any given job there will be only one mechanic working on it so the link will be a one to many and the key field of the employee record would be inserted into the Job file. The mechanic's name would then be redundant in the Job file and would be removed.

It would still be possible to find the mechanic's name by looking it up in the employees file, using the employee key to find the right record. Data modelling is unaffected by missing data. In the case of wanting to add an employee entity, it is only necessary to decide what the key field will be. It is not necessary to know what every field will be, as is the case with normalisation. If it is decided later to hold information about an employee's length of service this does not affect the data model at all. The additional data is just added to the list of attributes for that entity.

Data models are good for showing possible access paths through data. By following the arrows it is clear that it could be established which employees had been using any given part. Given a parts description a part number could be identified. This would be matched with the part number entries in the Quantity Used file to identify jobs which involved those part numbers. In turn the job numbers would identify the mechanics who had carried out those jobs.

In practice the analyst goes about designing the data model by establishing entities and assigning likely attributes to them. These assumptions are checked with people who are familiar with the processes. The analyst them asks the users to describe the sort of information they might want from the files. The analyst then tests to see if there is in fact an access path through the data model which would satisfy the query requirements.

Suppose the manager in this case felt that a requirement was to know what mechanic had serviced one particular car. The data model as it stands in Figure 13.7 could not supply this information. The entity vehicle type does not identify particular vehicles or their owners. The data model would need to have an additional entity for Owner and for Vehicle. The analyst would have to consider the relationship between owner and vehicle. Normally each vehicle has one owner, but a person or organisation may own more than one vehicle.

There is then the problem of how to link the job or mechanic to one particular vehicle. Each job only services one vehicle so the vehicle registration number could be stored in the Job file. Each vehicle has only one owner so the owner's name can be linked to Vehicle file. Each vehicle is one type only so the

Vehicle Type key could go into the Vehicle file. At this point the analyst might reconsider the use of the Vehicle Type entity and consider incorporating it as an attribute of the Vehicle entity or might add more attributes to it to hold data about what parts are used for particular Vehicle Types. The data model gets redrawn over and over as more requirements are added.

The resultant data model might look like Figure 13.8. As the model is developed, the analyst keeps testing the model to ensure that the access paths are available for all requirements and gradually evolves a robust model capable of handling all the processing.

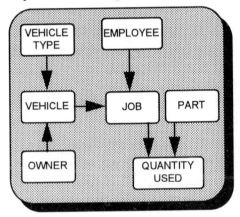

Figure 13.8

Once the logical requirements are satisfied, the analyst then has to consider how to turn the logical model into a physical implementation. This will normally follow the data model very closely with one file for each of the entities and relationships shown on the chart.

Each file would have as fields each of the attributes identified for each entity. In theory this should produce the optimum physical file design but in practice file may to be combined or split and compromises have to made between storage and processing. This process of 'tuning' occurs whether the data model was derived by normalisation or not.

The problems of drawing and amending data models are similar to those found when redrawing data flow diagrams. The solution is identical too. CASE tools are available which take all the drudgery out of modelling. They do the logic checking and maintain a data dictionary and make it possible to alter the models interactively.

Types of database

There are three basic types of commercial database: Hierarchical, Network and Relational. The hierarchical and network are older models which are being replaced by relational databases. Any data structure can be represented in any of the three ways but each type accommodates some structures better than others. Once the data structure is set up one way it is not easy to change it to another. The relational model is the most flexible for general use and has many advantages over the older types. However, in some circumstances relational databases tend to be less efficient and run more slowly than the older models.

Strictly speaking a data base should cater equally well for all types of files but current database technology only really caters for well structured data files. Other types of records such as text files, management reports, images and other badly structured files form a 'document base' and are not easily incorporated into today's database technologies. Object oriented databases are being developed and may prove a solution.

All database packages have to handle the four elements of physical storage, logical database design, application program design and end user accesses. Different software packages emphasise different aspects and some are better at some aspects than others. The relative importance of each aspect will depend on the size of the proposed database and the uses made of it. Most database management systems (DBMS) offer a wide variety of tools for the designer. One well known product, Oracle for example has a basic SQL query language, a screen painter, a forms designer which produces end user input and query screens automatically from the underlying tables, a menuing system and an easy to use report writer. Each DBMS has its own intended niche. A single user query oriented application will put more emphasis on ease of end user access than a high volume batch oriented application database. Small, microcomputer based applications tend to offer simplicity and graphical interfaces at the expense of efficiency. Large mainframe packages are concerned mainly with throughput and place their emphasis accordingly.

Relational databases

If the analyst chooses to use data modelling techniques then it is only a small step to designing a database. A database is basically just a collection of computer files, but computer files which are organised in a particular way.

Relational databases store the data physically according the conventions of the hardware being used. Logically however, a relational database is thought

262

of as storing all its data in tables. In a traditional data handling environmental the data structures closely follow the shape of the records being processed. In a relational approach all data structures, no matter how complex, are reduced to one form, the table. A table is a stylised conceptual view of a physical file, and data organised into a table according to certain rules is called a relation. At its simplest then, a relational database is a collection of data logically grouped into standardised tables.

The data structures produced by normalisation and data modelling can be used directly as relational database tables. A table represents either an entity and its attributes, or a relationship between entities. Note the difference between a relation and a relationship. A relation is a data structure which follows certain rules. A relationship is a logical association between two or more entities.

To model the job card data a table is set up for each entity and each relationship and then their columns are named for each attribute. Finally the tables are populated with the data items (Figure 13.9.)

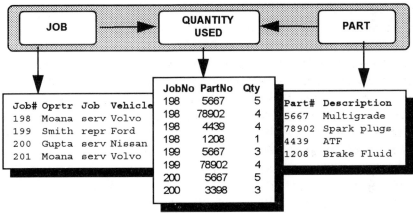

Figure 13.9

Logically, a relation is a two dimensional table made up of rows and columns in which :

- Each row (each record) is unique, there can be no duplicate rows

- Each entry in table represents a single data item, there are no repeating groups

- Every row has exactly the same structure. (Each record has the same fields of the same size in the same order).

- Each data item has a single value

263

- Each column is assigned a unique name

- All the values in a column are values of the same attribute, that is they all come from one predefined set of possible values.

- The order of the columns is immaterial

- The order of the rows is immaterial

- Both rows and columns can be viewed in any sequence at any time without affecting their information content.

At first sight it would seem that the table format is wasteful and clumsy to use. To find which parts were used on a given job involves reading the Quantity Used table to find the part number and then fetching the part description from the product table. However, in most cases the advantages outweigh the extra processing.

The table approach saves storage space. In the traditional file every time a part is listed its description is stored as well. In a large table there will be thousands of duplicated description fields, in the relational model the description is stored only once.

The table approach also allows the database to be expanded easily. Each table in the database is cross referenced to one or more other tables making it possible to 'navigate' a database going from table to table via the linking fields. The ability to link tables by the use of key fields is at the heart of the relational approach. The only links needed to support relationships are found inside the records of the tables which take part in that relationship. If the company wanted to know who supplied the parts, adding a supplier table would be easy. There would be one entity called SUPPLIER, and therefore one more table, and one relation showing the link PartNo,SupplierNo. Adding the same facility to a traditional file would mean storing the supplier details with each part and more duplication.

A relational database is perceived by its users as a collection of tables, and nothing but tables. The data in fact is not stored physically in a table format but visualising the files as if they were tables gives a better understanding of how a relational database operates. The end user does not have to know anything about indexes, pointers or any of the other physical storage details.

Database software

In a database environment there are three different kinds of database software in use.

The Data Base Management System

A data base management system is a collection of programs which manage the files which make up the data base. DBMS software allows users to store and retrieve data, and to modify it when needed, in an organised, efficient way.

DBMSs are commercial packages used by many organisations and will have been purchased complete. Some well known DBMSs include DB2, Adabas, MANTIS and Oracle. Any company will normally use only one DBMS.

The data files and tables

This is the collection of data elements organised into tables. Each particular company will create its own unique data set expressed as a logical data model. This model is described to the DBMS which then allocates the physical storage to hold the data. Typical database entries will be customers, products, sales orders and all the other things that the company wants to keep control over. There may be more than one distinct data base within a large organisation.

Database query software

These are programs written to extract information from the database. They typically produce printed reports for managers or display the results of a query. End users or programming professionals create these programs as they are needed.

Accessing a relational database

The most popular approach for manipulating data in a relational data base is the language called SQL (Structured Query Language). SQL is rapidly becoming the standard language for database programming because it is powerful and yet easy to learn. There is now a world standard for SQL called ANSI SQL, administered by the American National Standards Institute. Unfortunately most versions of SQL differ slightly from the standard because manufacturers add their own 'improvements' to the language. Effectively there is really an SQL standard core language with a whole series of non-standard additions to it. This also means that a program written in one manufacturer's specific version of SQL may not run on a different manufacturer's machine unless it is restricted to core SQL only, without any of the enhancements unique to that version. Nevertheless, since most DBMSs can recognise SQL instructions SQL makes it possible to access external data bases. For example SQL can provide the interface between products such as spreadsheets to a corporate database.

Summary of the relational database approach

1. The distinguishing feature of the relational model is the independence of the logical data model from the physical model. (Howe, 1983)

2. Tables are conceptually simple for users to understand and tends to lead to better data management.

3. The clarity of the table concept encourages discussion of the external model and more alternatives being explored.

4. Normalisation can be used as the basis for the external database design, or provide a simple check on database design.

5. High level languages such as SQL are available, which allow user friendly interfaces to be provided.

The database administrator

Controlling and administering a database is complex process and certain roles have to be performed. Perry and Lateer (1989) identify the main roles as Database Administrator, Systems Developer and End Users.

The person responsible for the control and management of a database is the database administrator or DBA. The DBA is the person who grants access to the data base and determines what privileges a user has and what restrictions are placed on them. Any system with more than one user needs a formal DBA; in single user systems the user acts as DBA by default. The duties of a DBA include

*   Defining the base tables

*   Authorising changes to the structure of the database

*   Ensuring back ups and recovery systems work

*   Monitoring the database's performance and efficiency

*   Preventing errors affecting the database

*   Checking data consistency

*   Moving data between the database and external files

*   Controlling the physical location of the database

These tasks are complex and time consuming and some form of central documentation must be built into every relational DBMS. This is the function of the data dictionary. It stores all the information relating to the database.

User names, user access rights, tables names, table attribute names, table storage information and auditing data for disaster recovery are all stored there. It would be impossible to manage the DBMS without this tool, since all users access the information in the data dictionary even if they themselves are not aware of it.

The systems developer

Systems developers create programs for others to use. These can range from simple data entry screens to complex applications involving multiple tables and remote sites. The programmer's tasks include

- Designing screens for end user accesses.

- Providing simple to use conditional query facilities

- Making peripheral devices available

- Exchanging data with other software packages

- Migrating the database to other hardware

Systems development has been transformed by the use of advanced manipulation tools such as fourth generation languages (4GLs), forms designers and screen painters. Applications can be produced in these non-procedural languages many times faster. It is the quality of these tools, their speed and ease of use, that differentiates the various relational DBMS products. Advanced tools make the developer's job easier and increase productivity. The best tools allow untrained end users to specify their own solutions directly.

The end user

Databases are ultimately judged by the quality of information provided to end users. It has to be fast, easy to understand, flexible and consistent. The end user interface needs to be as natural and non threatening as possible. Typical end user needs include

- Database queries

- Hard copy output

- Data exchange with other users

- Easy updates to the databases

- Simple application definition and automatic generation

The usefulness of databases

For all their power and ease of use, databases are complex to design, install and maintain. Bradley lists the following plus and minus features associated with databases, (Bradley, 1989)

Advantages of databases

Data independence: This means programs will still run correctly even if the structure of the files it accesses is changed. Data independence insulates programs from changes in the data files.

Maintenance: Data independence means fewer program changes and so leads to reduced maintenance overall.

Controlled redundancy: In a fully relational system data is stored only once. This leads to consistency of data and better quality reporting.

Cheaper programming: Since the file handling is all taken care of by the DBMS, programs which involve manipulating multiple files are easier to write.

Security: The generally high level of access protection within commercial DBMSs means that security is usually better than with in house systems.

Integrity: Database systems normally have extensive back-up and recovery sub-systems as standard, usually working automatically. The chances of accidental data loss is therefore reduced.

Query languages: Most relational DBMSs support high level query languages. These allow direct access to the database by end users and enhance the productivity of programmers.

Standardisation: Adopting a database approach usually means appointing a database administrator. The DBA in turn will ensure that standards are adhered to, rather than just being viewed as something found in a manual. (McFadden and Hoffer, 1988).

Disadvantages of databases

Software costs: Database management software tends to be expensive.

Hardware costs: A DBMS puts another layer of software between the user and the files. This layer is active all the time and so for any given application more processing is needed if a DBMS is present, often needing a larger machine to do the same job. The relational principle of data independence means file processing tends to be relatively inefficient compared to other, less flexible database structures. The relational approach is attractive for ad hoc multiple key query applications but is not always the best solution for high volume transaction processing.

Complexity: A relational database is a sophisticated software package and will usually need specially trained staff. If wrongly used the performance of a database system can degrade abruptly.

Centralisation: An integrated database can encourage a tendency to centralised management and control.

Vulnerability: If the central database fails for any reason then the whole organisation is affected immediately.

Summary

For the system designer the relational data base approach has many attractions. Deriving the data model is relatively straight forward. Much of the work of storage and access of data is automatic. Security and integrity are built in. Fourth generation languages make programming easier, and in particular make changes easy. Most products can work on a range of different vendor's equipment and can be scaled up or down. The flexible access paths to data makes prototyping an attractive option. It fits in well with the structured systems analysis methodology. It integrates well with CASE tools which often have data modelling capabilities built in and interfaced to a data dictionary.

Further Reading

Avison, D E (1985) Information systems development: A database approach. Blackwell Scientific, Oxford.

Bradley J (1989) An elementary introduction to data base management. The Dryden Press, Chicago

Finkelstein, C. (1992) Information Engineering: Strategic Systems Development. Pub Addison-Wesley, Wokingham, England.

Howe D R (1984) Data Analysis for Data Base design. Edward Arnold, London

McFadden , F. and Hoffer, J. (1988) Data Base Management. Pub Benjamin Cummings, Menlo Park, CA.

Chapter 14 System implementation

People centred change

Minimising resistance

To large extent the success or failure of a new design hinges on the skill with which it is implemented. No information system can work without the willing co-operation of the people involved so it is here that the main implementation effort needs to be concentrated. This is not to say that the technical aspects can be ignored, but that there are always ways of overcoming technical problems, human based problems take much longer to erase once raised.

In general, there are four main ways to minimise resistance to change. These are

1. Staff involvement

2. Incremental change

3. Flexible design

4. The socio-technical approach

Staff involvement

Most resistance to change stems from fear and misinformation about the nature and extent of changes which will follow a computerisation exercise. Obviously, the way to avoid this is to recognise that staff have a legitimate interest in any changes which affect their jobs and to keep them fully informed at every stage.

Another way of ensuring minimum resistance to allow the staff to see, by direct experience or through briefings, that changes are proposed in response to genuine operational difficulties which are having a negative effect on the organisation's efficiency. Whenever staff perceive the need for change clearly they are much more likely to react positively to it.

Incremental change

People are more concerned about rapid change than about gradual change and the systems designer can take advantage of this. Most computer systems are long-term applications and can therefore be implemented in small stages over a long period. Using this approach allows staff to become used to a series of small alterations.

None of these alterations are seen as threatening individually, but nonetheless they amount to a radical change in the longer term.

Flexible design

People today have all lived through periods of rapid changes in many aspects of their daily life and so are not usually resistant to changes just because they would prefer things to stay as they are. Change is regarded as normal and largely inevitable. What people do object to are changes which will affect them directly, perhaps adversely, and over which they have no control.

No systems designer should ever be committed to a system being designed in such a way that once started it cannot be altered. Given the time-lag which affects all projects, it is inevitable that the environment within which the application is being developed will change. In order to cope with this, the system should be designed to be flexible enough to meet these changes and to take advantage of any suggestions for alteration or improvement which may arise from staff involvement.

If the designer ensures that the project is open to revision and reconsideration, even after the detailed design stage has been approved then staff will tend to feel less isolated and more in control of their own destiny.

The socio-technical approach

The problems of technological change have been given a great deal of thought by managers and social scientists and several methodologies for implementation of change have been developed which are specifically designed to minimise resistance to it. These were discussed in detail earlier.

The principle of the socio-technical approach to implementation is the observation that a successful computer system is the outcome of the right mix of hardware, software, people and procedures. If any of these are designed in isolation, the other elements will suffer and the overall efficiency of the application will be adversely affected. The proponents of the socio-technical view believe that most computer applications are designed with too much emphasis on the technical aspects. Too often in the past, technically superior computer systems have failed in practice, because the human factors involved have been overlooked.

271

The socio-technical approach endeavours to think through the fundamental requirements of the organisation and to align all staff with these requirements. If a participative methodology has been adopted from the start then implementation should be that much smoother. This encourages the formulation of alternative designs for implementation. The perceptions of people have to be taken into account and an implementation plan drawn up which allows for enough time for the proposed changes to be discussed. The process of implementation involves consultation with the existing staff and designed to ensure that staff at all levels are fully conversant with the proposals.

Training for implementation

The personnel involved are a vitally important element in the success of any computer system and must be fully trained if they are to carry out their tasks effectively. However, training should not be seen as merely a way of teaching job skills. It also serves other useful purposes for the systems designer.

The purposes of training

- To enable staff to carry out tasks in support of efficient running of the new system

- To overcome any resistance to, and fear of change, e.g. lack of confidence that might adversely effect the efficiency of the system

- To convince users that the new system will be beneficial to them, and that overall it will be an effective and efficient system

- To save time later at the critical and costly 'live-running' implementation stage

Who needs training?

- All staff in the departments which are being computerised

- Any other staff affected, for example, by changes in manual procedures, or in the flow of work

- Management, who will have to understand the new procedures, and who will have to assess the effects on the existing organisational structure

- All computer room staff, e.g. operators, DP staff

- Auditors should be consulted at an early stage, and consulted as to the adequacy of training provided

Training methods

The analyst has a wide range of training methods available to use, each of which has its own specific strengths and weaknesses and which are particularly suited to particular training needs.

Lectures

DESCRIPTION

A formal presentation in a classroom situation by a trained speaker, using visual aids such as slides, films, videos and/or handouts

ADVANTAGES

Allows complete control of events by the presenter; takes trainees out of the work place; limits distractions

A cheap and effective method of influencing large numbers of people

DISADVANTAGES

The classroom atmosphere may alienate some trainees

Difficult to do well: needs a trained presenter

Can require a lot of preparation: not cost-effective for one or two lectures.

USES

Imparting a lot of factual information such as an overall presentation of a proposed computerisation and its likely effect on the organisation

RESOURCES

Can be presented by internal personnel such as the analyst or designer, or by external personnel such as consultants, manufacturers' representatives, or local colleges.

Needs suitable premises

Discussion meetings

DESCRIPTION

A formal or informal meeting of affected staff who undertake a general discussion under the leadership of an informed chairperson

ADVANTAGES

Can be located anywhere

Needs little notice

Needs little formal preparation

Very cheap to run

Allows full participation

Very flexible in content

Allows a full exchange of views

DISADVANTAGES

Can become unruly and out of control

Can become bogged down in trivia

Can turn into a vehicle for imposing narrow views on others

USES

An ideal method for identifying and dealing with staff anxieties prior to computerisation. Also useful for gauging opinion when evaluating alternative courses of action

RESOURCES

Can be led by internal staff or external consultants

Visits

DESCRIPTION

Members of staff are allowed time off work to visit another work-site or business premises where a similar set-up to that proposed for the organisation can be seen in operation

ADVANTAGES

Gives direct experience to staff who may not readily understand the concepts involved

Allows staff to talk informally with existing users

Can be combined with 'hands-on' experience

DISADVANTAGES

Can be very expensive in employee's time

There may be no suitable reference site to visit

Staff may gain a false impression by looking at different equipment

USES

Overcoming ignorance of basic computer applications

Eliminating resistance based on fear of the unknown

Stimulating positive attitudes towards new implementations

RESOURCES

Staff time, and often supervisor's time as well

Company magazines

DESCRIPTION

News-letters, notice boards, internal memos and professionally produced glossy magazines. Normally a full description of proposed events can be given well in advance to allow staff in all departments to be kept informed of events happening in the company

ADVANTAGES

Promotes a good image
Staff have time to assimilate material and discuss it with colleagues
A great deal of factual information can be conveyed
Normally a very cheap method

DISADVANTAGES

Often regarded as propaganda by employees
Can be used as an excuse for not allowing full staff participation
Frequency of publication may be too seldom

USES

Good for passing on progress reports where a large number of staff are likely to be affected

Self-managed learning

DESCRIPTION

A method of training where one person follows a course of instruction on their own, and at their own pace, using specially prepared materials

ADVANTAGES

Information can be taught to any desired level of complexity

No need to involve any other staff

Training can be done anywhere, any time

DISADVANTAGES

Requires a high level of motivation on the part of the trainee

May have to be combined with supervision or monitoring

The preparation of materials has to be particularly meticulous

USES

Any type of training from basic computer appreciation to high-level instruction, such as learning a computer language or operating an application package

RESOURCES

A wide variety of materials is available including:

- Video cassettes
- Audio cassettes
- Programmed learning packages
- Programmed learning books
- Simulation packages
- Computer based training (CBT)
- Computer aided teaching packages (CAT)

On-the-job training

DESCRIPTION

Staff are trained in how to do a job by actually handling the machinery they will be required to operate, and learning as they go.

ADVANTAGES

Gives staff immediate familiarity with the equipment they will be using

Builds confidence very rapidly

Avoids any hint of the 'back to school' atmosphere engendered by formal lectures

DISADVANTAGES

Often ties up machinery and personnel resources for great amounts of time

Training cannot start until the hardware is installed and tested

USES

All forms of practical skills learning. Commonly used for teaching data preparation operators, computer operators, programmers, etc.

RESOURCES

Full access to suitable hardware and software

Staff needed to show newcomers how to do the job

Can be combined with secondment to manufacturer's premises

Can be so complex as to involve guided projects and action learning, or as simple as 'sitting next to Nellie'.

Can be combined with role-playing techniques

Training manuals

DESCRIPTION

These are basically handbooks detailing how each of the tasks of the new application is to be carried out

ADVANTAGES

Often produced as a by-product of the systems specification

Should always be up-to-date in a properly run organisation

Can be used to train new staff or as reference for existing staff

DISADVANTAGES

Frequently badly written and out-of-date

If they are the only means of training provided, they do not allow a newcomer to gain from the practical experience of existing staff

USES

Should allow any member of the computer staff to be trained to carry out day-to-day jobs

Communication principles

Making a presentation

Analysts have to make presentations frequently, and to all levels of staff within an organisation. The main elements which contribute to successful presentation are:

- thorough preparation
- restricted content
- competent delivery

No analyst should have any difficulty making a good presentation if these elements are mastered. Each person will rapidly develop an individual style but the following observations should prove useful in most circumstances.

Preparation

The primary requirement is always to prepare well. If you are to make a good presentation you must always know more than just the bare facts to be put across. The analyst should therefore be well briefed, not only on the subject in hand, but also on the wider issue concerning its application, or this will soon become apparent in the presentation. If the presenter does not appear to know very much about even a few aspects of the subject, the audience will very quickly pick this up and begin to doubt the validity of even the most incontrovertible facts put forward by the presenter.

Content

The mistake most commonly made by presenters is to try to put across too much at one time. A good presentation is one which presents only a limited amount of information. The presenter can then concentrate on how best to get the information across in a clear at memorable way.

A presenter thinks about the needs and interests of the audience first and tailors the contents of the presentation accordingly. This means that to a certain extent the presenter has to try to get to know the audience beforehand, must start from where they are, and must slant the material in a way that is likely to be of most interest to them.

The presenter must also think carefully about whether to provide supporting material and handouts for the audience, and whether illustrate the presentation with diagrams, etc. Different audiences come with different backgrounds, expectations, education and attitudes. These must be taken into account.

Delivery

Anyone can make a speech, but not everyone will be willing to listen to it. The primary principle of good delivery is first to establish, and then to maintain, contact with your audience.

This means that the presenter must be willing to depart from the plan whenever the audience shows that it is more interested in one aspect of the presentation than another. It also means that the presenter must be willing and able to vary the length (and speed) of the presentation to fit in with the audience's attention span. No one audience will be exactly like another.

A good presenter can actually control the audience without their being aware of it. Skilled speakers manipulate the attention span by using neat, arresting and informative visual aids. To do this it is vital that the visuals can be clearly seen and easily understood.

The presenter can also hold the audience's attention by varying the approach, perhaps by involving the audience in some sort of action. There is an old saying:

I hear and I forget; I see and I remember; I do and I understand

The presenter needs feedback from the audience to see how well the material is being received and so needs to make frequent eye contact with members of the audience and constantly monitor how the material is going over, addressing his or her remarks as if to one particular person.

From these general considerations can be extracted a short set of rules for effective presentations.

Rules for making a presentation

- Use diagrams wherever possible-one picture is worth a thousand words

- Do not be afraid to repeat yourself. 'Tell them what you are going to tell them, tell them, then tell them what you've just told them' is still good advice!

- Stop your narrative at frequent intervals to summarise the material you have covered.

- Go over the main points several times if necessary.

- Always put the needs of the audience first.

- Do not read from prepared notes if you can avoid it.

- The main points of your presentation should be summarised and provided for the audience as handouts for later examination.

- Be natural, enthusiastic and retain eye contact with the audience.

- Encourage your audience to interrupt if they do not understand a point.

- Invite questions, especially if audience needs to participate.

- Do not be afraid to digress from the point you want to put across if the audience's interest lies in another direction.

- Do not assume any particular level of knowledge or expertise in your audience.

One-to-one communication

The points made in the discussion of how to make good presentations to a group of people will also apply when you are conducting a one-to-one communication. However, in a one-to-one situation the close nature of a two-way interchange will lead to greater immediacy and virtually instantaneous feedback.

Better communication

In general all of the rules given for presentations should be observed. The following additional rules will prove useful in achieving better one-to-one communication.

- Always try to use simple direct language.

- Determine the listener's way of thinking and identify with it.

- Use the listener's phrasing where possible, rather than your own.

- Use as many different channels of communication as possible: in other words, draw diagrams, demonstrate with models and show pictures to support the spoken word.

- Attempt to eliminate all distractions and environmental noise.

- Put forward ideas in *general* first before developing them in *detail*.

- Do not try to impart too much information at one meeting.

- Do not rely on the listener's memory

- Check frequently that your listener understands what you are saying and is following your line of argument.

Technology centred change

Implementation

Implementation is the name given to that part of the systems design cycle which lies between formal approval of the specification for the proposed new system and the final handover of a working application.

It is a major undertaking and always requires careful planning. A good analyst will have been thinking about implementation and its problems even while considering design alternatives and so will have already formed at least an outline implementation plan at an early stage. Implementation requires the management and co-ordination of a whole range of different functions including programming, personnel selection, training, building supervision, test scheduling and trouble shooting. The only person with the necessary in-depth knowledge of the new system and its needs is the systems analyst, and so they usually assume responsibility for all aspects of implementation.

The main stages of system implementation

Planning
Implementation of a large system may take anything up to 2 years and so can not be approached in a haphazard way. The analyst normally has to set up some sort of formal planning committee whose function will be to direct and co-ordinate the actions of the various functions and departments involved. In addition it is usual to adopt some form of planning methodology such as critical path analysis (CPA) as an aid to day-to-day management.

Installing equipment
The physical acceptance of the hardware also has to be planned well in advance. Large computers have to be ordered in advance and consideration has to be given to the siting of the machine, access to it, power supplies, stationery stores, staff facilities and so on, all of which can take a long time and require considerable political skills.

Testing the system
Once the hardware has been installed it has to be tested to ensure that all peripheral devices are working to specification and that the whole system functions smoothly with no interfacing problems. Once the analyst is satisfied that the hardware is operating correctly then the programs have to be tested, singly and in combination. This requires the preparation of test plans and test data well in advance.

281

Training and communication

A good working system is a careful balance between its component parts: hardware, software and people. If the personnel involved are to play their part effectively in the new design they will have to be trained, and the analyst will have to provide adequate documentation for them to carry out their duties once training has been completed.

File conversion

Whether changing from a manual system to a computer system, or converting an existing computer application to a more advanced one, there is always the problem of carrying over the old systems records to the new system. This is frequently a major task and requires a separate planning stage of its own.

Changeover strategy

The data processing function is at the heart of most modern businesses and so any operation which could threaten disruption to that function must be handled with great care. A number of different strategies have been developed to simplify the task of moving smoothly from one system to the other. Part of the analyst's planning tasks will be the choice of which strategy to adopt for the particular application being converted.

Although they are not strictly speaking stages of implementation, there are two other main aspects of implementation which are usually considered under the following headings

Implementation strategy

Modern analysts recognise that they are working within a social environment and cannot concentrate solely on the technical aspects of their work. Several different social approaches to the design of new systems are available, and whether consciously or not, the analyst must adopt one or more of them as part of the implementation scheme.

Documentation

The implementation stage as a whole can only be regarded as complete when, as well as providing a working system, all the necessary system documentation is also complete. Too often in practice, the provision of good documentation is neglected particularly where there is pressure to get the processing working as quickly as possible and the analyst and programmers are moved on to other, more urgent tasks.

Hardware installation

The hardware installation process is relatively straightforward.

Hardware acquisition

Select vendor

Negotiate price and delivery terms. Place order

Order accessories, furnishings, etc.

Consider standby equipment

Site preparation

Select site: consider security, physical movement of records, physical storage of data

Prepare site: consider power requirements, weight distribution, environmental controls, communications links, planning for delivery, physical access path

Engineering standby

Equipment installation

Inform all affected parties of time-table

Physical installation. Consider: the need for engineering personnel, work disruption, timing

Evaluation

Prepare test schedule

Undertake individual hardware testing

Undertake trial run of system

Implement acceptance procedures

Network analysis

Project control

One of the main problems associated with the implementation of a computer system is the difficulty of co-ordinating all its various elements. A number of management aids have been developed to help in these complex tasks. The most commonly used of these is **critical path analysis** (CPA).

283

The basic idea behind CPA is that any complex task can be broken down into a number of smaller component parts. The individual parts are easier to manage when treated separately because they can be examined in isolation. This examination aims to produce a detailed plan of operation, including an estimated time scale for completion for each sub-task.

The problem then arises of how to ensure that each of the many sub-tasks are carried out in the right order and at the right time. Additionally, there is the problem of presenting the detailed schedule in a clear and informative way.

CPA gets round these problems by using a graphical technique to link the sub-tasks and to show the inter-relationships between them.

Critical path analysis

Any project can be reduced to smaller sub-tasks known as activities. These activities are nothing more than convenient units which appear to the analyst to be a smaller part of the system as a whole. For example, systems analysis can be thought of as comprising separate activities such as the feasibility study, the fact-finding phase, the programming phase and so on.

CPA diagrams also have to show events. These mark the points in time where some activity starts or stops. In any project the analyst will aim to produce a listing of all the activities which go to make up the project, with an estimate of the time required to complete each of them and a note of the other activities which must have been completed before that activity can begin.

A simple example

Suppose you wanted to have a glass of water. The activities involved in this might be:

> Fetch glass
> Fill with water
> Drink water

Now suppose also that having drunk water many times you know that it takes one minute to get the glass, ten seconds to fill it with water and fifty seconds to drink the water. This could be presented as follows:

Activity number	Description	Preceding activity	Duration (seconds)
A	Fetch glass		60
B	Fill with water	A	10
C	Drink water	B	50

The total time to complete the project 'Drinking the water' would therefore be two minutes (60 + 10 + 50 = 120 seconds).

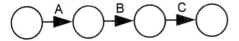

Figure 14.1 CPA for drinking a glass of water

Figure 14. 1 shows the CPA diagram for drinking a glass of water. The circles ('nodes') represent events. The one on the left is the start event (every sequence must have a starting point) and the circle on the right is the finish event. The circles are linked by arrows representing activities. There is always one arrow for each activity. In this case the activities all follow one another in order. The activity B, 'Fill with water', follows activity A, 'Fetch the glass', and C follows B. There are event circles between A and B because you cannot pour the water until the glass is in position. Getting the glass in the right position is therefore the 'event' which lets you begin to pour the water. Until the preceding activity is finished you cannot begin the next one. Suppose you want to drink a cup of coffee. The schedule might be like this:

Activity	Description	Preceding activity	Time (sec)
A	Fill kettle		30
B	Boil kettle	A	360
C	Fetch mug		60
D	Put coffee in mug	C	10
E	Fill mug	B & D	20
F	Stir coffee	E	10
G	Drink coffee	F	50

How long would it take to make and drink the coffee? In the case of the glass of water the answer was found by simply adding up the times for the individual activities. However with the coffee project some activities can be carried out simultaneously. This is shown in Figure 14.2.

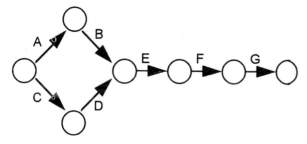

Figure 14.2 CPA for drinking a cup of coffee

This time the activities are not laid out in a straight line. An examination of the diagram shows that the filling and boiling of the kettle follows a different path from fetching and putting coffee in the mug, but they join again at the pouring activity. This makes estimating the completion time more difficult.

Once the basic diagram has been drawn we can add information about the times of the various activities and try to get a figure for the duration of the whole project. Figure 14.3 shows the activity arrows with the times for each activity written below the line.

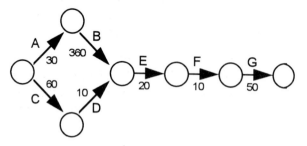

Figure 14.3 CPA with times added

This diagram has more information than the previous one but it still doesn't state very clearly how long it will take to make the coffee, although it does show clearly how each of the activities relates to one another, and the sequence in which they are to be performed. Nor does this diagram show which of two possible paths is the most important. A further refinement is needed.

The Figure 14.4 shows a more complete version of the CPA for the coffee-making project.

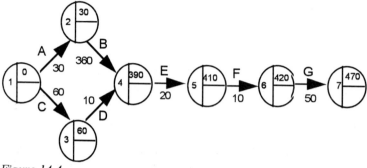

Figure 14.4

In this version the event circles have been divided into three parts. The left hand part has been used for numbering the events (1 2,3 ... etc.) but can be left blank if you want to avoid cluttering the diagram.

You will see that the upper right hand side of event circle now contains a number. This number represents the earliest possible start date for that event.

By convention, CPA diagrams always start from right now, that is from time zero, so event node i (circle 1) shows a zero.

If you follow the upper path, going from the start event through activity A then you will see the number 30 shown in the upper right section of event 2. This is the minimum time needed before being able to start activity B, that is, activity B cannot begin any earlier than 30 seconds after starting the project. Similarly activity E cannot be started less than 390 seconds from the start, and activity F must wait 410 seconds to begin (30 + 360 + 20).

If we follow the lower path, by similar reasoning, activity D can only start after 60 seconds. However, following on from D to E the figure in event 4 shows the previously calculated number 390,. Y you might think would be the correct number to follow on from event 3 would be 70 (60 + 10). Why isn't it?

The correct number is in fact 390. Activity E (Fill the mug) cannot be done until both B (Boil the water) and D (Put coffee in mug) have been done. This means that E cannot really start until the preceding activity with the longest time requirement has been completed. This gives rise to an important general rule.

> Where there is more than one path available to get to an event node, calculate the time along every possible path, and insert the highest number into the event node.

By following this rule through all the nodes we can calculate that this project will take not less than 470 seconds.

The critical path

The path through ABEFG is called the **critical path.** This is because any delays in any of the activities making up this path will inevitably result in the whole project being delayed. An. delay in activities not on the critical path will not affect the overall time to completion, unless they are excessive.

Consider the effect on the project of doubling the time taken to put the coffee in the mug. Raising it from 10 seconds to 20 seconds will not affect the overall duration of the project. Even doubling activity C's time will have no appreciable effect on project completion time, as long as it is finished before activity B is completed. On the other hand, increasing activity F by 5 seconds to 15 seconds will immediately increase the whole project time by the extra 5 seconds.

By how long could the combined times of activities C and D be increased before there would be any increase in the overall project duration?

Identifying the critical path

In this example it is easy to tell, just by inspection of the diagram, which is the path with no 'allowance' on it - the critical path, and which path has some time to spare.

In more complex examples it is not so easy to tell. In order to identify the critical path, another calculation of times is done, this time working backwards and calculating the latest time an activity could be started and still allow the whole project to finish on time. These calculations are shown in Figure14.5, where they are added to the lower right side of the event circles.

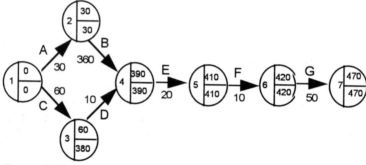

Figure 14.5

The values in the lower right-hand side of the event nodes are found by considering the latest start time for each activity. Starting with event seven, obviously the latest time is the same as the earliest time, so 470 is entered. Working backwards, the latest time you could start activity G, and still finish on time, would be 420 seconds after the beginning of the sequence (470 - 50). Similarly we can work backwards through nodes 6,5 and 4 without difficulty.

Nodes 2 and 3 present problems. If we calculate along path 4, 2, 1 we get a latest start time of zero (390 - 360 - 30). If we follow the path 4, 3, 1 we get the latest start time of 320. However, since node 1 is the point in time for starting both activity A and activity C, node 1 must have a start from zero or the project cannot finish in time. Zero is therefore entered in node 1.

In order to simplify these conflicting figures another rule can be used in order to choose the right number when there are two paths to a node.

Where there are two or more paths backwards to a particular node, you calculate the longest path back from the finish node and enter that figure, that is to say the smallest number is entered.

The critical path is then easily identified as the one where the upper and lower right hand numbers are identical. It is the path where the earliest start times of each activity are equal to the latest start times. There is no slack involved.

Slack time
Consideration of the path through C and D to E shows that there is time to spare. This is known as 'slack time', or sometimes just 'slack'. Activity D could start at any time between 60 seconds and 380 seconds and so has 320 seconds of slack. Activity C could start at any time between 0 and 320 seconds and also has 320 seconds worth of slack. (In fact it is more accurate to say that the chain of events 1, 3, 4 has 320 seconds slack, because we could allocate the slack in any combination between the two activities, but could not give the 320 seconds slack to each).

Try giving slack values of 320 seconds to each of the activities C and D and see what the overall effect would be.

The final version
The path with no slack on it is the critical path; in order to make the critical path stand out clearly, the final version of the CPA diagram is drawn out as shown in Figure 14.6, with the critical path central and shown as a double line.

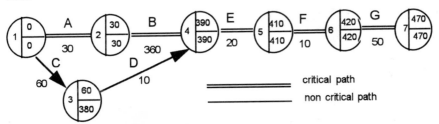

Figure 14.6 The final CPA

Rules for drawing up CPA diagrams

1. Every CPA diagram must have only one beginning event.

2. Every CPA diagram must have only one ending event.

3. All activities must eventually lead to the ending event.

4. Concurrent activities can not be represented on the same arrow.

5. There must be at least one critical path through the diagram.

6. There can only be one occurrence of any individual event.

7. Time is shown going from left to right.

8. Where there is more than one path available to get to an event node, calculate the time along every possible path, and insert the highest number into the event node.

9. Where there are two or more paths backwards to a particular node, you calculate the longest path back from the finish node and enter that figure, that is to say the smallest number is entered.

Gantt charts

A Gantt chart is a simple visual aid to planning. These diagrams offer an alternative to CPA networks for showing linked activities, their relationships, and the time taken to complete them. Gantt charts, more commonly called bar charts, can be used on their own or in conjunction with CPA network diagrams.

A Gantt chart uses lines (or bars) to show the amount of time needed by an activity. The length of the line is proportional to the length of time the activity takes to complete. The position of the line is important too.

Its start shows the earliest point in time from which the activity can start. The end of the line shows the earliest time that the activity can end. An example should make this clearer.

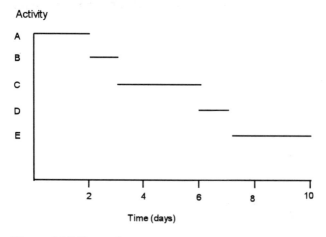

Figure 14.7 Gantt chart

Figure 14.7 shows a simple Gantt chart with five activities, A to E. Activity A takes 2 days, activity B takes 1 day, and so on. This type of chart can be a little confusing, however, when it is made up of lines. A better form is shown in Figure 14.8, where the lines have been replaced by bars.

It is now very much clearer to read off where any particular activity begins and ends. If further clarification is needed, then the duration of each activity can be displayed by writing the appropriate figure inside the bar.

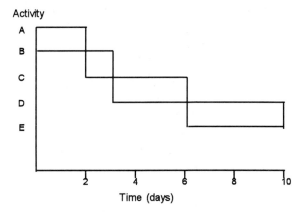

Figure 14.8 Bar chart

The series of bars shown in Figure 14.8 implies that C cannot begin before B ends, and B cannot begin until A is complete, exactly like a CPA network chart. A bar chart can be used in a similar way to a CPA network to show which activities are critical and which activities are not critical. Figure 8.9 shows the bar chart for the coffee-making problem discussed in the previous section.

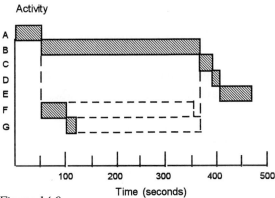

Figure 14.9

291

The critical path ABEFG is shown in Figure14.9 as a series of connecting bars, each drawn to scale and shown opposite the activity identifier (in this case the letter). The activities not on the critical path are shown as being clearly separate from those activities which are.

The bar for activity C is shown starting at the earliest possible time after completion of activity **A.** The vertical dotted line is there to make this relationship absolutely clear. The fact that activity C is not critical means that it has some slack. This is indicated by the rectangle of dotted lines to the right of the bar for activity C. The dotted rectangle shows the limits of the space within which activity C can be scheduled, that is, the amount of slack available. Within this space the project manager is free to move the start time of activity C to fit in with other demands and constraints. Similarly, activity D is shown joined to C, and with its slack space outlined with another dotted rectangle. A vertical dotted line shows that D must be completed before activity E begins.

This idea of sliding the start times of non-critical activities around within their slack space and so varying the start and finish times can be used to schedule the application of resources in a project. Consider the following example.

Activity	Preceding activity	Duration (days)	Personnel required
A		2	8
B	A	4	8
C	A	5	11
D	B	4	9
E	C	5	3
F	E	3	3
G	D,F	4	10

Construct a critical path analysis diagram for this example. What is the minimum time required for completion? Which is the critical path? How many people will be needed on the project?

The finished CPA diagram for the example is shown in Figure 14. 1 0. Check your answer against this.You should have had no trouble in establishing the critical path, ACEFG, or in calculating the total time needed, 19 days. However, it is unlikely that you would have managed to find the correct number of workers without using a bar chart.

Construct a bar chart for the example given using the model shown in the text as a guide. Can you still trace the critical path? Can you now tell how many people will be needed on the project?

A bar chart for the example is shown in Figure 8.1 1. Your answer should be substantially similar. Figure 8.12 shows the same information rearranged vertically. This type of bar chart is known as a **histogram.**

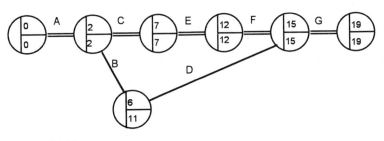

Figure 14.10

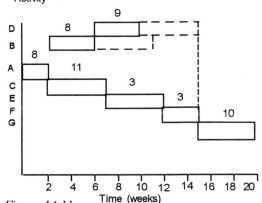

Figure 14.11

Scheduling with a bar chart

How many workers will be needed? Reading the bar chart as it is set out in Figure 14.12 will reveal that the total number of staff needed will vary from 3 in weeks 10 to 15 to as many as 20 in week 6. In fact neither of these figures is correct.

A closer look at how Figures 14.11 and 14.12 are made up will show that the numbers can be reduced considerably. In week 3, for example, activity C will need 11 workers, and at the same time activity B will need 8 workers, giving a combined total of 19. But it is not essential to carry out activities B and C simultaneously: B can be rescheduled. The same is true of activity D: it does not need to be done at the same time as activity E.

Figure 14.13 shows one way that the project activities might be rearranged to minimise the number of personnel needed on the project at any one time.

Again this information is summarised in a histogram (Figure 14.14), where the height of the bars represents the approximate number of workers needed in each week.

Number of employees

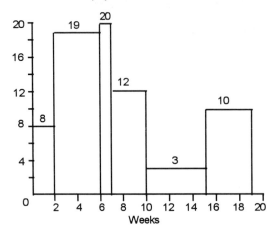

Figure 14.12

Activity

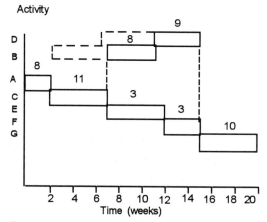

Figure 14.13

Rules for the Gantt chart

1. The bars on the critical path should be continuous or otherwise clearly shown to be consecutive

2. All bars should be labelled with the event letters

3. The length of the bars should be drawn to scale

4. Each activity not on the critical path should lie within its earliest and latest start times

5. The resource requirements should not exceeded at any time

6. The Gantt chart should accurately reflect the given situation

7. A histogram of the resource allocations should be shown at the foot of the Gantt chart

Number of employees

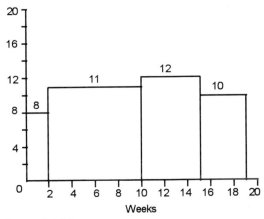

Figure 14.14

System testing

The main purposes of testing

A new computer system is much too important to the organisation for anything to be left to chance, and so extensive testing is necessary to ensure that the installed application will perform to its specification.

Any computer system consists of five parts:

- The hardware: the computer, printers, terminals etc.

- The software: systems and applications

- Data: input and output

- User documentation: operators and users

- Clerical procedures: associated manual processes

295

All these five parts need to be tested. This is known as system testing and serves more than one purpose. As well as merely verifying that the system delivered is as ordered, testing can also be used to:

- Prove that the new system will perform the tasks it has been designed to achieve

- Give added confidence to the design term

- Inspire confidence in the users, who are often very reluctant to use the new system initially, by demonstrating that the system does actually meet their requirements

- Prevent hold-ups and frustration during implementation by ensuring that individual units operate correctly before integrating them

- Reduce the need for remedial maintenance

- Encourage acceptance by the computer operations and programming maintenance staff by showing that it functions correctly on a routine basis

The main procedures of testing

Many people are misled by the term 'system testing' and think that system testing and program testing are the same thing. In fact program testing is a part of system testing.

Program testing

This is known as **internal testing.** It is concerned with testing the computer processing of individual programs. These tests are normally done by the programmers themselves before the finished programs are implemented into a system.

System testing

This is known as **external testing** because its primary objective is to test how well the system as a whole works. It aims to test the linkages between programs, input preparation procedures, output production, and error handling routines.

It should not be carried out by programmers, nor by the organisation responsible for developing the system, if that is an external service. It should instead be done by the internal analyst or designer in conjunction with the user staff.

296

Testing practice

The actual design of tests will depend upon particular circumstances but a good general testing scheme would be expected to include most of the following procedures.

- Test the system with predetermined 'clean' data

- Test with the same 'clean' data, but with additional data containing known errors

- Test using greater volumes than expected during operation

- Test particularly any special monthly or period-end routines

For all of the above, compare the actual results (output) with expected results.

- Test recovery procedures separately

- For more extensive testing, go on to use combinations of pre-prepared program test data and data copied from live cases. Move from simple, artificial tests and data to more complex, related ones, finally using both live data and exceeding operational loads.

- To facilitate future program maintenance, the original test data and results should be retained and not discarded

- Test the interfaces of sub-systems, and interfaces between computerised and clerically-operated sections thoroughly

File conversion

The main methods of converting files

One of the major problems of systems implementation is always that of accurately converting existing records, from whatever form they are currently held in to a form suitable for the new system to handle.

The degree of difficulty of this operation depends to a large extent on the number of records involved and on the type of transfer being attempted. In general, transfers can be classified into four broad types. These are where the organisation is trying to:

- Computerise a completely new system

- Convert from a manual to a computerised system

- Upgrade an existing computer system

- Replace one computer with a different make

Problems with file conversions

Completely new system

This form of conversion has both attractions and problems. For instance there are no reconciliation problems since there are no previous records to match up with. There are no staff conversion problems since of course there are no previous processing techniques to unlearn. There are no problems of parallel running since there is no previous system to maintain in action.

On the other hand there are quite serious problems to overcome. There are often externally fixed deadlines to meet, especially since this type of application is often initiated in response to external pressures such as impending legislation. Another problem is that there is, of course, no backup system available if the new application should go wrong: this type of application probably goes wrong more than most because the applications tend to be unique and complex rather than simple.

Computerising an existing manual system

Converting existing records is often a major operation. Extensive staff training is needed and ensuring that the new records are kept in phase with the development of the new system can be a very tedious and time-consuming task. This is particularly so where the number of records in the old system is very large. In small companies, finding the staff to carry out the job of conversion can be a further problem.

By way of example, consider the steps involved in computerising a fairly straightforward manual system.

1. Ensure that the original records are accurate and up to date.

2. Decide which data needs to be converted.

3. Ensure that user and computer staff understand and can use any new coding systems and are fully trained in procedures for conversion.

4. Ensure control systems have been tested and work satisfactorily in order to establish the completeness and validity of converted data.

5. Record the old data on input documents specifically designed for new system.

6. Transcribe the completed input documents on to magnetic media.

7. Ensure that verification of transcription is done.

8. Use specially written programs to create and check the new files.

9. Print out files for visual verification.

10.   Check printout against the old files and input documentation.

11.   Retain the old files and input documents for file security and undisclosed errors.

Upgrading an existing computer system

This is usually the most straightforward conversion because there should be a sizeable group of experienced staff already in place and user resistance should be minimal. The deciding factor as to the degree of difficulty involved is the extent to which the existing computer-readable files need to be changed. If the existing files can be used almost unchanged then the upgrading is usually relatively uncomplicated. However, if the files are to be substantially amended or if they are to be combined into a database then problems can be expected.

Changing from one computer make to a different make

This is very often the most difficult conversion of all because, although the company will have experienced staff to carry out the conversion process, the file conversions can be very complex.

File conversion techniques

The physical changeover from a set of manual records to a new, computerised system can be accomplished in a number of ways.

Iteration transfer

The new master is created by copying the old records. In substantial files, by the time that the last record has been transferred some of the old records may have been altered by transactions that have taken place during the transfer period. The new records may therefore contain outdated information errors as well as transcription errors. To eliminate both of these, a second pass is made through the file comparing the new with the old and correcting differences a they are found. Of course new transactions are coming in all the time: the second pass file will still have some inaccurate records, but many fewer since the second pass is much faster. A third pass is therefor made and so on until the new file is an exact copy of the old file. This method is frequently used in parallel-running changeover.

Selective transcription

This is the name given to the technique of file conversion used on some large manual files. In these files the overall hit-rate is variable but low: some records have many more accesses than others, and some are completely dormant.

File conversion proceeds by transferring a record to the new master file only when a transaction is received for that record. In this way only active records are transferred and the file effectively 'cleans' itself of dead records. The advantages are that: file control totals can be maintained at all times; and the new system runs with manageable file size in its very early stage which aids error tracking and allows high seasonal businesses to have a 'running in' period in the quiet season. Once a substantial proportion of the file has been transcribed, decision can be made as to whether to transfer the rest as and when time allows or to leave them in the manual system indefinitely. This method is used in conjunction with phase in/phase out changeover procedure

Transaction capture

This is the process of file creation used where a totally new system, or one which is substantially different from the existing system, is to be installed. Master files are set up by examining past transactions and identifying likely candidates for inclusion. Alternatively, once the system is running a master record is created for each transaction received until duplicate avoidance becomes too cumbersome. This method allows the capture of data not currently held anywhere in the organisation.

One-shot transfer

This transfer method is used where the old file a relatively simple structure and a high hit-rate, or where every record must be transferred, as in accounting applications. All the non-volatile fields of the old master record are transferred over and verified. At a convenient point, usually at close of business immediately prior to changeover, the details of the variable fields are filled in. When the file totals have been verified the new file is ready for use. This method is usually used in conjunction with direct conversion methods.

Selecting a suitable conversion method

The appropriate conversion method will depend largely on the size and complexity of the files to be converted and to a certain extent on the changeover method envisaged. The following is a list of the major features of each method and should indicate which method is most suitable for any particular circumstance.

Iteration transfer

Used with large numbers of manual records. Useful where the records are complex. Suitable for fast-changing application. Allows for periodic checking and complete accuracy. Needs a great deal of clerical work.

Associated with parallel running.

Selective transcription
Used with large manual files. Useful when the hit rate is variable or low. Conversion rate exactly matches the activity level. Allows for a smoothly managed conversion Allows live running with small files to start with.

Associated with phase in/phase out changeover.

Transaction capture
Used when creating totally new file types. Allows the capture of data not held elsewhere. Can use data from past transactions. Can use data from incoming transactions.

Associated with direct changeover.

'One-shot' transfer
Used where records are simple in structure. Suitable where every record has to be carried over. Allows partial transfer, with intermediate checking Implementation is usually very swift.

Associated with direct changeover.

Changeover procedures

There are four basic changeover procedures, one or other of which is used during the process of actually moving from the old system to the new:

- Direct
- Parallel running
- Phased implementation
- Pilot working

Direct changeover

This is the simplest form of changeover. involves introducing a complete new system in its entirety on a specific date as a total replacement for the old system. Once the new system has been completed and all the programs judged to be working properly the old system is abandoned and the new takes over.

Parallel running

This is probably the commonest method of changeover used commercially. The new system replaces the existing system after running alongside it for a trial period. During this time the outputs of the new system are compared with the outputs from the old system. Any discrepancies are immediately investigated and corrected. This process continues until a sufficient period has passed in which there are no discrepancies and there is perfect correspondence between the outputs of the two systems. This period also allows the staff to gain experience of operating the new system and to have confidence that new system is working adequately.

Phased implementation

The new system replaces the existing system by converting one part of the old system at a time until all the procedures have been replaced. In many systems it is possible to break the implementation task down into separate functional areas which are then dealt with one by one.

For example, a company might convert the order collection first, then the invoice printing, and then the updating of the stock master file, and finally the automatic updating of the individual customer balances.

Another way of using phased implementation is divide an application into several parts artificially and implement those. For example, a large stock-control application might divide the inventory into bought-in items and in-house manufactured items and treat these separately although they are dealt with identically by all the processing applications.

Pilot working

This method can be used in conjunction with any of the others. It is used where an organisation consists largely of fairly identical operating units, such as a chain of shops or the branches of bank. A typical unit is chosen to develop the new system. Once the new way of working has been tried out and tested successfully then all the other units can be converted very quickly using the proven system

Selecting the right changeover strategy

Each of the four methods has its own advantages and disadvantages and very often a combination of methods is used.

Direct conversion
ADVANTAGES

- Limits the number of systems staff needed
- Cheap-only one system operating at any one time.

DISADVANTAGES

- Unpredictable loadings from technical, staff and work flow problems
- Relies too heavily on thorough pre-testing
- High risk of damaging failure
- Used on small systems only
- Removes the safety net of the existing system

USE

Simple, single purpose applications.

Phased implementation
ADVANTAGES

- Eases the training load
- Can solve operational problems without total shutdowns
- Extends the implementation period as long as needed
- Reduces the risk of lack of continuity

DISADVANTAGES

- The constant changes may confuse the staff
- Only appropriate where functions are distinct
- Can cause confusion where artificial divisions are used.

USE

Large multi-function applications.

Parallel running
ADVANTAGES

- Useful where accuracy is critical
- Useful when replacing a manual, paper-based system
- Always the security of back-up of existing system
- No danger of loss of continuity

DISADVANTAGES

- There is the danger of overloading staff resources
- Greater costs due to duplicated processing.

USE

Accounting, high-security applications.

Pilot working
ADVANTAGES

- Can be proved under real-life conditions without serious results if failures or errors occur.
- Less risky because allows concentration of resources
- Several different systems can be tried at the same time
- Branch staff can train other staff
- The conversion time can be as long as needed.

DISADVANTAGES

- Loss of contact with, and suspicion from, staff in other branches
- Possibility of chosen sites not being truly representative

USE

Branch banking, chain stores, building societies.

Exercise

The head office of a firm of double-glazing installers intends to buy several microcomputer software packages. They will use a data-base program to keep track of sites and sales prospects, a word-processing package to generate standard letters to customers and an integrated accounting suite. Justify your choice of strategy for changeover from the present fully manual system to the new micro-based one.

Further reading

Eliason, A. (1990) Systems Development: Analysis, Design and Implementation. Pub Scott, Foresman/Little, Brown. Glenview, Ill.

Kendall, P. (1990) Introduction to Systems Analysis and Design: A structured approach. Pub Wm C. Brown, Dubuque IA.

Schultheis, R. and Sumner, M. (1992) Management information systems: The manager's view. Pub Irwin, Homewood, Ill.

Chapter 15 Standards and documentation

Advantages of standards

Maintenance and documentation standards

The work of the analyst is not finished until all the documentation needed for the system is complete and delivered. However, it happens all too often that commercial pressures on analysts encourage them to concentrate solely on producing a working system at the expense of all else. Thus documentation is often allocated a very low priority and in the end even neglected as the analyst is moved on to another job.

This lack of documentation means unnecessarily difficult maintenance, extended learning times and expensive duplication of effort in subsequent years. To combat these effects various attempts have been made to establish standardised documentation, called simply standards for short. Many different types of documentation standardising schemes now exist. The most widely used of these in Britain is probably the National Computer Centre (NCC) scheme.

The NCC is the main body responsible for setting standards for computer applications. The NCC gives the following reasons for maintaining standards in all aspects of system analysis. Standards are an aid to:

1   Analysis

2   Design

3   Control

4   Completeness

5   Communication

6   Training

What are standards?

Standards are a preplanned set of specified documents to be prepared and maintained in the normal course of work during systems analysis and design. The adoption and maintenance of standards within a systems design environment is a costly and time-consuming business but is in reality very cost-effective as the effort is more than repaid in reduced system maintenance costs over the lifetime of the new system.

Why have standards?

To encourage and record formal **communication** between analyst and user, analyst and programmer, other analysts, and management in general. Also to act as an introduction to the system to others who will come along after, perhaps many years after, the analyst has left the job.

To facilitate **designing the system**. A good documentation scheme will enable information to be found easily for checking and so on, and will also enable several analysts to work simultaneously on different parts with minimum coordination problems.

Complete documentation is needed if operators and other system users are to gain the maximum benefit from the system. It promotes efficient and trouble-free running and **maintenance** of the system.

Standards aid greatly in **locating problems** and their speedy resolution.

The documentation has to act as a sort of bridge to provide **continuity**. It works against loss of contact arising, for example, from staff resignation, transfer, or the use of temporary staff.

The act of completing the documentation itself **disciplines the analyst** to produce systems information in the most desirable format for all interested parties rather than in the way the individual thinks fit.

Documentation is a great aid to **analysis**. Systems analysis is concerned with the acquisition and recording of masses of information and to derive maximum utility this information must be recorded and processed in a systematic and professional way.

Standards aid **control**. If there is an agreed code of standards operating on a particular project, this provides a convenient means of monitoring the progress of the work. Every stage of analysis and design has its own recognised output and completion of the documentation means completion of the stage. The standards in use provide a listing of expected outputs from the analysis and design work: control can be exercised by comparing planned completion dates against the actual dates on which finalised documentation is handed over.

Standards aid **completeness**. Where there is a recognised standard scheme in operation completion of all the documentation means that every stage has been tackled and none inadvertently overlooked.

Documentation plays an important role in facilitating **training**, and aids learning both in preparing and implementing the new system.

Documentation can act as an aid to **security**. It is very common for magnetic media to be accidentally lost and a system of regular documentation can prove valuable backup protection.

Minimum system documentation

The main documents created and maintained for a normal system will be:

1   The terms of reference

2   The feasibility report

3   The system specification

The following are derived from the systems specification:

1.   Program specifications and documentation (done by the programmers)

2.   Hardware specification and manual

3.   Software manual(s)

4.   Training manual

5.   User's manual

6.   Operating procedures manual

7.   Clerical procedures manual

8.   Operations log (history of new system)

Main systems documents

Terms of reference
This is the document which lays down the objectives of the new systems, the scope of the system study, the resources and constraints to be observed. It specifies who is to be involved, what is to be investigated, how long is to be spent and how much of the organisation's resources can

be allocated to the task. It also defines the boundaries within which the analyst must work.

Feasibility report

This document is outcome of the feasibility study stage. It is effectively the result of a mini systems investigation designed to discover whether the objectives specified in the terms of reference can actually be met by applying the resources allocated within the constraints given. It details the probable hardware configuration, the processing requirements and gives an informed opinion as to whether the existing resources of the organisation will be able to carry out the proposed project successfully. It contains a list of all the likely costs associated with the project, a list of the benefits and finishes with a cost-benefit analysis.

Functional specification

Otherwise know as a 'logical specification', this document is the outcome of an analysis of what the system must do, rather than how it is to be done. The mechanics of turning the logical specification into a working reality is the subject of the systems specification. The functional specification document contains a detailed breakdown of every procedure which has to be carried out by the system if it is to do its job properly, and a definition of the various data items and files which act as links between the procedures. The document very often consists of extensive data-flow diagrams and a data dictionary.

Systems specification

The major document produced by the systems analyst at the end of the systems study stage. It provides complete details of the analyst's proposed solution to the problem outlined in the terms of reference. It is the key document of the system and is used to justify the continued implementation of the system. It is also a principal reference source during the implementation stage.

Program specification

This is a document, produced by the programmer, which specifies precisely what each program does and how it does it. Each program is described in several ways. There is a description of the input requirements and how the data is to be validated, a description of the output and the various choices of output format available. There are details of all the files used and a description of the relationship between the program and the files. There will also be a description of the internal organisation of the program showing the relationship between the various modules and demonstrating the overall structure. There will also of course

308

be a complete source-code listing for each program. The main purpose of the program specification is to allow other programmers to carry out maintenance easily and quickly when the original programmers are no longer available.

Hardware specification

This describes all aspects of the hardware used in the system, including clerically operated equipment. The operation of the machinery is described, as are any user-servicing routines required. It also specifies who to contact when anything goes wrong.

Software specification

This is similar to the program specification in that it describes how to operate the program. However, this document is designed for the non-technical user, that is, someone who needs to use the computer but would not be expected to have any knowledge of programming.

It describes how to get into the system, how to call up the program wanted and how to use the program to carry out information handling.

Training manual

This is a document drawn up by the implementation team prior to the system going live. Its purpose is to act initially as a step-by-step guide to all staff who will have to operate the computer, including those who will only use the computer to access information, the users.

Training manuals should cover every aspect of computer use, for every possible class of user. As well as elementary and introductory matters, many manuals incorporate more advanced sections for experienced users often including quite technical aspects of the computer operation.

Some manuals will also often incorporate tests and drills so that staff can test themselves to ensure that they have reached an appropriate level of expertise.

User manual

A document produced by the systems analyst designed to allow the users of the system to obtain the maximum benefit from it. It explains how to enter the system, the facilities available, where to get help, what the error messages mean, etc. Generally it tries to be as helpful as possible for people who are not familiar with the operation of the computer. Very often it shows pictures of the screen displays and explains what each of the data items show signifies. Some user manuals act as a step-by-step tutorial, others also will give quite technical information for the more advanced user.

Procedures manuals

These can be either for Operating procedures or for Clerical procedures, or a mixture of both. The documents are prepared by the systems analyst during the design and implementation stages.

The main purpose of the clerical procedures manual is to inform the clerical staff how to integrate their work with the new computer system. It details all the computer tasks which link to the non-computerised, manual parts of the systems. The document specifies the clerical jobs to be done, the order in which they are to be done and the exact nature of the interface between the manual procedures and the computer procedures.

The operating procedures manual specifies the skills, knowledge and aptitudes required of the computer operations staff. In it will be found details of the jobs of all the various staff. It will set out precisely how and when and in what order tasks are to be carried out.

The procedures manual is both a training document for new staff and a work of reference for more experienced staff. It will give details of all the possible error conditions and how to correct them, security measures, diagnostic tests and many other aspects affecting the normal daily routines of work in the computer department.

Chapter 16 Case Study: Polyfloor Vinyl Coverings

The problem

Polyfloor is a large organisation which owns a chain of carpet shops - 87 branches - and operates in all the major cities of the UK. The main warehouse is at head office in Kidderminster in the Midlands and the shops replenish their stocks by telephone orders placed with the central warehouse.

These orders are met if stock is available but in recent times the warehouse has been persistently running out of stock of many of the less popular items although there is a sophisticated manual stock control system in operation. This has resulted in delays in supplying the branches and the branch managers are blaming the fall in sales on the poor head office service.

You have been called in as consultant to the sales director to determine whether it is feasible to overcome the problem by installing a computerised solution.

Early investigations have determined that the shops are correct in their complaints of poor service. The buyer has revealed that he is under pressure to reduce stockholding to the barest minimum because of cash flow constraints and has pointed out that the central warehouse can now only supply the less popular items against a firm order and can no longer be expected to keep stocks of them.

The sales and marketing department have concluded that the reduction in stocks held need not necessarily mean a further drop in total sales through the shops. They believe that they can overcome the smaller choice offered in the shops by selling from samples at a very keen price, and in this way actually increase the range that each shop can handle.

They have made arrangements with 15 different suppliers who will each provide samples of 25 designs in six colours and between one and three textures. The warehouse will continue to stock 1,000 separate items.

The shop managers are enthusiastic about the new scheme but have pointed out that there could easily be problems arising from changes in prices. It would be very tedious for them to have to update a very long price list every time a supplier changed his price or a special offer was announced.

The Board of Directors is very keen to use modern methods and wants you to recommend a computer arrangement which will solve the current problem and avoid any similar problems in the future.

In addition, the marketing manager would like to have more information regarding sales performance for each branch. The central warehouse manager would like a system which would allow him to identify surplus stock in a branch so that it can be sent to another branch which needs it, without having to buy more in. The finance manager is worried that this will complicate his bookkeeping.

The administration manager has said that his staff is unable to keep up with the typing and correspondence as it is and doesn't think that his staff will be able to produce regular price lists for the sample ranges in addition to their normal duties. Finally, the chairman says that he will want to be shown areas where savings might be made before he would even think about implementing any new system.

Requirements

Produce a report which covers the points listed below.

1   Describe in outline a computerised system which will satisfy the above requirements.

2   Draw a systems run chart for the main sub-systems to illustrate your ideas, showing clearly input, output, and file content.

3   Describe in general terms the kind of hardware you would need.

4   Describe in detail three different data-capture methods which could be used in the branches.

5   Indicate the data security controls you would incorporate into the new system.

Getting to the solution

Problem definition

In order to clarify the problem, the requirements of the design are listed below.

1   Minimise the amount of stock held in the central warehouse

2   Minimise the stock held in the individual branches

3   Streamline the reordering processes

4   Increase the variety offered by each shop

5   Eliminate the need for each branch to continually update a list of current prices

6   Improve sales reporting from the branches

7   Allow transfers between branches of surplus stocks

8   Avoid excessive bookkeeping

9   Avoid burdening head office administration staff

10   Demonstrate areas where savings can be made

Analysis of the existing system

Identifying the subsystems
The overall problem breaks down into three smaller areas.

1   The problems associated with maintaining adequate stock levels in the central warehouse, and dealing with shop orders and enquiries.

2   The problems of maintaining adequate stock levels in individual branches, and the procedures for dealing with customer orders, direct sales, enquiries and reporting these back to head office.

3   The problem of finding out what stocks are held at other branches, and the administration of the interbranch transfers.

Another way of looking at this organisation is to consider it from the point of view of the customer sales operation.

Direct sales
Some sales will be for items which are normally always in stock in the individual branch, and the customer will expect to see the items on display, select and pay for them, and have them delivered with a day or two. This type of sale requires no interaction with the central warehouse except to reorder the items sold in the normal course of events. Only branch records are involved and all procedures are internal.

313

Special orders

These will involve items which are not normally stocked in any branch and are always ordered through head office for delivery to the customer in some weeks time. Customers normally select from samples and pay only a deposit. The branch has to maintain records of outstanding orders, customer details and also to notify the central warehouse.

Out-of-stock orders

These are sales of items which should normally be available from stock at a particular branch, but which for some reason have sold out temporarily, or for items which are stocked by some branches and not others. In this case the shop will have to identify the nearest branch which does have some stock and arrange a transfer. The customer would expect to take delivery in a few days time. This is the most complicated of the three cases as it requires the shop to keep records of the customer's unfilled orders, to access external records to identify a shop with stock and organise the paperwork to record the transfer details.

Operational requirements

Analysis of the problem suggests that the most useful approach would be to treat each of the three sub-systems separately and then try to find a design which will integrate them all into a unified system.

The procedure requirements of the shops

In considering possible designs it is probably best to start with the needs of the shops since they are the most important elements in the problem because there are so many of them. If the requirements of the shops can be met then the bulk of the problem has been solved. It is assumed that every part of the company will be under head office central control and would operate normal commercial accounting procedures.

For the purposes of analysis the shops can all be regarded as identical. The minimum data requirements will be as follows.

For a *direct sale* the shop must maintain records of:

- Customer transaction number
- Products stocked
- Current prices
- Quantities in stock

Details of these have to be reported to head office periodically.

314

For a *special order sale* the shop must maintain records of:

- Customer transaction number

- Customer details

- Deposit paid

- Sample range

- Current prices

- Lead time for delivery

Some provision will also have to be made for reporting the special orders to head office or the central warehouse, monitoring outstanding orders and notifying customers of delivery times. Some form of access to central warehouse records will be needed in order to check on stock availability.

The data requirements for *out-of-stock orders* will be identical to those for the direct sale order, but will require each branch to be able to access the stock records of every other branch. There will also have to be some procedure for compensating the other branch for using its stock.

The central warehouse processing requirements
The work of the central warehouse will fall into three main areas.

1. Procedures arising from direct sales

- Bulk stock requests:

    Recording incoming orders from the shops

    Despatching the stock

    Charging shops for supplies

- Bulk purchases

    Issuing bulk reorders to suppliers

    Maintaining a list of suppliers

    Maintaining a cost-price list

    Forecasting demand from shops

2 Procedures arising from special order sales

- Maintaining a list of products

- Maintaining a list of suppliers

- Maintaining a current cost-price list
- Recording orders from shops
- Monitoring progress of orders
- Despatch of supplies
- Charging of supplies to shops

Procedures arising from out-of-stock sales are purely shop-to-shop transactions so the warehouse will not be involved in them.

3 Procedures for management reporting

- Periodic analyses of sales
- Periodic analyses of stock holding
- Sales forecasting

The hardware

Advances in technology make it possible to utilise many different types of computer. Each comes with a different specification and can be adapted to do a variety of jobs. Networks of micro-computers can be linked together to use shared peripherals and can perform complex tasks cheaply and reliably. Minicomputers offer much of the power of mainframes at a fraction of the cost, and mainframes are getting ever more powerful.

In order to choose the right hardware many factors have to be taken into consideration such as the size of the company, its precise needs (does it need just stock control or does it want total automation?), the resources available (staff, capital, size of buildings) and the time-scale.

The proposed solution

Polyfloor is a large company, with 87 branches/shops and a warehouse/central office, selling a wide range of products (over 1,000 items stocked, over 7,000 available) and will employ a relatively large workforce. It follows that the data processing task will not be simple either and that the best system for this company will be a mixture of centralised design to aid security and control and a distributed design to minimise costs and maximise flexibility.

The design can be considered as being in two parts. There are two major areas of data storage in the proposed design (warehouse and individual branches) and one major interface. These will be described separately.

316

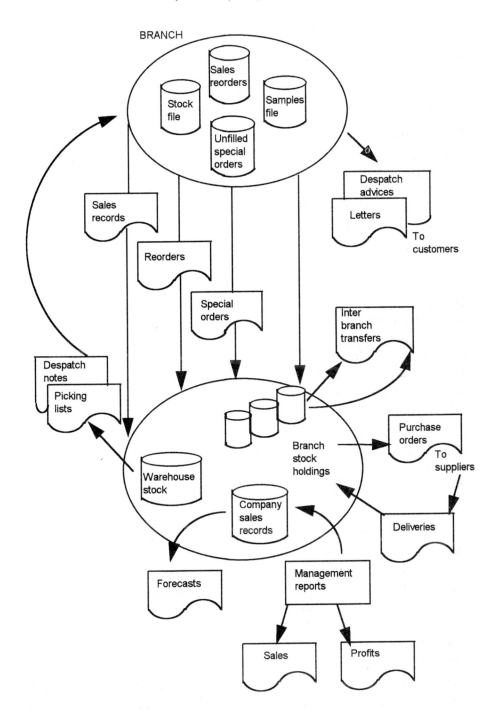

Figure 16.1 The information requirements

The warehouse system

The largest task is that of warehouse recording and processing. The main files and principle output documents are shown on the diagram and the contents of these can readily be established by considering the functional breakdowns shown in the section on operational requirements.

Given the data volumes envisaged, it seems likely that either a minicomputer or a mainframe is needed mainly because of the size of the company and the number of its widespread branches. Both types of computer can work at very high speeds and as well as having good processing capacity; they can both cater for on-line multi-user environments should it later be felt that this is what is needed in the organisation in order to secure tighter control.

An appropriate-sized central computer working on-line will require immediate access magnetic backing storage to be used. The most appropriate type would be a system based on exchangeable disk packs or high capacity fixed disks.

The warehouse installation will also require printers to produce the output documents shown in Figure 16.1, will require a suitable communications set-up in order to interface directly with the branches and would have terminals for the input of data and to allow warehouse staff to interrogate the data base.

The branch computer system

As shown in Figure 16.2 most of the data will be input at branch level, and only summaries will normally be sent to the central computer. Each branch would have its own computing facility consisting of a terminal, hard disk storage of perhaps 300 Mb, a printer and communications modem.

In normal operation the point-of-sale terminal would operate in three modes. In sales-recording mode the terminal would be program-driven and would prompt the salesperson to enter the details required for each type of sale and file a record of the sale. Alternatively, the terminal can be used to investigate the stock position, whether to display details of the complete sample range or to examine the current position of the shops own stocks. For out-of-stock sales the terminal would go into its communications mode allowing it to access the central warehouse computer and through it find out if and where any unused stock is being held.

The branch computer would also be used for non-sales purposes. Since it is a complete computer system it will be able to run software packages and could be used by the shop managers to reorder stock, prepare forecasts, wordprocess letters, print confirmation notes etc.

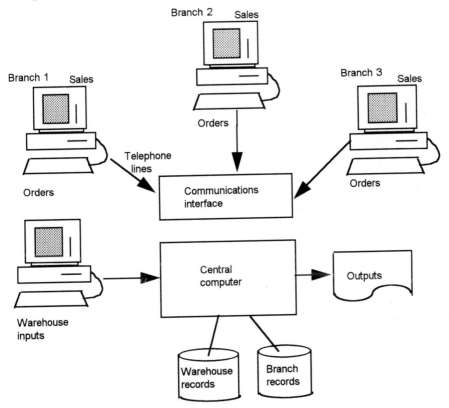

Figure 16.2 The branch computer system

The communications facility would also be used to send data to the central computer in batch mode. Each evening after the close of business the terminal would be used to call up the central computer and would download the day's sales data. The central computer would then amalgamate all the branch data into a daily master file for the whole company. While the branch and the warehouse were connected the warehouse would update the branch samples files with any changes in prices or availability of stock. This facility could also be developed to accommodate records of goods received at the branches, or to allow for an overnight electronic mail service.

The branch computers would obviously be smaller than those in the warehouse, but would still have to be powerful enough to be able to process data and run programs. The best machines for this purpose would be microcomputers. Modern microcomputers are getting more powerful all the time. A typical configuration would have a user friendly graphical operating system, 8Mb of RAM and a hard disk capacity of over 200Mb. One of these would enable the branch staff to handle the transactions easily and efficiently. A second might be used to handle routine administration.

Printers would also be needed at all these sites but can be obtained fairly inexpensively. The shops do not have to involve themselves in large volumes of paperwork so only one printer capable of producing near-letter quality (NLQ) printing need be used, although a good case could be made for having two interchangeable models for backup purposes.

Communications

One of the most important parts of the system is the communications package needed to bring the whole system together. This will include modems and operating software which enable all the branches to communicate with the central computer via communications lines.

These communication lines come in different forms including microwaves, fibre optics and satellites but by far the cheapest and most efficient way would be to use existing telephone lines. This form of communicating data between two different computers is widely used, and packages and data bases exist for machines ranging from small micros to large mainframes. To minimise costs, branches need not be on-line to the warehouse at all times, but can use a dial-up facility as and when needed.

Changeover considerations

The introduction of a system such as the one proposed is a major undertaking and must be carefully planned. As the business comprises a number of essentially similar branches and one central warehouse it would be sensible to equip a few of the branches first and use them as pilot sites.

While these sites were being evaluated and the programs and procedures for them being refined, the warehouse systems could be installed with view to operating them in a stand-alone mode. There will be some difficulty in transferring stock records from the manual system to the computer system.

320

This will be a very big job and should be spread over as long a time as possible. With machines of this size great care in servicing and operation is needed. Trained personnel will have to be brought in or existing personnel trained up. A totally new department will have to be created, specialising solely in data processing and supplying data to other departments. A job like this would probably need two years to complete.

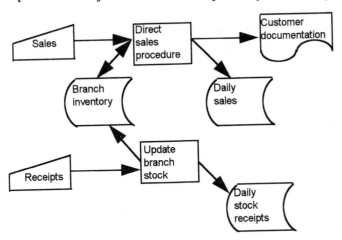

Figure 16.3 Flowchart for branch direct sales

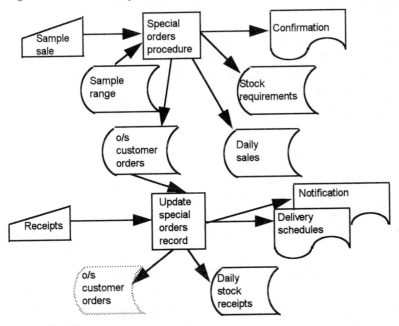

Figure 16.4 Flowchart for special orders

Systems flowcharts

Figures 16.3-16.8 show systems flowcharts for the main subsystems: branch direct sales, branch special sales, branch out-of-stock sales, daily warehouse update, warehouse reordering procedure, management information system.

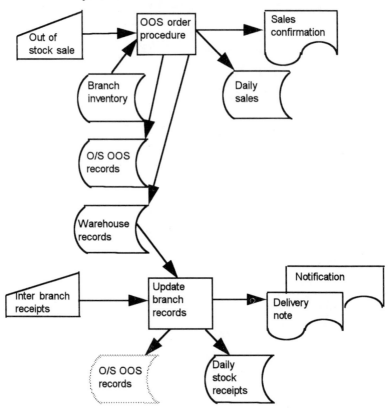

Figure 16.5 Flowchart for out of stock sales

Data capture methods

VDU using intelligent terminals

A VDU can be used for both input and output. It can handle a variety of applications including transmission of data between locations, time-sharing facilities, random enquiry facilities, on-line ordering and stock control.

A VDU looks like a television screen with a keyboard; some are capable of processing data and are said to be 'intelligent'. The monitor can produce images of both text and graphics and data can be seen on-screen once it has been entered. As these terminals display everything that is entered it becomes very easy to detect typing errors which can quickly be corrected. Errors can be detected by using resident validation programs which can make sure that the data is in its correct format before being processed. These terminals are versatile and can accept a large number of 'add-ons' which increase their value as input devices.

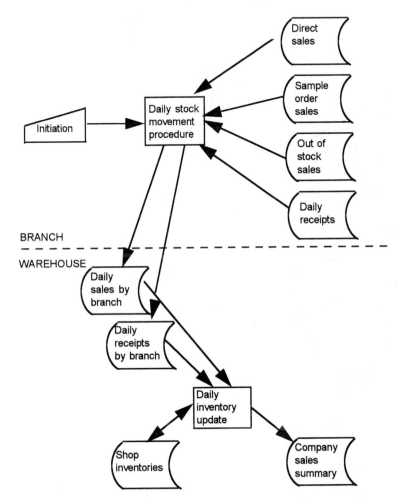

Figure 16. 6 Flowchart for daily warehouse update

Bar codes

Bar codes using article numbering are now being used in the retail business sector with much success. A bar code is made up of a series of bars and spaces of varying width which are laid out in accordance with predetermined standards. The bar code includes an article's product number (in this case a carpet or a carpet sample) which is unique to that product and which can only be read by the use of low intensity laser scanners or light pens. The advantages of using bar codes include faster and easier selling of goods; the unique bar code numbering system makes stock-control more efficient which in turn helps to increase sales.

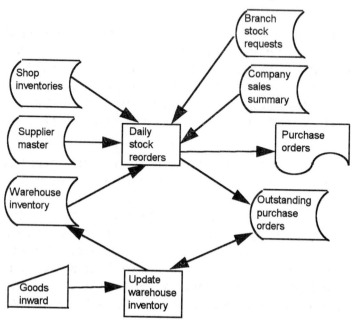

Figure 16. 7 Flowchart for warehouse reordering

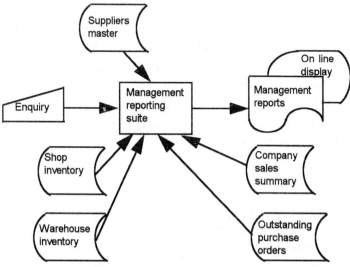

Figure 16.8 Flowchart for management information system

324

The shops which want to make use of this system would only require terminals capable of accepting light pens. The light pen is a very simple tool which scans light or shade of varying width and with the help of software converts this into suitable information ready for validation and processing.

Input by 'Mouse'

'Mouse' is the name given to a small electronic analogue device used in data input . The mouse consists of a hand-held plastic case with two buttons which is connected to a computer via a cable or infra-red link. The mouse uses a unidirectional ball which is attached to the underside of the case and which, when slid across a smooth flat surface, makes a cursor move across the screen where it is usually displayed in the shape of an arrow.

This arrow or cursor is positioned over special graphical characters displayed on the screen know as icons and one of the buttons pressed in order to start the task which that particular icon specifies. This could include anything from calling up a particular program through to file handling and operating system prompts. The same results can be achieved by typing instructions onto a keyboard but a mouse is quicker. Of course jobs involving great amounts of text capture which need packages such as word processors would still require a keyboard, so the mouse will never be the complete answer, and keyboards will not go totally out of existence.

Control and security in the proposed system

A modern computer system represents the investment of many thousands of pounds in hardware and software and in the amount of time spent by development staff. This investment will not be properly utilised unless control is exercised over the whole system at all times.

The control of data processing is a very complex subject and only some aspects of it can be considered here. The following list gives some of the major controls necessary in this system.

- Hardware controls

- File security

- Auditing

- Confidentiality of information

- Software controls

Hardware controls

It is important to maintain hardware by regular servicing in order for it to function efficiently and avoid too many interruptions due to breakdowns. Breakdowns within a system can at best cause the loss of invaluable processing time; at worst complete loss of data can occur. Most hardware controls are built in to the system by the manufacturer and so the analyst's responsibility is largely confined to ensuring that they are adequate for the job.

File security

One common type of file security is called **generation technique** because it creates several generations of files in the sequence grandfather, father, son - a term used to describe the several stages of a file. The purpose of file security is to develop generations of old master files in order to keep up-to-date copies of data files in case of data loss or corruption. Breakdowns or malfunctions within systems can cause data to be lost but if backups are kept of previously correct and processed files, these can be used to restart processing. This technique can be used for both disks and tapes.

Another type of file security is known as the **dumping** or **copying technique**. This works by 'dumping' copies or 'images' of individual records onto a separate disk just before they are updated. In the event of data loss the spare disk can be brought into use as it would contain all the records as they were just before the data loss.

Auditing

This is an important aspect of data control which is conducted by auditors either from inside or outside the organisation. The purpose of auditing is to check out all the data within the system to ensure that it complies with expected results. In this way errors in the system can be detected and corrected. the auditors must have some knowledge of computers but they need not be experts. They should also be familiar with programming techniques and with systems development if they are to know which controls they should recommend for incorporation into the system.

In a well-designed system the audit checks should be able to detect any discrepancies within that system automatically by using internal checking and should therefore catch errors before they lead to major processing problems or even fraud.

326

Confidentiality of information

Information, in the form of files and hard copy, must also of course be systematically protected. Access to files by unauthorised personnel should be totally avoided and can be controlled by certain simple techniques. This is a further aspect of file security.

Information can be kept confidential by the use of **passwords** which have to be entered by the users at their terminals before the system can be entered. The password is then transmitted to the computer for validation, and only if it is acceptable is the user let in. Passwords can be used to define several levels of security so that access to certain files is only given to those with a given security status within the organisation. File security can also be achieved by using scrambling techniques when writing data onto magnetic media; special decoding keys are used to unscramble it. Both of these security techniques are used widely in many business environments and could be particularly useful for this organisation because of its size.

Data validation

The object of data validation is to detect errors in data as quickly as possible before processing takes place. In our case on-screen checking with the aid of a special editing package would enable us to detect any incorrect data. Data validation would be widely used within the system in programs and is one of the main tools used by the auditor.

There are several types of checks that can be used in order to detect these errors. Some of the more common ones are as follows:

Check digits

These test for errors of transcription. A check digit is a single value which when appended to a code number, such as a product number or customer number, makes the resulting longer number self-checking. The check digit is itself found by a simple calculation involving all the other digits in the code number. This means that if the relationship between the digits is disturbed, for example, by getting the digits out of order or inserting a spurious digit, then the value of the check digit will also be altered. This alteration is easily detected; most common errors of transcription can be eliminated by this means.

Range tests

It is possible to set minimum and maximum values for all data entering the computer system. Any data which falls outside these predetermined values will be automatically rejected. For example in a payroll application the only acceptable values for the hours worked field would be those between zero and say 60. Any attempt to enter a value outside this range, such as 300, would be rejected as impossible.

Field size

Some data items will always be of a predetermined size. A product code, for example, may always need to be five digits long, while on the other hand the amount of the product ordered maybe represented by a number between one and four digits long, depending on the exact quantity wanted. The data entry program can be designed to test for the field length and so catch input errors as soon as they arise.

Validity tests

This type of test compares input data against a table held in memory or on disk to check whether the actual value is a valid one. For example a customer number can be searched for in the customer master file to ensure that the customer record actually exists before doing any further processing.

References

Anthony, R. (1965) Planning and control systems: A framework for analysis. Division of Research, Graduate School of Business Administration, Harvard University, Boston.

Antill, L. and Wood-Harper, T. (1984) A multiview approach to business. Soft January 1984

Argyris, C. (1980) Some inner contradictions in management information systems. From The Information Systems Environment. (Eds. Lucas et al), North-Holland, 1980.

Avison, D. E. (1985) Information Systems Development: A database approach. Blackwell, Oxford

Baronas, A-M.K. and Louis, M.R. (1988) Restoring a sense of control during implementation: How user involvement leads to system acceptance. MIS Quarterly March 1988

Benbasat, I et al. (1984) A critique of the stage hypothesis: Theory and empirical evidence. Communications of the ACM. Vol 27 pp 476 - 485.

Bowers, D S (1988) From data to database. Van Nostrand Reinhold (UK) Ltd, Wokingham.

Bradley J (1989) An elementary introduction to data base management. The Dryden Press, Chicago

Checkland, P. (1981) Systems Thinking, Systems Practice. Wiley, New York.

Checkland, P. and Scholes, J. (1990) Soft systems methodology in action. Wiley, New York.

Codd, E F (1970) A relational model of data for large shared data banks. Communications of the ACM.

Colter, M.A. (1984) A comparative examination of systems analysis techniques. MIS Quarterly March 1984

Davis, G.B and Olson, M.H. (1990) Management information systems McGraw-Hill, New York.

Dearnley & Mayhew (1983) In favour of system prototypes and their integration into the SDC Computer Journal 26(1) 1983

deMarco, T. (1978) Structured Analysis and System Specification. Yourdon Press, New York.

Desanctis, G. and Courtney, J.F. (1983) Toward friendly user MIS implementation. Communications of the ACM Vol 26 No 10

Dickson, G.and Wetherbe, J. (1985) The Management of Information Systems. McGraw-Hill, New York.

Dos Santos, B.L.and Hawk, S.R. (1988) Differences in analyst's attitudes towards information systems development: evidence and implications. Information and Management Vol 14 1988 p31-41

Er, M.C. (1986) Classic tools of systems analysis - Why they have failed. Data Processing Vol 28 No 10

Fertuck, L. (1992) Systems analysis and design with case tools. (Pub Wm C. Brown, Dubuque, IA)

Finkelstein, C. (1992) Information Engineering: Strategic Systems Development. Pub Addison-Wesley, Wokingham, England.

Fitzgerald, G., Stokes, N. and Wood, J. (1985) Feature analysis of contemporary information systems methodologies. The Computer Journal. Vol 28, No 3 1985

Gane, C.and Sarson, T. (1979) Structured Systems Analysis. Prentice Hall.

Hirschheim, R., Earl, M., Feeny, D. and Lockett, M. (1988) An exploration into the management of the IS function.: Key issues and an evolving model. Proceedings of the Joint International Symposium on IS (March 1988).

Hirschheim, R. (1985)Office automation: A social and organisational perspective. Wiley

Howe D R (1984) Data Analysis for Data Base design. Edward Arnold, London

King, J and Kraemer, K. (1984) Evolution and organisational information systems; An assessment of Nolan's staged model. Communications of the ACM. Vol 27, pp 466-475.

Mackay, H., Lane, S. and Jenkins, A. (1989) Systems analysts and the social shaping of technology. Paper for the 7th annual UMIST/Aston Conference on the Organisation and Control of the Labour Process. Manchester, March 1989

Mahmood, M.O. (1987) Systems development methods: A comparative investigation. MIS Quarterly September 1987

Markus, M.L. (1981) Implementation politics: top management support and user involvement. Systems, Objectives, Solutions North-Holland 1981

Martin, J. (1982) Application development without programmers. Prentice-Hall Inc. (Engelwood Cliffs, New Jersey)

Martin, J. (1985) Fourth generation languages Volume II: Survey of representitive 4GLs. Savant Research Studies, England. 1985

Mason, R.E.A. and Carey, T.T. (1983) Prototyping interactive information systems. Communications of the ACM Vol 26 No 5 May 1983

Mayhew, P.J. and Dearnley, P.A. (1987)An alternative prototyping classification. The Computer Journal Vol 30 No 6 1987 p481- 484

McFadden , F. and Hoffer, J. (1988) Data Base Management. Pub Benjamin Cummings, Menlo Park, CA.

McFarlan, W. and McKenney, J. (1983) Corporate Information Systems Management. Irwin Inc. Homewood, Illinois.

Methlie, L.B. (1980) Systems requirements analysis - methods and models. The Information Systems Environment Eds. Lucas et al. (North-Holland, 1980)

Misra, S.K. and Subramanian, V. (1988) An assessment of CASE technology for software design. Information and Management Vol 15 p213-228

Mumford, E. (1983) Designing Human Systems. Pub Manchester Business School.

Munro, M.C. and Davis, G.B. (1977) Determining management information needs: a comparison of methods. MIS Quarterly June 1977

Naumann, J.D. and Jenkins, A.M. (1982) Prototyping: the new paradigm for systems development. MIS Quarterly September 1982

Nolan, R. (1973) Managing the computer resource: A stage hypothesis. Communications of the ACM. July 1973 p399-440

Nolan, R. (1979) Managing the crisis in data processing,. Harvard Business Review, March/April pp 115-126.

Peacham, D. (1985) Structured methods - ten questions you should ask. Data Processing Vol 27 No9 November 1985

Perry, J.T. and Lateer, J.G. (1989) Understanding Oracle. Sybex, Alameda, CA.

Peters, G and Naughton, J (1985) Comparing systems approaches. Technology: A third level course. Block V Units 19/20 Complexity, management and change - applying a systems approach (The Open University, Milton Keynes, England)

Pratt P and Adamski, J (1987) Database systems: Management and design. Boyd and Fraser, Boston.

Rock-Evans, R. (1981) Data Analysis (IPC Press, A Computer Weekly publication, Sutton, Surrey 1981)

Rockart, J.F. (1979) Chief executives define their own data needs. Harvard Business Review March/April 1979.

Senn, James A. (1990) Information systems in management. Wadsworth, pub, Belmont, CA.

St John-Bate, J. and Vadhia, D. (1987) Fourth Generation Languages under DOS and Unix. (BSP Professional Books, London) 1987

Sumner M. and Sitek, J. (1986) Are structured methods for systems analysis and design being used? Journal of Systems Management. June 1986. pp18 - 23

Tasker, D.(1987) In search of fourth generation data. Datamation 1st July 1987 Page 61

Tasker D A (1989) Fourth generation data. Prentice Hall, Englewood Cliffs.

Ward, J., Griffiths, P. and Whitemore, P. (1990) Strategic Planning for Information Systems. Wiley, Chichester.

Wood-Harper, A., Antill, L. and Avison, D. (1985) Information Systems Definition; The multiview approach. Blackwell Scientific Publications, Oxford.

Yourdon E. (1986) Whatever happened to structured systems analysis? Datamation. 1st June 1986.

Index